The Rise of Mutual Funds

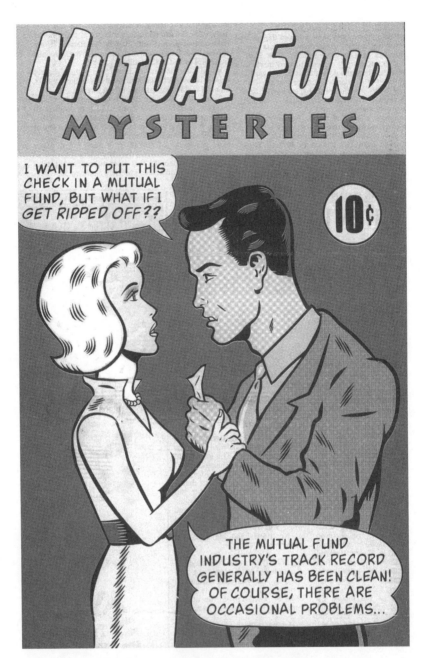

Copyright *Los Angeles Times*. Reprinted with permission.

The Rise of Mutual Funds

An Insider's View

Matthew P. Fink

OXFORD

UNIVERSITY PRESS

2011

OXFORD

UNIVERSITY PRESS

Oxford University Press, Inc., publishes works that further
Oxford University's objective of excellence
in research, scholarship, and education

Oxford   New York
Auckland   Cape Town   Dar es Salaam   Hong Kong   Karachi
Kuala Lumpur   Madrid   Melbourne   Mexico City   Nairobi
New Delhi   Shanghai   Taipei   Toronto

With offices in
Argentina   Austria   Brazil   Chile   Czech Republic   France   Greece
Guatemala   Hungary   Italy   Japan   Poland   Portugal   Singapore
South Korea   Switzerland   Thailand   Turkey   Ukraine   Vietnam

Copyright © 2011 by Oxford University Press

Published by Oxford University Press, Inc.
198 Madison Avenue, New York, New York 10016

www.oup.com

Oxford is a registered trademark of Oxford University Press

Library of Congress Cataloging-in-Publication Data
Fink, Matthew P.
The rise of mutual funds : past, present, and future / Matthew P. Fink.
p. cm.
Includes bibliographical references and index.
ISBN 978-0-19-975350-5 (pbk. : alk. paper) 1. Mutual funds—History. I. Title.
HG4530.F527 2011
332.63'27—dc22   2010011753

2 4 6 8 9 7 5 3 1

Printed in the United States of America
on acid-free paper

To Ellie

Acknowledgments

I received assistance from numerous individuals and organizations.

Tom Harman, Jared Minsk, and Joelle Frank of the Washington, DC office of the law firm of Morgan, Lewis & Bockius provided extensive research support. Terri Brooks, the Investment Company Institute's director of Library Services, guided me though the association's archives. Brian Reid, the institute's chief economist, his staff, and Michelle Kretsch, the manager of Member Services, provided statistics. Janet Zavistovich, the institute's design director, prepared the illustrations. Hans-Peter Guttman provided much-needed computer support.

I selected individuals from different backgrounds to review my drafts. From the U.S. Securities and Exchange Commission, Bob Plaze and Doug Scheidt. From the Financial Industry Regulatory Authority, Angela Goelzer and Tom Selman. From mutual fund companies, Jack Brennan of Vanguard, Tim Forde of American Funds, and Craig Tyle of Franklin. From law firms, Joel Goldberg of Willkie Farr & Gallagher, Marty Lybecker of WilmerHale, Dick Phillips of Kirkpatrick & Lockhart Preston Gates Ellis, and Irv Pollack of Fulbright & Jaworski. From academia, Joe Franco of Suffolk University Law School, and Emily Martz of the history department at the University of Delaware, and Lisa Ragen of the George Washington University School of Law. My final draft was reviewed by my longtime boss and mentor, Dave Silver.

Contents

Preface

Remember, the inevitable ineffectiveness of regulation.

—Louis D. Brandeis

Since publication of the first edition of this book in October 2008, the financial world has been traumatized. House prices have fallen sharply, major banks, securities firms, and insurance companies have failed or been rescued by government, unemployment has soared, and the stock market has plummeted (though it subsequently rallied).

The economic crisis, the worse since the Great Depression, had its origins in a record run up in home prices, followed by the bursting of the housing bubble. I did not say a word about home prices in the first edition. Had I considered the matter, I might have predicted that home prices were due for a fall. I never would have guessed that the decline would devastate the financial system and the economy as a whole.

During the years leading to the crisis I did express concern that regulators were not keeping up with developments. I led the mutual fund industry in calling for regulation of asset-backed pools, hedge funds, and rating agencies. Not only did these suggestions fall on deaf ears, but policymakers moved in the opposite direction, jettisoning some controls (e.g., the exemption by the Securities Exchange Commission (SEC) of asset-backed pools from regulation), weakening others (e.g., the SEC's lessening of capital requirements for broker-dealers), and declining to apply others (most famously, the Federal Reserve Board's refusal to raise interest rates as the housing bubble grew). Actions and nonactions by regulators produced the economic crisis. *The story of the 2008 meltdown was not the failure of financial laws, but rather the failure of regulators to properly apply those laws.*

Fortunately, during the good years of the 1980s and 1990s the mutual fund industry resisted the siren song of deregulation. Basic mutual fund controls, such as required diversification, strict limits on borrowing, and mandated daily marking to market were not eliminated or weakened. Therefore, while the 2008 storm hit mutual funds hard, they were not nearly as shaken as institutions that had never been regulated (hedge funds) or that had been deregulated (banks and securities firms). In this new edition I discuss the impact of the 2008 meltdown on mutual funds generally, as well as specific areas such as money market funds, the fate of the SEC, and 401(k) plans.

Looking ahead, I have relatively few worries about the mutual fund industry. The industry and its regulator, the SEC, still seem intent on retaining and strengthening core controls (see the SEC's recent caveat on leverage via derivatives), while modernizing fund regulation (such as recent prospectus reform).

I am far more concerned about the financial system generally. The 2008 crisis was followed by a national debate over financial reform. There were those in the academy, in the media, in Congress, in the Obama Administration, and even in the financial industry who called for fundamental reform that would impose strict statutory limits on the activities and size of financial institutions, so that none would be "too big to fail." But the administration and Congress rejected this advice. Instead, they opted for a massive 2,319-page law that grants regulators, who had helped produce the crisis, even more authority. The Dodd–Frank Act provides the SEC and the Federal Reserve Board with greatly expanded powers and creates entirely new regulatory bodies such as the Consumer Financial Protection Bureau and the Financial Stability Oversight Council.

I hope that this reliance on regulation works. Experience indicates that it won't.

I fear that we are headed toward a world of giant financial conglomerates that are impossible to manage or to regulate, riddled with conflicts, and periodically in need of massive government bailouts.

MPF

Chevy Chase, Maryland
October, 2010

The Rise of Mutual Funds

Introduction

There are a lot of things that can be said in favor of investment trusts, but they make less interesting reading than the things that can be said against them.

—Fred Schwed Jr.

On the morning of July 23, 1993, I was about to testify on the state of the mutual fund industry before the U.S. House of Representatives Subcommittee on Telecommunications and Finance. I planned to begin my testimony by referring to mutual funds as "a great American success story." Before the other witnesses and I testified, Subcommittee Chairman Ed Markey beat me to the punch by declaring in his opening statement that mutual funds were "a genuine American success story."

Chairman Markey and I were correct. American mutual funds have been phenomenally successful. More than 88 million Americans own mutual fund shares. Almost half the assets of 401(k) plans and individual retirement accounts are invested in mutual funds. Mutual funds are the largest financial institutions in the world, with assets of over $10 trillion.

Today, this success may seem inevitable. But no one expected it. In 1940, when the modern mutual fund industry began, mutual funds had assets of only $450 million.[1] Since then, there have been constant predictions that the mutual fund industry has matured and its growth years are over.

- In 1949, when fund assets were less than $2 billion, some observers concluded that mutual funds "have reached the peak of their growth."

- In 1973, when fund assets had grown to $47 billion, Donald Pitti, president of Weisenberger Services, then the statistical bible of the investment company industry, stated that "the fund industry as we know it today is likely to disappear."

- In 1977, when fund assets amounted to $50 billion, Harvard Business School Professor Martin Marshall declared, "The mutual fund industry has seen its great growth years."

- In 1987, when fund assets had grown to $4 trillion, Harvard Business School Professor Michael Porter predicted, "The bottom line is that the structural attractiveness of this industry is inevitably going to decline. 1993 may be the peak. Maybe it's 1994. But it's inevitably going to decline."

- In 2000, when over 83 million Americans owned funds with assets of $6 trillion, Forrester Research forecast "the coming demise of mutual funds," and *Red Herring* proclaimed "the death of mutual funds."

- In 2008, when fund assets exceeded $9 trillion, Celent, a research and consulting firm, declared "mutual funds in peril."[2]

Despite these repeated gloomy predictions, the mutual fund industry has continued to thrive. This book describes the specific events that by design or good fortune have produced this long history of success.

Countless books have been written about investing in mutual funds, there are a number of textbooks for use in law and business schools, and many works criticize mutual funds generally or recount the histories of specific fund companies. But the only history of the mutual fund industry, Hugh Bullock's *The Story of Investment Companies*, was published almost half a century ago.[3] Thus, this book is the first modern history of the mutual fund industry.

This book differs from most industry histories in that much of it is a personal narrative. My discussion of developments from 1971 to 2004 reflects my own firsthand experience. I spent my career representing the mutual fund industry before Congress, the U.S. Securities and Exchange Commission, and other federal and state government agencies. My selection of key events stresses the importance of developments in which I participated in Washington, rather than those that took place in Boston, New York, or elsewhere. I spent my career at the industry's trade association, the Investment Company Institute, and I give great weight to the role played by that organization in shaping events. Most important, I am a fan of mutual funds. I believe that they have been and remain by far the best way for the vast majority of Americans to save and invest for their futures. It would be surprising if this bias is not reflected in my account of mutual funds' history.

In some areas, such as the creation of the first mutual funds, I rely heavily on works by earlier writers, although I provide my own analyses. In other cases, I seek to relate developments in other areas, such as legislation authorizing the creation of various types of retirement plans, to the mutual fund experience. Finally, in many areas I discuss events that have not been covered elsewhere. I tend to provide greater detail on developments relating to issues that are still with us today, such as money market fund safety, use of fund assets for distribution, and disclosure to participants in 401(k) plans.

Most if not all of the developments covered in this book deserve more extensive discussion and analysis than is possible in a general history. I hope this book will whet readers' appetite for more information about mutual funds and will lead other writers to cover specific matters in greater detail. I am certain that others will disagree with some of my opinions. I hope that they will express their views. In fact my principal hope is that this book will spur analysis, discussion, and additional publications dealing with mutual funds. Mutual funds are vital to millions of Americans and their families as well as to our nation's economy. Therefore, mutual funds and their history merit serious analysis and informed debate.

It would have been more fun to write (and certainly to read) a book about mutual fund personalities, or about the ten best funds, or about allegedly shocking abuses. But such works tend to entertain rather than enlighten. My goal is to help educate readers so that they will be in a better position to understand and, if they desire, to participate in informed public discussion of mutual funds.

Nomenclature

Books and articles dealing with mutual funds employ a variety of terms to describe pooled investment vehicles that invest in securities, including investment trusts, investment companies, investment funds, funds, closed-end funds, open-end funds, mutual investment companies, mutual funds, unit investment trusts, fixed trusts, exchange-traded funds (ETFs), and hedge funds.

The original British pooled investment vehicles were organized in trust form and therefore were called *investment trusts*. They were later required to incorporate under the British Companies Act, so that they became *investment companies*. However, the term *investment trust* stuck to British investment companies and was also used to describe the first American ones. There is general agreement that this term is a misnomer. Fortunately, the phrase has gone out of style, but it was used in much of the older literature referred to herein.[4]

Therefore the proper term to generally describe pooled vehicles that invest in securities is *investment companies*. I use this term, as well as the word *funds*, to describe the broad universe of pooled vehicles that invest in securities.

Generally investment companies that operate in the United States are regulated by the Securities and Exchange Commission under the Investment Company Act of 1940. However, the 1940 act excludes many types of investment companies from regulation. Investment companies that are regulated under the 1940 act can be divided into three basic types.

First, there are "fixed trusts" or "unit investment trusts," vehicles that invest in a predetermined portfolio of securities that generally cannot be changed.

Second, there are "closed-end investment companies" or "closed-end funds," funds that invest in portfolios that are managed. The fund's own shares trade in the market at prices that may be greater or less than the value of its portfolio. For example, a closed-end fund might have a portfolio valued today at $100 and five shares outstanding. If the fund were to be liquidated today, each share would receive $20. But the shares might trade at $23 (a $3 premium) or at $18 (a $2 discount).

Third, there are "open-end investment companies," "open-end funds," or "mutual funds." The word *open-end* signifies that the fund is open to redemption, that is, a shareholder can tender shares to the fund at any time and receive proceeds based on the current value of the fund's portfolio (in the foregoing example, $20). As a matter of practice, most mutual funds also continuously offer new shares to investors.

Recently, new types of open-end investment companies, "exchange-traded funds" (ETFs), have been developed. An institutional investor deposits a prespecified basket of securities with an ETF in exchange for a creation unit consisting of ETF shares. The institutional investor can either keep the ETF shares or sell them on a stock exchange. Thereafter investors can purchase and sell ETF shares on the exchange. The institutional investor can redeem a creation unit by returning ETF shares to the ETF in return for a basket of securities. If ETF shares are trading at a discount or premium, an institutional investor can create or redeem ETF shares to take advantage of the spread. This provides an arbitrage mechanism that, in theory, helps to keep ETF trading prices in line with the current value of the ETF's portfolio

Hedge funds are types of investment companies that are excluded from regulation under the Investment Company Act, either because they have 100 or fewer shareholders or because all of their shares are owned by wealthy investors.

I hope that the foregoing explanation is helpful. In any event, I have tried to make clear in the text which particular type of investment vehicle is under discussion. I am responsible for any ambiguities and errors in this and other areas.

1

Beginning the Foundation

Miracles do happen, but one has to work very hard for them.
—Chaim Weizmann

Many developments in recent years have contributed to mutual funds' success, including generally rising securities markets, a growing middle class, the creation of new types of funds and new ways to distribute fund shares, and laws designed to encourage Americans to save for retirement. However, the foundation of mutual funds' success was laid early, in the 1920s and 1930s. Beginning with the creation of the first fund in 1924, mutual funds used redeemable shares and a simple capital structure that did not result in leverage. In 1934, a federal agency, the U.S. Securities and Exchange Commission (SEC), was established that was devoted exclusively to administration of the federal securities laws. In 1936, a law was enacted providing favorable tax treatment for funds and their shareholders. The only missing element was the enactment of a law, discussed in chapter 2, mandating practices that were voluntarily followed by the original mutual funds.

As is the case of much American history, the mutual fund story began in Europe.

Foreign Antecedents

In 1822, King William I of the Netherlands formed the Société Générale des Pays-Bas pour favoriser l'industrie nationale in Brussels to perform a number of financial activities. Over time it gave up its banking functions and focused on facilitating small investments in foreign government loans. Many scholars credit it as being the world's first investment company—that is, an arrangement by which a number of persons pool their funds primarily for investment in securities. A recent publication maintains that the concept goes back even further, to Amsterdam in 1774. In any event, investment companies were not common in continental Europe in the nineteenth century.[1]

Investment companies became popular in England and Scotland in the latter part of the nineteenth century. These companies, known as investment trusts, resembled what Americans now call closed-end funds. The fund issued securities to the public and used the proceeds to acquire a managed portfolio of securities. The fund's own shares then traded in the market at prices that reflected supply and demand for the shares, and that thus could be greater or less than the value of the portfolio.

British investment trusts were organized in a way that was almost universal—the trust did not have its own employees but instead "the management of the Trust and its financing are performed by another organization, which might be called the management company or the fiscal agent, or a combination of both." The advantage of such external management was that there could be "a number of Trusts grouped together under control of one fiscal agent. This has the tendency to reduce the financing cost of each trust in the group as well as the management cost."[2]

British financial writers welcomed the investment trust principle of providing small investors with the same diversification and professional management available to the wealthy investor. However, there were a number of abuses involving many investment trusts, including lack of disclosure to investors, insufficient portfolio diversification, excessive leverage by borrowing through the issuance of senior securities, funds engaging in underwritings and other noninvestment activities, and the issuance of cheap "founders' shares" to the funds' promoters. There was a speculative bubble in the late 1880s as one fund after another came to market. The *Economist* warned that speculative periods are often followed by depressions and falling prices. There was a major crash in 1890, and to regain investor confidence, British investment funds adopted more conservative policies.[3]

U.S. Experience in the 1920s

Investment companies first became popular in the United States during the bull market of the 1920s. All of these funds, like their British antecedents, were closed-end funds whose shares traded at premiums or discounts from the value of their portfolios. The first mutual funds, funds that issue redeemable shares, began in Boston in 1924. During the late 1920s, closed-end funds were far more popular than mutual funds. But the 1929 crash proved to be near-disastrous for closed-end funds, spurred public acceptance of mutual funds, and led to calls for government regulation of all types of investment companies.

Closed-End Funds and Their Problems

Many closed-end funds of the 1920s had characteristics that later proved important.

First, their shares often traded at premiums above the actual values of their portfolios. As John Kenneth Galbraith explained: "The only property of the investment trust was the common and preferred stocks and debentures, mortgages, bonds, and cash that it owned.... Yet, had these securities all been sold on the market, the proceeds would invariably have been less, and often much less, than the current value of the outstanding securities of the investment company."[4] By mid-1929, "the average investment trust was selling for 47 percent above the liquidating value of its portfolio."[5]

Second, closed-end funds engaged in leveraging by borrowing. Galbraith explained, "Leverage was achieved by issuing bonds, preferred stock, as well as common stock to purchase, more or less exclusively, a portfolio of common stocks. When the common stock so purchased rose in value...the value of the bonds and preferred stock of the trust was largely unaffected....Most or all of the gain from rising portfolio values was concentrated on the common stock of the investment trust which, as a result, rose marvelously."[6] Some closed-end funds took leverage several steps further through pyramiding, whereby a leveraged fund invested in another leveraged fund that invested in another leveraged fund, and so on. In addition, many investors borrowed money from banks to purchase fund shares. A historian of the 1929 crash has written, "Since the trust also purchased securities on margin, the speculator was, in effect, piling margin on margin on margin on margin; his true equity was extremely small; the slightest rise in stock prices would be magnified many times over."[7]

Third, many closed-end funds were organized and sold by securities firms. The SEC later reported, "In particular, houses of issue, brokers, and security dealers sponsored and undertook the distribution of the securities of investment company after investment company, these types of sponsorship accounting, on the basis of assets, for over 60% of management investment companies in 1929."[8] Many observers warned that securities firms might be tempted to dump slow-moving or questionable securities held in their inventories or that they were underwriting into their funds.[9]

The First Mutual Funds and Their Advantages

In 1924, a new type of investment company, known as an open-end fund or mutual fund, was introduced. Open-end funds, in contrast to closed-end funds, were prepared to buy back (redeem) their shares at a shareholder's request at a price based on the current value of the fund's portfolio (current net asset value, NAV) and continuously offered new shares based on that price. While the first three mutual funds started in Boston and were associated with old Boston families, Edward G. Leffler, who first came up with the distinguishing characteristic of these funds (daily redeemability and continous offering of new shares at current NAV) was a salesman of Swedish descent from Wisconsin. He was instrumental in starting two of the original three Boston funds and later spearheaded the sales effort for the third.[10]

On March 21, 1924, Leffler organized Massachusetts Investors Trust (MIT), the first mutual fund. MIT was managed by its own trustees, issued only common stock, and continuously offered new shares to investors. A redemption feature was added in September.

On July 29, 1924, apparently unaware of the creation of MIT, Paul C. Cabot and two associates formed State Street Investment Corporation. The fund was managed by its own officers and issued only common stock. Initially the fund was not offered to the public. In 1927 the fund began continuously offering new shares to investors and added a redemption feature.

On November 23, 1925, Leffler and a group of Bostonians (in the form of Parker, Putnam, & Nightingale) organized a fund, Incorporated Investors, and Parker, Putnam, & Nightingale contracted to manage the fund. The fund issued only common stock and continuously offered new shares to investors. A redemption feature was added in 1928.

Thus in a relatively short period of time, the three Boston funds had all of the major characteristics of today's mutual funds.

- All three issued only redeemable securities—that is, an investor could tender shares to the fund at any time and receive proceeds based on the fund's current net asset value. Therefore, shares of the three funds, unlike shares of closed-end funds, did not trade at premiums or discounts.

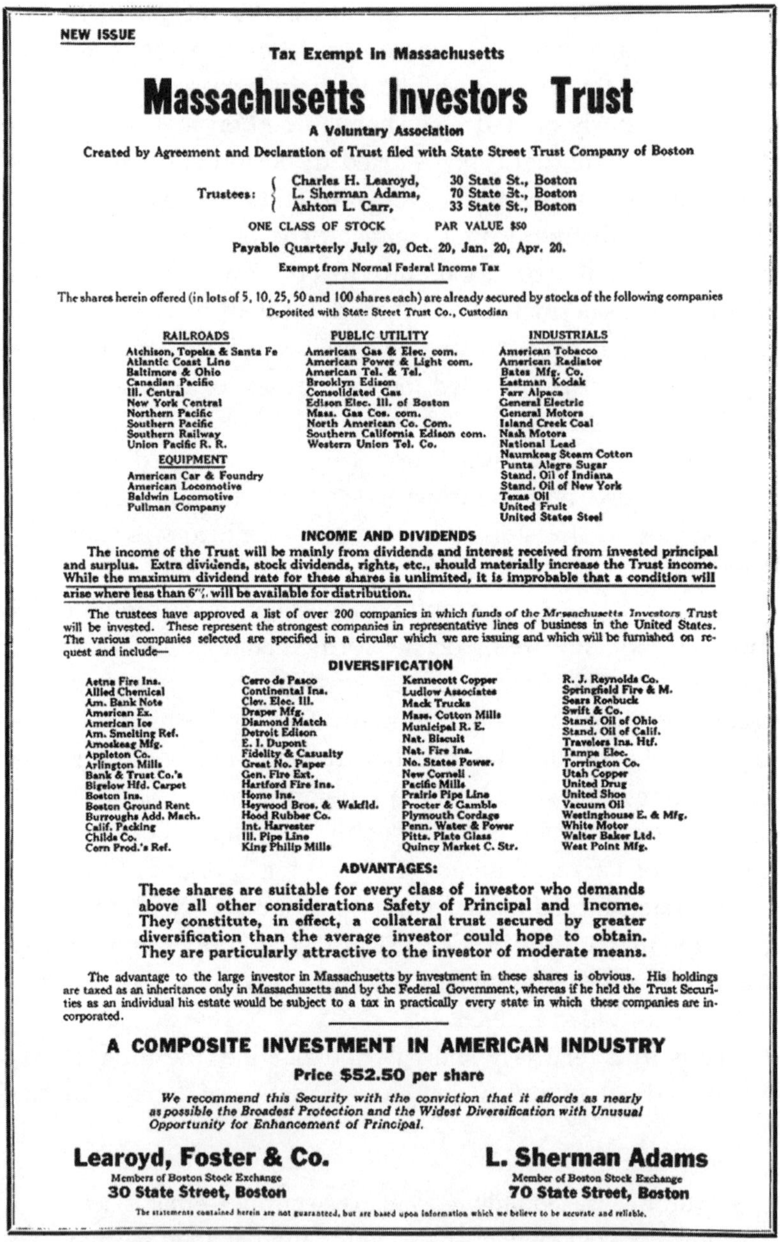

NEW ISSUE

Tax Exempt in Massachusetts

Massachusetts Investors Trust

A Voluntary Association

Created by Agreement and Declaration of Trust filed with State Street Trust Company of Boston

Trustees:		
	Charles H. Learoyd,	30 State St., Boston
	L. Sherman Adams,	70 State St., Boston
	Ashton L. Carr,	33 State St., Boston

ONE CLASS OF STOCK PAR VALUE $50

Payable Quarterly July 20, Oct. 20, Jan. 20, Apr. 20.

Exempt from Normal Federal Income Tax

The shares herein offered (in lots of 5, 10, 25, 50 and 100 shares each) are already secured by stocks of the following companies

Deposited with State Street Trust Co., Custodian

RAILROADS	PUBLIC UTILITY	INDUSTRIALS
Atchison, Topeka & Santa Fe	American Gas & Elec. com.	American Tobacco
Atlantic Coast Line	American Power & Light com.	American Radiator
Baltimore & Ohio	American Tel. & Tel.	Bates Mfg. Co.
Canadian Pacific	Brooklyn Edison	Eastman Kodak
Ill. Central	Consolidated Gas	Farr Alpaca
New York Central	Edison Elec. Ill. of Boston	General Electric
Northern Pacific	Mass. Gas Cos. com.	General Motors
Southern Pacific	North American Co. Com.	Island Creek Coal
Southern Railway	Southern California Edison com.	Nash Motors
Union Pacific R. R.	Western Union Tel. Co.	National Lead
EQUIPMENT		Naumkeag Steam Cotton
American Car & Foundry		Punta Alegre Sugar
American Locomotive		Stand. Oil of Indiana
Baldwin Locomotive		Stand. Oil of New York
Pullman Company		Texas Oil
		United Fruit
		United States Steel

INCOME AND DIVIDENDS

The income of the Trust will be mainly from dividends and interest received from invested principal and surplus. Extra dividends, stock dividends, rights, etc., should materially increase the Trust income. While the maximum dividend rate for these shares is unlimited, it is improbable that a condition will arise where less than 6% will be available for distribution.

The trustees have approved a list of over 200 companies in which funds of the Massachusetts Investors Trust will be invested. These represent the strongest companies in representative lines of business in the United States. The various companies selected are specified in a circular which we are issuing and which will be furnished on request and include—

DIVERSIFICATION

Aetna Fire Ins.	Cerro de Pasco	Kennecott Copper	R. J. Reynolds Co.
Allied Chemical	Continental Ins.	Ludlow Associates	Springfield Fire & M.
Am. Bank Note	Clev. Elec. Ill.	Mack Trucks	Sears Roebuck
American Ex.	Draper Mfg.	Mass. Cotton Mills	Swift & Co.
American Ice	Diamond Match	Municipal R. E.	Stand. Oil of Ohio
Am. Smelting Ref.	Detroit Edison	Nat. Biscuit	Stand. Oil of Calif.
Amoskeag Mfg.	E. I. Dupont	Nat. Fire Ins.	Travelers Ins. Htf.
Appleton Co.	Fidelity & Casualty	No. States Power.	Tampa Elec.
Arlington Mills	Great No. Paper	New Cornell.	Torrington Co.
Bank & Trust Co.'s	Gen. Fire Ext.	Pacific Mills	Utah Copper
Bigelow Hfd. Carpet	Hartford Fire Ins.	Prairie Pipe Line	United Drug
Boston Ins.	Home Ins.	Procter & Gamble	United Shoe
Boston Ground Rent	Heywood Bros. & Wakfld.	Plymouth Cordage	Vacuum Oil
Burroughs Add. Mach.	Hood Rubber Co.	Penn. Water & Power	Westinghouse E. & Mfg.
Calif. Packing	Int. Harvester	Pitts. Plate Glass	White Motor
Childs Co.	Ill. Pipe Line	Quincy Market C. Str.	Walter Baker Ltd.
Corn Prod.'s Ref.	King Philip Mills		West Point Mfg.

ADVANTAGES:

These shares are suitable for every class of investor who demands above all other considerations Safety of Principal and Income. They constitute, in effect, a collateral trust secured by greater diversification than the average investor could hope to obtain. They are particularly attractive to the investor of moderate means.

The advantage to the large investor in Massachusetts by investment in these shares is obvious. His holdings are taxed as an inheritance only in Massachusetts and by the Federal Government, whereas if he held the Trust Securities as an individual his estate would be subject to a tax in practically every state in which these companies are incorporated.

A COMPOSITE INVESTMENT IN AMERICAN INDUSTRY

Price $52.50 per share

We recommend this Security with the conviction that it affords as nearly as possible the Broadest Protection and the Widest Diversification with Unusual Opportunity for Enhancement of Principal.

Learoyd, Foster & Co.
Members of Boston Stock Exchange
30 State Street, Boston

L. Sherman Adams
Member of Boston Stock Exchange
70 State Street, Boston

The statements contained herein are not guaranteed, but are based upon information which we believe to be accurate and reliable.

Figure 1.1. Massachusetts Investors Trust 1924 offering circular.

- To offset redemptions and increase assets, all three funds continuously offered new shares to investors. In contrast, most closed-end funds only issued shares at the time of their creation.

- All three funds issued only common stock. Therefore the funds, unlike closed-end funds, did not use leverage through the issuance of senior securities. (State Street did purchase portfolio securities on margin.)[11]

- Like closed-end funds but unlike fixed trusts, all three had managed portfolios.

- Incorporated Investors was managed by Parker, Putnam & Nightingale, the firm that had created the fund. Although State Street initially was managed by its own officers, it soon changed to management by an outside firm to better allocate expenses and fees among the fund and other clients.[12] MIT made the change to external management years later.

Thus, mutual funds retained the core advantages of closed-end funds—portfolio diversification and professional management—but avoided the defects of shares trading at premiums or

Figure 1.2. A typical mutual fund complex. Virtually all funds do not have employees. Instead, their operations are conducted by affiliated organizations and independent contractors. Courtesy of the Investment Company Institute.

discounts and leverage through the issuance of senior securities. The basic mutual fund characteristics of daily redemptions and sales at current NAV and little if any leverage were responsible for much of mutual funds' future success, but no one foresaw this at the time. In May 1929, Paul Cabot authored an article in the *Atlantic Monthly* in which he sharply criticized three characteristics of closed-end funds—shares trading at premiums, excessive use of leverage through the issuance of senior securities, and sponsors dumping securities into their funds—but he did not go on to discuss mutual funds nor predict their future. In 1930 a leading financial journalist, John T. Flynn, excoriated closed-end funds in his book *Investment Trusts Gone Wrong!* Although Flynn praised MIT and State Street, there is no indication that he realized that they were so qualitatively different than closed-end funds that they represented the start of a new industry.[13]

Following the creation of the first three mutual funds, others were formed in Boston in the late 1920s, including Scudder Stevens & Clark's Investment Counsel Trust; Shaw, Loomis, and Sayles Mutual Fund; and Century Shares. Mutual funds were formed in other cities as well—such as Wellington Fund in Philadelphia.

There was a fierce rivalry between mutual funds, generally located in Boston, and closed-end funds, centered in New York. Merrill Griswold, the head of MIT, took great delight in praising mutual funds at the expense of closed-end funds. Cabot, head of State Street, contrasted "the reputation of the old Boston conservative trustee" versus "the reputation of the slick Wall Street fellows who take the shirt off your back." The Boston newspapers joined in the fray, "intensifying an inter-city and intra-industry rivalry."[14]

The Late 1920s: The Boom in Closed-End Funds

During the bull market of the late 1920s, there was a boom in the investment company business. From 1927 through 1929, shareholders increased more than ninefold, from 55,000 to 525,000; the number of funds grew from 75 to 181; and assets quadrupled from $600 million to over $2.7 billion. Annual sales soared from $188 million in 1927 to over $1.6 billion in 1929. But the boom was largely a closed-end fund phenomenon. At year end 1929, there were only 19 mutual funds versus 162 closed-end funds. Mutual funds accounted for just $89 million of the over $1.6 billion in sales in 1929. Although mutual fund assets grew from $47 million in 1927 to $140 million in 1929, they actually declined as a percentage of total mutual fund–closed-end fund assets, decreasing from 8 percent in 1927 to 5 percent in 1929.[15]

Investors preferred closed-end funds to mutual funds because closed-end funds offered the possibility of greater returns due to their use of leverage and the history of their shares trading at premiums. Two English writers noted, "In a prospering economy, with incomes and profits rising, the gearing [leveraging] of the pyramided (a capital structure of senior and junior securities) closed-end trusts produced a more than proportionate rise in their equity income. In a highly speculative era the demand for trust securities raised their prices far above their net asset value."[16]

But there were dangers. First, just as closed-end shares could trade at large premiums when investors were irrationally exuberant, shares could go to deep discounts when investors' moods soured. Second, although leverage benefited common shareholders in good times, there could be reverse leverage in bad times—a steep decline in portfolio values could wipe out the value of a fund's common shares.

Many closed-end funds had other problems. Hugh Bullock, an industry leader, later wrote: "Bonus stock and stock options frequently went to promoters, cost of raising capital was often high, hidden profits were occasionally present, capital structures were unduly complicated, inter-company holdings were apt to be like a Chinese puzzle.... Sponsors would not always use the pool of money under their aegis in the best interest of stockholders; sometimes it would prove a convenient resting place for unmarketable securities or a source of too-frequent stock exchange commissions."[17] Concerns were expressed by a number of parties, including state securities regulators, the Investment Bankers

Association of America, and the New York Stock Exchange. In his *Atlantic Monthly* article, Cabot warned: "I strongly believe that unless we avoid these and other errors and false principles we shall inevitably go through a similar period of disaster and disgrace [as occurred in England]. If such a period should come, the well-run trusts will suffer with the bad as they did in England forty years ago."[18] However, Cabot opposed regulation, preferring to rely on education and publicity.

There were those who called for government regulation. In 1928 the New York State attorney general proposed legislation subjecting investment companies to regulation under the state's banking laws. Investment companies, for the most part, were in favor of the legislation. But it was not enacted because some feared that "to place investment trusts under the superintendent of banks would be to imply official sanction for their activities," whereas others "contended that the powers of the superintendent of banks, under the proposed legislation, did not go far enough."[19] Some thought was given to federal regulation. George V. McLaughlin, a former New York State superintendent of banks, argued "that national legislation is preferable to state legislation, because of the interstate character of [the] investment business." Others contended that federal regulation might be unconstitutional, and that in any event, "the suggestion for Federal action has little likelihood of early acceptance and is of academic interest only."[20]

The entire situation—including the roaring bull market, the public's overwhelming preference for closed-end funds, and the lack of interest in regulation—was about to change.

The 1929 Crash Spurs Mutual Fund Growth

The stock market reached its high in September 1929 and crashed in late October 1929. The Dow Jones Industrial Average finished the year down 28 percent from its 1929 peak. Worse was yet to come. The Great Depression was marked by record unemployment, failures of thousands of banks, and continued declines in stock prices. In 1932 the Dow Jones was down over 80 percent from September 1929.[21]

Mutual fund share prices fell along with the market. From September 1929 to year end 1932, MIT was down 75 percent, State Street 71 percent, and Incorporated Investors 81 percent.[22]

But closed-end fund shares fared far worse. From the height of the market on September 5, 1929 to the 1931 low (October 25), American International stock's price fell from 84 to 6, Goldman Sachs Trading Corp. from 110 to 2.5, and U.S. and Foreign Securities from 64.5 to 1.875.[23]

Closed-end shares fell to a much greater degree than the stock market and mutual fund shares due to the twin effects of reverse leverage and shares moving to deep discounts from their asset values.

As to reverse leverage, the SEC later reported: "Over the period as a whole, the market experience of the common stocks of closed-end leverage investment companies was much worse than that of the common stocks of non-leverage companies. By the end of 1937, the average dollar which had been invested in July 1929 in the index of leverage investment company common stocks was worth 5¢, while the non-leverage dollar was worth 48¢."[24] As to the discount phenomenon, the SEC reported: "The aggregate market values of shares in investment companies following the close of 1929 was approximately 35% less than the actual value of the assets of these companies."[25]

Given the huge losses suffered in closed-end funds, it is not surprising that the phrases "investment trust" and "management" became dirty words to investors. Many sponsors of these funds, particularly securities firms, exited the business. In 1930 and 1931, investors reacted by avoiding any type of managed fund—closed-end fund or mutual fund—and instead purchased shares of fixed trusts, which are investment companies holding predetermined portfolios that generally are not subject to change.[26]

As the economy began to recover in 1932, investors started investing in mutual funds. Two British writers noted:

> With the revival of trade in the early thirties came a revival of interest in management. What many investors appeared to be seeking was a trust form which avoided

gearing [leveraging], had a managed diversified portfolio, and the…[redeemable] feature of the fixed and semi-
fixed…trust. Without gearing, the shares of the trust would
be less volatile and less speciisative [sic] with [a] soundly
managed diversified portfolio, the average investor would
share in results better than he could secure for himself or
in a fixed trust; and the obligation of management to repur-
chase shares should the investor wish to sell ensures ease
of selling at a share price related to the value of the underlying securities. These became the three main features of
open-end trusts and accounted for their popularity.[27]

The three original mutual funds ramped up their sales
efforts (in 1932, Leffler began working for State Street). New
funds were started in Boston (including Fidelity and Eaton &
Howard) and in other cities (including Calvin Bullock and Lord,
Abbett in New York, Selected American Shares in Chicago, and
Keystone in Philadelphia). From year end 1929 through 1940,
mutual fund assets increased from $140 million to $450 million,
whereas closed-end fund assets fell from $2.6 billion to $784
million. Thus, mutual funds moved from constituting 5 percent
of total managed investment company assets in 1929 to 36 percent in 1940.[28]

The years of the Great Depression had been a trial by fire
for all types of financial institutions. Mutual funds not only
survived but gained ground.

Calls for Regulation

Investors' heavy losses resulted in calls to impose governmental controls on investment companies. Some, like John T. Flynn,
advocated subjecting investment companies to stringent regulation. Initially, Flynn called for state regulation, but subsequently
he urged federal legislation providing that "no corporation
should be permitted to own stock in any other corporation,"
although "Investment trusts might well be permitted to buy and
own the stocks of other corporations subject to certain drastic

limitations, such as, for instance, a rule against investing more than one per cent of the trust's funds in any one corporation or owning more than one-half of one per cent of the stock of any one corporation."[29] Some, like Felix I. Shaffner, an instructor of economics at Harvard University, and Frank A. Vanderlip, former head of First National City Bank (now Citibank), wanted to go further and, because of the problem of dumping, flatly prohibit securities firms from managing investment companies. Finally, others, like Barnie Winkelman, a Philadelphia attorney, wanted to go further still and outlaw all investment companies:

> After careful consideration, the writer finds little justi-fication for investment trusts of any kind....The plea of diversification is without merit. An investor with only a few hundred dollars can diversify if he desires by buying single shares of several corporations. Even a purchase in a single large company means diversification, because practi-cally every large railroad, utility, or industrial company has substantial investments in other corporations. The entire plan of the investment trust is a snare for men of small means. The basis of management fees is without foun-dation as there is little work of management. Legislation against holding companies should properly include every set-up which embraces the investment trust idea.[30]

Leaders of the investment company industry could see that a major battle over government regulation of the industry was on the horizon. But investors' anger was not limited to investment companies. The 1929 crash and the onset of the Great Depression ignited public demand for government regulation of all aspects of the securities markets.

Creation of the SEC: An Agency Devoted Exclusively to Securities Regulation

The mutual fund industry and its shareholders have been for-tunate in having funds regulated by the SEC, a federal agency whose sole responsibility is administration of the federal securities laws in the interest of investors. The SEC has long been regarded as perhaps the most effective agency of government. Former SEC Chairman and Supreme Court Justice William O. Douglas recalled, "I told FDR over and over again that every agency he created should be abolished in ten years [because] eventually they are transformed into spokesmen for the interest groups....The SEC was not like this in the early days." He also said, "Forty years after the SEC was established it still had the best professional staff of any agency in Washington."[31]

A principal reason for the this success is that the SEC is a relatively small organization whose sole responsibility is the administration of the federal securities laws. Former SEC Chairman James Landis observed: "By creating a new Commission...it was possible to have individuals in charge whose single concern was the problem of securities regulation. They were thus not required to dissipate their energies over a wide periphery by being responsible for the determination of problems of equal public importance but which bore no discernible relationship to securities regulation."[32] However, the creation of an agency devoted exclusively to securities regulation was not preordained. In fact, President Franklin Roosevelt and his fellow New Deal supporters opposed the creation of the SEC, and instead wanted the securities laws to be administered by the Federal Trade Commission, an agency with broad responsibilities in many other areas.

Origins of Federal Securities Regulation

Calls for federal regulation of securities date back at least to the Pujo Report issued by a subcommittee of the House Banking Committee in 1913. The report urged mandatory disclosure regarding new issues of securities and federal regulation of the New York Stock Exchange. Due to concerns over the authority of the federal government to regulate these areas, the report proposed placing regulatory authority in the Post Office Department because the Constitution gives the federal government exclusive authority over use of the mail.[33] Legislation to implement these recommendations was introduced in the House of Representatives. But the Wilson Administration did not endorse the bill, and it was not voted on. Thus, proposals for federal regulation of new offerings of securities and the New York Stock Exchange, like many other Progressive era ideas, were put away into the back of the national medicine cabinet and forgotten.[34]

The 1929 stock market crash and the onset of the Great Depression revived interest in these ideas. Reformers reached into the medicine cabinet and took out the prescriptions. In 1932 A. Newton Plummer, editor of *Finance*, urged the establishment of a national commission to regulate the sale of new securities. During his 1932 presidential campaign, Franklin Roosevelt called for a series of financial reforms, including truth telling in the sale of securities and "the use of Federal authority in the regulation of...exchanges." However, he did not specify which agency of government was to administer these programs. After the 1932 election, Roosevelt and his advisers considered a number of different approaches.[35]

Samuel Untermyer, who had been counsel to the Pujo Committee twenty years earlier, drafted a bill that addressed both securities disclosure and exchange regulation. But the proposed bill had a major defect. Raymond Moley, a leading policy adviser to FDR, wrote, "This bill would have placed the regulatory machinery in the Post Office Department, an obvious attempt to guarantee the measure's constitutionality. I had told Untermyer—and Roosevelt agreed—that it would be unwise to burden what was essentially a service organization with such a complex system of regulation."[36]

The Securities Act of 1933

A second bill was prepared by Huston Thompson, a former chairman of the Federal Trade Commission (FTC). Thompson's bill dealt solely with the sale of securities, did not address regulation of the exchanges, and placed regulatory authority in the FTC. The Senate passed a revised version of the Thompson bill. However, hearings before the House Commerce Committee convinced committee chairman Sam Rayburn and the White House that the Thompson bill was overly severe, for example, granting the FTC authority to revoke a security's registration if it found the business was "not based on sound principles." A third bill was prepared by James Landis, a professor at Harvard Law School, and Benjamin Cohen, general solicitor of the Public Works Administration. Like the Thompson bill, the Landis-Cohen bill dealt solely with the sale of securities and utilized the FTC as the regulator. The Landis-Cohen bill, with revisions, was passed by the House.

A Senate-House Conference Committee reconciled the two bills, and on May 27, 1933, President Roosevelt signed into law the first federal securities law, the Securities Act of 1933. The 1933 act differed from the original Thompson and Landis-Cohen bills in a number of substantive areas. There had been no objections to both bills' designation of the FTC as the regulatory body, and the 1933 act placed the FTC in that role.

The Securities Exchange Act of 1934

The administration turned to the second area of securities regulation that Roosevelt had advocated during his 1932 presidential campaign—regulation of the stock exchanges. Two very different approaches were considered. First, the president appointed a committee chaired by Assistant Secretary of Commerce John Dickinson. The committee's report called for licensing of the exchanges by a new federal regulatory authority that would also take over administration of the Securities Act of 1933 from the FTC. One of the seven members of the authority would be a representative of the exchanges. The report stated that "self-regulation should be emphasized...and...the governing boards of the exchanges should, in the first instance, formulate...fair rules, subject to the veto of the Federal Regulatory Authority."[37] A very different approach was taken in legislation drafted by a group of New Dealers including I. N. P. Stokes of the FTC,

Telford Taylor, and Benjamin Cohen. Their draft did not call for the creation of a new federal authority that would only have the power to veto rules adopted by the exchanges, but instead would have granted the FTC direct regulatory authority over the exchanges in such areas as price manipulation, segregation of broker and dealer functions, and the power to set margin requirements higher than those specified in the bill.

The bill was introduced in both houses of Congress and was greeted with a barrage of criticism from the New York Stock Exchange, regional exchanges, brokerage firms and their employees, corporate issuers, and others. The New York Stock Exchange opposed the use of the FTC as the regulatory body and testified in favor of the creation of a new commission. The Federal Reserve Board objected to granting the FTC authority over margin.

The wave of criticism drove the New Dealers back to the drawing board. They came up with modifications that softened a number of provisions dealing with regulation of the exchanges. In addition, the revised bill granted authority over margin to the Federal Reserve Board. It retained the FTC as the regulator of exchange practices. The modifications failed to mollify the stock exchanges, who continued to oppose both substantive provisions and the designation of the FTC as the regulatory body. The Senate and House committees struggled to reach consensus.

Senator Carter Glass, a Democrat from Virginia, was one of the most respected members of Congress on financial matters. Glass had been the principal congressional author of the 1913 legislation that created the Federal Reserve System (Fed) and often was called the father of that system. He saw himself as a protector of the Fed, and in particular he wanted to keep it free from any involvement with the stock market. Although personally friendly with the president, he opposed much of the New Deal, and, like the exchanges, he was distrustful of the reformers at the FTC. Glass offered a proposal in the Senate Banking Committee to create a new agency, a three-person Securities Exchange Commission, to replace the authority proposed in the bill for the Fed and the FTC. Glass's proposal was an attempt to kill two birds with one stone: first, the Fed, by not having authority over margin, would be kept free from entanglement with the stock market; second, the reformist regulators at the FTC would be replaced by an agency of technical specialists in the securities markets. The Senate Banking Committee, over the objection of its chairman, Senator Fletcher, adopted Glass's proposal by a ten to eight vote, and the Senate passed a stock exchange bill providing for the creation of the SEC.

President Roosevelt opposed the creation of the SEC. Joel Seligman, the leading historian of the SEC, has written:

> Roosevelt and Fletcher...made a final attempt to restore the FTC as the administrative agency....Ignoring long-standing custom, Fletcher chose not to name senior Banking Committee members Glass and Robert Wagner to the Conference Committee, since both favored the new Securities Exchange Commission....Nearly simultaneously, Roosevelt informed a press conference that he "personally" preferred...FTC enforcement....
>
> The move to reinstate the FTC misfired badly.... Roosevelt, embarrassed by accusations that he had attempted to influence the Conference Committee and had not originally objected to Glass's proposal for a new com-mission, awkwardly retreated, informing the press that it was "not a frightfully important thing, one way or the other" which agency enforced the stock exchange bill.[38]

In fact, "FDR saw credit [rather than the particular regulatory agency] as the key to reform. 'Speculative trading must be very greatly curtailed,' he told Henry Morgenthau, Jr., '[and] that means...the requirement of very large margins and sufficient flexibility in some agency of government to increase margin requirements if the minimum amount provided in the bill... does not ... greatly curtail speculative trading....'"[39]

The Conference Committee reconciled the bills passed by the Senate and House, and on June 6, 1934, President Roosevelt signed into law the Securities Exchange Act of 1934.

The 1934 act created a new federal agency, the Securities and Exchange Commission, to administer the Securities Act of 1933 as well as the 1934 act. The 1934 act gave the Federal Reserve Board the authority to establish margin requirements. The 1934 act gave the SEC some (but not all) of the direct federal control over the exchanges that the New Dealers sought. The final results reflected a number of ironies.

- Senator Glass proposed creation of a new commission so that it, rather than the Fed, would have authority over margin. But the 1934 act lodged margin authority in the Fed.
- The exchanges sought creation of a new commission because they feared regulation by FTC officials. But Roosevelt proceeded to appoint leading FTC officials as three of the SEC's first five commissioners.
- The exchanges sought creation of a new commission in the hopes that they could influence its decisions. But the SEC proved to be among the most independent of agencies.
- Although President Roosevelt and his fellow New Dealers are often credited with the creation of the SEC, credit actually belongs to Senator Glass, a leading opponent of the New Deal.[40]

Importance of the 1933 and 1934 Acts to Mutual Funds

The 1933 act had relatively little impact on mutual funds. It mandated disclosure regarding new issues of securities by means of prospectuses. Because mutual funds continuously offered new shares to investors, the 1933 act required funds to continuously provide disclosure to investors through the delivery of current prospectuses. However, mutual funds reported that the law had little impact on them because they had always voluntarily provided full disclosure.[41] The 1934 act did not regulate mutual funds. Instead, it protected them and other investors by regulating the markets in which they invested.

However, the 1934 act proved to be vitally important to the mutual fund industry by creating an independent agency whose sole responsibility is the administration of the federal securities laws in the interest of investors. SEC regulation has been critical to public confidence in the securities markets in general and the mutual fund industry in particular. In 1935, in the Public Utility Holding Company Act, Congress directed the SEC to study the investment company industry and submit recommendations to Congress.

The Revenue Act of 1936: The Most Important Event in Mutual Fund History

Although investment companies in the mid-1930s faced a host of problems, including the likelihood that the SEC would recommend stringent federal regulation, the continuing Depression, and angry investors, one bright spot was the tax area. The federal income tax law provided a 100 percent exclusion for dividends received by one corporation from another corporation. Therefore, investment companies did not pay any tax on dividends they received from corporations in which they invested. Investment companies passed these corporate dividends on to their shareholders, who paid tax as they would on any dividends they received.

In June 1935, President Roosevelt, as part of his efforts to discourage holding companies, proposed taxing intercorporate dividends. In his message, the president stated that there might be an exemption for investment companies that submitted to "public regulation" and that offered "small investors...the benefit of diversification."[42]

Congress proceeded to reduce the intercorporate dividend exclusion from 100 percent to 90 percent, but did not, as Roosevelt had mentioned, provide an exemption for investment companies. Therefore investment companies became subject to tax on a portion of the dividends they received, and fund shareholders bore a tax burden that was not imposed on them if they held securities directly. Investment companies feared that they would be taxed out of existence.

In March 1936, President Roosevelt proposed an entirely new tax scheme aimed at taxing undistributed corporate profits: corporate tax rates would be increased, but there would be a full deduction for dividends paid to shareholders. Corporate America and the financial community rose in vehement opposition to the proposal for fear it would pressure corporations to distribute all of their earnings.

Mutual funds reacted quite differently. In the words of Merrill Griswold, head of MIT, mutual fund leaders saw the president's proposal as a "godsend" that could solve their tax problem.[43] Griswold developed a theory under which an investment company is regarded as a mere conduit between fund shareholders and the securities in which the fund invests. Under this theory, the fund is ignored for tax purposes and shareholders are treated as though they own the securities directly. Griswold, Paul Cabot of State Street Investment Trust, and Tudor Gardiner of Incorporated Investors met with Senator David Walsh, a Democrat from Massachusetts and a member of the Senate Finance Committee, to discuss a statutory exemption for mutual funds based on the conduit theory. They then met in Washington with other members of Congress and officials in the Bureau of Internal Revenue and the Treasury Department.[44]

On June 3, the group saw President Roosevelt. Just as they entered the Oval Office, the president received an urgent phone call. When the ten-minute call ended, an aide entered the room to say the meeting was over because the president's next visitor had arrived. Cabot could not contain himself and blurted out, "Mr. President, this is a damned outrage. It is true we were promised only ten minutes, but you wasted the entire ten minutes talking to that man on the telephone." The president laughed and said, "All right, boys, you can have another ten minutes." Cabot later recalled: "I gave him my speech 'A.' He pulled just one sheet out of his drawer, and it had the whole summarized tax bill that was up for consideration. I told him what we wanted and why. And he understood what it was all about better than anybody—mind you I was prejudiced against the guy—he understood it better and quicker and asked more intelligent questions about it than anybody I had talked to in Washington and I was amazed."[45]

The result of these efforts was the Revenue Act of 1936, which provided that if a mutual fund met a number of tests, it would be exempt from tax, and fund shareholders would be taxed on distributions they receive, thus putting fund shareholders on a par with direct investors in securities.

A number of the tests were of the type one would expect to find in a tax law. The act sought to ensure that a mutual fund would be an investment company, rather than an operating company, by mandating that it derive at least 95 percent of its income from dividends, interest, and gains on the sale of securities. To guarantee that fund shareholders would pay tax, the law required that the fund distribute at least 90 percent of its income to shareholders as taxable dividends during the current year.

The 1936 act also contained tests that reflected New Deal regulatory concerns. The *Wall Street Journal* reported that "the law, in its application to investment companies, seems to show what the New Deal wants in such corporations."[46]

First, President Roosevelt's 1935 message on intercorporate dividends indicated that the New Deal wanted to provide small investors with the ability to diversify. Therefore the 1936 act required that not more than 5 percent of a fund's assets could be invested in any one corporation.

Second, as Griswold later wrote, the New Deal wanted to "protect investors against speculative activities."[47] Therefore the 1936 act provided that not more than 30 percent of a fund's gross income could be derived from gains from the sale of securities held for less than three months.

Finally, Griswold stated that the New Deal "wished to prevent the possibility of an investment company acquiring control of any company in which it invested."[48] Therefore the 1936 act provided that a fund could not own more than 10 percent of the stock of any corporation.

Enactment of the Revenue Act of 1936 was the most important event in mutual fund history for the following reasons.

- First, the act granted conduit tax treatment to mutual funds, thus putting fund shareholders on a par with direct investors in securities. Without such treatment, it is doubtful if mutual funds would have continued to exist, much less flourish.

- Second, the Revenue Act was the first time that mutual funds were subjected to federal regulation, albeit in the form of a tax bill, to protect investors and further other public policy concerns. Most important, the Revenue Act required mutual fund portfolios to be diversified.

- Third, as will be explained in the next chapter, by providing tax relief only to mutual funds and not closed-end funds, the Revenue Act of 1936 was instrumental in leading to enactment of the Investment Company Act of 1940, the statute that governs the structure and day-to-day operation of mutual funds and other investment companies.[49]

2

Completing the Foundation:
The Investment Company Act

It would have made things easier if it had been written in English.

—Ray Garrett Jr., former SEC chairman

The Investment Company Act of 1940 generally is regarded as a model regulatory statute, one that strikes a careful balance between the need to impose uniform standards of fiduciary behavior and the desire to encourage experimentation, change, and innovation. The 1940 act was enacted due to a highly unique set of circumstances, including closed-end funds' desperate need to be regulated to obtain tax relief, the willingness of both the Securities and Exchange Commission (SEC) and the industry to accept reasonable compromise, and a good deal of luck.

While the mutual fund tax issue was being resolved, the SEC continued work on its study of investment companies mandated by the Public Utility Holding Company Act of 1935. On March 14, 1940, a bill of over 100 pages drafted by the SEC was introduced in both houses of Congress.

From the Doghouse Into the Pound?

Figure 2.1. *Barron's*, March 18, 1940. Courtesy of Dow Jones & Company.

The press was unanimous in predicting that the bill was unlikely to be enacted into law, mainly due to the expectation of strong industry opposition. The headline in the March 18 edition of *Barron's* declared, "Investment Trust Law Unlikely This Year," and the story stated, "the bill's best chance of enactment lay in the possibility that the SEC and the investment trusts could agree on a bill which would provoke no controversy. The bill…made this possibility a very slim one." Similarly, the *New York Times* of March 24 reported that "the chances of passage of the bill at this session are said to be slight."[1] Predictions grew even more pessimistic after the Senate Banking Committee concluded hearings. On April 27, the *Wall Street Journal's* story began, "Enactment of legislation for federal regulation of investment trusts is no longer considered as even a fair prospect this session."[2] But the press was wrong. Within a few months, the Investment Company Act, with revisions from the SEC's original bill, was enacted into law with strong industry support. The 1940 act has been a cornerstone of the mutual fund industry.

Million of words can and have been written about the 1940 act. I address three questions here. First, why, despite unanimous predictions to the contrary, did the investment company industry support the 1940 act? Second, what were the most important differences between the SEC's original bill and the final act? Third, what were the most important provisions of the act?

Why Did the Industry Support the 1940 Act?

It appears that in one respect the press was correct—had the industry opposed congressional action, it is likely that legislation would not have been enacted. By 1940, the New Deal had run out of steam, the SEC was under attack, and the nation was focused on the war in Europe and American defense preparedness. Moreover, even supporters of legislation, such as the *New York Times,* believed that the SEC's bill had gone too far.[3] Robert Taft, a leading Republican Senator, advised the industry to hang tough and not negotiate with the bill's sponsors: "If you think you can sit down with those Democratic bastards and get anywhere, well your [sic] nuts."[4]

The investment company industry surprised Senator Taft, the press, and other observers and worked aggressively for the enactment of legislation. Why did an industry that apparently could have defeated legislation subjecting its members to stringent regulation instead seek its enactment?

The explanation is fairly clear in the case of the smaller segment of the industry, mutual funds. Mutual fund leaders had long been concerned about abuses. Paul Cabot wrote a landmark article in the *Atlantic Monthly* before the 1929 crash on problems in the investment company industry. Mutual funds viewed federal regulation as a way to address abuse and restore public confidence. They were already subject to a degree of federal regulation under the Revenue Act of 1936. The industry became even more comfortable with legislation when the SEC's bill was revised to remove or modify provisions they found most objectionable. Massachusetts Investors Trust stated that the final 1940 act "called for very few changes in the business methods of our Company, and these changes were relatively unimportant." *Time* magazine reported, "So similar were M.I.T.'s bylaws to the Investment Company Act of 1940, which laid the ground rules for the funds, that M.I.T. had to change only a few commas."[5] In short, mutual fund companies had much to gain and little to lose by enactment of the revised bill into law.

The situation of closed-end funds was more complex. On one hand, closed-end funds, like mutual funds, wanted to end abuse and saw federal regulation as a way to restore public confidence. On the other hand, the proposed legislation focused heavily on closed-end funds because that was where most abuses had occurred. When the SEC presented its bill to Congress, an estimated 80 percent of the its testimony was devoted to closed-end funds. The SEC's bill would have outlawed both closed-end funds' use of leverage and securities firms' ability to sell securities to their funds. It is by no means clear why closed-end funds, with these factors in mind, should have concluded that it was in their best interest to support legislation.

There was an additional factor that helped lead closed-end funds to back legislation—the need to become subject to public regulation to obtain favorable tax treatment. Because the Revenue Act of 1936 granted special tax treatment solely to mutual funds, closed-end funds found themselves at a competitive disadvantage versus not only direct investors in securities but also their long-standing rivals, mutual funds. The tax discrepancy between closed-end funds and mutual funds was well known and widely publicized. A humorous 1940 book on the stock market noted, "The rate of tax on investment-trust profits is now a ripe and juicy 18 per cent," with a note explaining, "Not true of 'open-end' trusts." Mutual funds, which had amounted to only 5 percent of managed investment company assets in 1929, were gaining an increasing market share, growing to 25 percent in 1936 and 36 percent in 1940.[6] Closed-end funds were convinced that a major factor contributing to this trend was the disparity in tax treatment. Closed-end funds concluded it was essential that they, too, obtain conduit tax treatment. A closed-end fund witness at the Senate hearings declared, "The problem of future tax treatment for closed-end investment trusts is most important."[7]

Closed-end funds realized that to obtain tax parity with mutual funds, they would have to become subject to "public regulation", and they saw the 1940 act as a vehicle to accomplish this result. Closed-end fund companies adopted a two-step strategy—first, public regulation via enactment of the 1940 Act, and then tax relief. A witness from a closed-end fund company at the Senate hearings stated, "We urge that the basis for this taxation be laid in this bill." Similarly a witness told the House committee, "We are very hopeful that with the passage of this bill and with these companies placed under regulation the Treasury will see fit to go into this problem."[8]

Closed-end fund companies undertook a series of steps to implement their strategy. First, they put aside their long-standing rivalry with mutual funds, and the two groups formed a joint task force to work on the legislation. Second, closed-end funds obtained SEC support for their two-step approach. This was not difficult. The SEC knew that closed-end funds were desperate to obtain tax relief and used that desperation to obtain closed-end funds' support for the Investment Company Act. In fact, the SEC refused to support legislation that would grant full tax relief for closed-end funds until passage of the Investment Company Act was assured. A 1937 internal SEC memo stated:

> In case that no complete regulatory bill can be passed at the coming session of Congress, we will, by common agreement, have to propose to Congress an interim solution in the form of an extension to the great majority of all bona fide investment companies of the special tax treatment now granted to mutual investment companies. It appears essential to me that in doing so we do not give to these companies all of the benefits which we may be willing to grant them in connection with the passage of the regulatory act. We have to continue holding at least some piece of the bait before them after the Revenue Act of 1938 is passed and until the regulatory bill is on the statute books. Should we omit this elementary precaution we may be certain that, with very few exceptions, none of the representatives of the industry will have the slightest interest in furthering the passage of the bill once they have got what they desire with respect to tax treatment. [9]

Third, closed-end companies urged that the Senate and House committee reports accompanying the legislation spell out the need for extending special tax treatment to their funds.

Now that both mutual funds and closed-end funds supported legislation, the two industries acted in concert to achieve enactment. First, witnesses for both testified in strong support of reform legislation while stressing specific defects in the SEC's bill. Next, the joint industry task force prepared a detailed outline of suggestions for legislation within the structure of the original bill. The SEC was amenable to change, and it and the task force reached agreement on the framework for a revised bill. The *first page* of the SEC-industry framework stated: "The Commission and the industry unite in the earnest suggestion to the Senate committee that it call attention to the tax problem and to the desirability of providing special tax treatment not merely for certain classes of open-end investment companies as under the present law, but for closed-end investment companies as well."[10]

The SEC–industry framework was used as the basis for a new bill that was reported by the Senate and House committees, with the report of the Senate Committee on Banking and Currency stating:

> Representatives of the Securities and Exchange Commission and of the industry…called…attention…to the serious tax problem affecting investment companies. It appears that the nature of these companies in many respects, constituting a conduit for distribution of income to the smaller investor, is such that they should not be subjected to the same type of taxation as the ordinary business corporation. This has already been recognized in respect of certain classes of open-end companies which receive special tax treatment under existing Federal tax laws. The record before the committee indicates that the tax problem is acute with respect to closed-end companies of the type classified in this bill as "diversified". If this bill is passed, the committee believes

National Committee of Investment Companies

Testimonial Dinner in Honor of

DAVID SCHENKER

**Retiring Director of Investment Company Division
of the
Securities and Exchange Commission**

The Waldorf-Astoria   **July 2, 1941**

Figure 2.2. Invitation to National Committee of Investment Companies dinner in honor of David Schenker.

that the tax problem of these companies should receive prompt consideration.[11]

The new bill was passed unanimously by both houses, and the Investment Company Act was signed into law by President Roosevelt on August 23, 1940. As closed-end funds hoped, the next major tax law, the Revenue Act of 1942, extended conduit tax treatment to closed-end funds.

Senator Sheridan Downey, a Democrat from California and a member of the Senate Banking Committee, called the SEC–industry agreement on the 1940 act a "miracle." Many observers credited the fund industry with great statesmanship for supporting enactment of the Investment Company Act. For example, on July 2, 1941, the industry sponsored a dinner in honor of David Schenker on his retirement from the SEC, and Leslie Gould, a leading financial columnist, wrote, "The trust people got together and worked out with the SEC and Congress…a regulatory law that was acceptable. The trusts are the one section of the financial business that have come out of Washington with their shirt intact." Others have argued that revelations of abuse made legislation all but inevitable. The legislative history makes it clear that the industry's own self-interest , closed-end funds' desperate need for tax relief, rather than industry statesmanship or revelations of abuse, played the critical role in producing this miracle.[12]

What Were the Major Differences between the Original Bill and the Final Act?

At the hearings on the SEC's bill, mutual fund and closed-end fund witnesses expressed support for reform legislation but stressed specific problems in the bill. In response, the joint SEC-industry agreement called for a number of significant changes that were reflected in the final act. Four of the most important changes related to a proposed limitation on the size of funds, a proposed restriction on the number of funds one person could organize, a series of proposed prohibitions regarding affilia-tions, and a provision permitting fund organizations to estab-lish the sales loads charged by broker-dealers.

First, the SEC's bill would have limited the size of any fund to $150 million. I suspect that the SEC's position reflected a generalized concern over what Supreme Court Justice Louis Brandeis called "a curse of bigness." Moreover, there were alle-gations that one cause of the 1929 crash was investment compa-nies dumping securities on the market.[13] In its testimony, the SEC warned, "If you were to have a run on...[a mutual fund]—and it is no different from a run on a bank...you will get a program of liquidation [of portfolio securities] which may result in...an undesirable effect upon the stock market in general...[and a fund] stockholder...may find himself with an illiquid stock and...may not be able to get his asset value."[14]

Mutual fund witnesses testified in strong opposition to any size limitation. Merrill Griswold stressed that there was abso-lutely no basis for the run-on-the-bank analogy:

> There is nothing in the 16-year record of the open-end trusts that gives the slightest reason for the belief that "runs" on them would take place. There were no such runs in 1929 or the early 1930s during the heaviest security liq-uidation that ever occurred in this country. There were no such runs during the violent market decline of 1937. The reason for this is fundamental. The shares of an open-end trust are not a bank deposit. They are an investment. And a difference of opinion always exists as to the attractive-ness of any investment at any given moment. That's why there are always buyers and sellers. That is what makes a market. It is conceivable that all of the depositors of a bank might decide at the same time that it was wise for them to withdraw their funds. But it is inconceivable that all the holders of an open-end trust would simultaneously decide to liquidate their investment. The very market action that would cause some holders to liquidate would cause others to hold or increase their investment.[15]

The final act removed the size limitation. Instead, section 14(b) authorized the SEC to study at its discretion the effects of any further increase in the size of investment companies and make recommendations to Congress.

Although the SEC never again proposed to limit the size of investment companies, the run-on-the-bank concern has reappeared again and again. In 1959 in a cover story on mutual funds, *Time* reported the "charge that, in a falling market, millions of panicky, inexperienced shareholders would redeem their shares, forcing the funds to liquidate huge blocks of stock and collapse the market." In 1960 a life insurance company executive predicted that "a run on mutual funds similar to a bank run could readily develop. In this event, the funds would have little or no choice but to dump their shares in a declining market and further aggravate the decline." In 1994, Henry Kaufman worried that when the stock market broke, millions of new fund shareholders would panic and redeem en masse, causing funds to dump billions of dollars of securities onto the market. Kaufman's proposed solution is discussed in chapter 8.[16] I have no doubt the issue will arise again.

Second, the SEC's bill provided that any person who had organized one fund could not organize another fund for a period of five years. The SEC's official explanation was that this provision was designed to prevent "switching" from one fund to another to generate sales charges: "They organize one investment trust. The security of that investment trust loses its sales appeal. Thereupon they organize another investment trust, and what do they do? Then they start switching from one investment trust to another, and our record indicates... that there were as many as six switches from one to another."[17] However, this explanation made little sense. If switching was the problem, the answer was for the legislation to address switching, not prohibit the creation of a number of funds. Again, I suspect that the SEC's true motivation was a generalized uneasiness over size—in this case, a single person managing a number of investment companies. The industry criticized the proposal as preventing a person from organizing a number of funds with distinct portfolios and investment objectives. One witness testified:

> Is there any reason why a person managing, let us say, an investment company maintaining a highly diversified portfolio should not organize another investment company devoted entirely to securities of one industry such as, for example, aviation or chemicals? Is there any reason why the organizer of an investment company placing its principal emphasis on common stocks should not also manage one whose portfolio is primarily in bonds?[18]

The final act deleted this restriction and section 11 directly addressed the problem of exchange offers.

Third, the SEC's bill sought to prevent numerous types of affiliations. From the time of its enactment, the Investment Company Act has been criticized for being overly complicated and virtually unreadable. A 1941 article in the *Georgetown Law Journal* stated, "The existing big companies have legal departments quite capable of handling the situation; but on careful consideration one wonders if new men would not take one look at the voluminous statute, teeming with hundred-word sentences, and then call the whole thing off."[19] As convoluted and difficult to read as the final act may be, section 10 of the SEC's original bill dealing with affiliations takes the grand prize for complexity. This was due to the fact that the SEC drafted this section to address numerous types of relationships that could give rise to conflicts of interest. Among other matters, this section sought to:

- require that a majority of a fund's directors have no relationship with the fund's adviser and principal underwriter (the company responsible for distribution of the fund's shares);
- prohibit an investment banker or broker from serving on the board of more than one group of funds;
- prohibit a firm from managing more than one group of funds;
- prohibit a bank director or officer from managing a fund;

- require that a fund's adviser and principal underwriter be unaffiliated; and

- prohibit a fund director or officer from serving as a director or officer of any company whose securities are owned by the fund.

Industry witnesses criticized many of these provisions, particularly those requiring a majority of outside directors and prohibiting a fund director or officer from serving as a director or officer of a portfolio company. Cabot was caustic: "The result will be that investment trusts will be forced to elect outside directors—and the bill requires that these shall be in the majority—from among those individuals who have no business affiliations, connections, or property of their own; and the boards will be filled with artists, architects, musicians, doctors, and the like."[20] The final act replaced most of these complex provisions with the simple requirement that at least 40 percent of a fund's directors must be unaffiliated with the fund's adviser, and if the fund has a principal underwriter, a majority of directors must be unaffiliated with the underwriter. (The act also limited board service by regular brokers for the fund, investment bankers, and bankers.)

The mutual fund industry certainly would be very different had major changes not been made to the original bill. It is difficult to see how the industry could have agreed to the SEC's proposed limitations on fund size and number of funds. Fortunately, the SEC never offered convincing rationales for these restrictions, thus making it easy to withdraw them. There was undoubtedly strong evidence to support many of the proposed provisions regarding affiliations. Had these various provisions been broken out into separate sections, many of them possibly would have been enacted into law. By rolling all of these provisions into one incredibly complex section, the SEC inadvertently created an easy target for criticism. One senses that the SEC itself may have been relieved when the section was simplified. When David Schenker, the chief counsel of the SEC study, presented the revised section to the Senate Banking

Committee, he stated: "Section 10 has been simplified substantially. You remember it was quite a complicated provision in the previous draft." Senator Robert Wagner's reply indicated that he certainly felt relieved by the simplification: "We heard a lot about section 10. I thought about it in my sleep."[21]

The fourth major change from the original bill was the addition of a new provision. The SEC's bill did not set forth how the amount of sales charges on sales of mutual fund shares was to be determined. The industry suggested and the SEC-industry framework added section 22(d), which provides that fund shares are to be sold "at a current public offering price described in the prospectus." The section is contrary to general antitrust concepts in that it permits a manufacturer (the fund organization) to set the price that retailers (dealers) can charge.

I tend to agree with Mark Roe, who has surmised that the SEC agreed to inclusion of the provision as a quid pro quo exchange for the industry going along with other parts of the bill:

> Although resale price maintenance has been illegal in antitrust (but attacked as not necessarily good policy), the mutual fund industry had federally-mandated noncompetition among dealers: the advisor sets the load, dealers cannot cut it. Price competition among mutual fund dealers is a criminal offense. *These elements can be seen as part of the political payoff to the mutual fund industry for the operating restrictions.*[22]

It is unclear why the industry wanted such a provision. The best explanation seems to be that prior to 1940, fund organizations had agreements with dealers that obliged the dealers to charge the single price set forth in the fund's prospectus. Noncontract dealers would purchase shares from investors for slightly more than the redemption price and then offer to sell the shares for less than the published sales price. This bootleg secondary market caused many contract dealers to cancel their agreements with fund organizations and thus disrupted the continuous offering of fund shares. A leading law review article on the subject concludes: "The advocates of enacting Section 22(d) sought to curtail this type of competition in order to prevent discrimination among purchasers and to insure the orderly distribution essential for a security having the unique feature of continuous redeemability. The passage of Section 22(d) was the legislative antidote."[23]

The SEC and its staff have proposed repealing section 22(d) on a number of occasions, most recently in the staff's 1992 report on investment company regulation.[24] Each time, the industry vigorously opposed repeal on the grounds that it would disrupt orderly distribution of fund shares, and each time the SEC did not push for legislation.

What Are the Most Important Provisions of the 1940 Act?

The goal of the drafters of the act was to permit investment companies to continue to operate and innovate without a recurrence of the abuses of the 1920s. As one observer has noted, "The purpose of the Investment Company Act of 1940 was primarily regulatory. The main objectives were to prevent abuses of position, fraud, and conflicts of interest that had occurred in prior periods."[25]

It would take volumes to discuss how the act sought to deal with numerous potential abuses and conflicts. But it is instructive to examine how it addressed the major problems that had occurred in the 1920s. As discussed earlier, those problems were fund shares trading at substantial premiums over actual portfolio values, excessive use of leverage through borrowing, and securities firms dumping securities into funds they managed.

First, the drafters of the act did not attempt to address the premium issue, presumably because there is no way to prevent an investor from paying $2 for a fund share when the liquidation value is only $1.

Second, section 18 of the SEC's bill offered a simple way to end the problem of excessive leverage. It flatly prohibited closed-end funds and mutual funds from issuing *any* senior securities. The idea of a total ban on senior securities did not present a problem for mutual funds because their core concept of daily redeemability rested on the existence of only one class of securities, common shares. But closed-end funds criticized the SEC's position as overkill.[26] Instead of imposing a total ban on senior securities, section 18 of the final act severely limited leverage by closed-end funds by requiring any issue of bonds to have asset coverage of at least 300 percent and preferred stock to have asset coverage of at least 200 percent. Section 18 totally prohibited mutual funds from issuing senior securities and limited bank borrowings to those with asset coverage of at least 300 percent. These provisions have been extremely effective. Since 1940, leverage has not threatened the solvency of any mutual fund or closed-end fund. In contrast, the major hedge fund debacle to date, Long-Term Capital Management, was attributable to the fund's excessive use of leverage, which reached a ratio of debt to capital of thirty-four to one, a ratio that would have been the envy of the most speculative closed-end funds of the 1920s.[27]

Third, although the problem of dumping led many observers to call for prohibiting securities firms from managing and distributing investment companies, the act permitted them to remain in the business but addressed specific problem areas. First and foremost, section 17(a) flatly prohibited a fund adviser from selling securities to or buying securities from the fund it manages. Thus, a fund manager can never deal with its fund as principal, no matter how fair the transaction may be. Second, in the case of underwritings, section 10(f) went further and prohibited an investment company from purchasing securities being underwritten from any party in the underwriting if the fund's adviser is one of the underwriters. Sections 17(a) and 10(f) have proved extremely effective in eliminating dumping, one of the major abuses of the 1920s.

There is a fourth provision that in certain ways is the most important part of the Investment Company Act. The law could have been written in a short and simple manner, setting forth broad general standards and leaving it to the courts and the SEC to provide specifics. Alfred Jaretzki Jr., an attorney who represented the closed-end fund industry during the legislative process, noted that under such an approach, "the industry would have been left in complete uncertainty as to its rights and duties," and the drafters rejected this approach. Jaretzki explained, "It therefore became necessary to formulate rather elaborate and perhaps complicated provisions to curtail, if not eliminate, the possibility of abuses."[28]

The net result was an extremely detailed statute that laid down a series of very specific do's and don'ts. The approach was successful in identifying and outlawing specific types of abuse and enumerating permissible activities, but by setting forth such detailed standards it easily could have stifled change and innovation. To counteract this tendency, many sections of the act gave the SEC the authority to grant exemptions from their requirements, either to specific companies by order or across the board by rule. In addition, section 6(c) granted the SEC sweeping general exemptive authority:

> The Commission, by rules and regulations upon its own motion, or by order upon application, may conditionally or unconditionally exempt any person, security, or transaction, or any class or classes of persons, securities, or transactions, from any provision or provisions of this title or of any rule or regulation thereunder, if and to the extent that such exemption is necessary or appropriate in the public interest and consistent with the protection of investors and the purposes fairly intended by the policy and provisions of this title.

The drafters of the act were well aware of the tremendous importance of these exemptive provisions and of the extraordinary authority they gave to the SEC. Jaretzki observed, "Without these exemptive powers and without a wise exercise of discretion thereunder, the Act would be unworkable, unduly restrictive, and would cause unnecessary hardships."[29] He and others who were "present at the creation" realized that the future of the industry would depend on SEC-industry cooperation in identifying needed exemptions and on the SEC's wise use of its exemptive authority to permit change and innovation in the interest of investors.

Over the past seven decades, the exemptive process has worked perhaps even better than Jaretzki and others who helped draft the act had hoped. Many of the innovations in investment products and services that have produced the mutual fund industry's success have been based on SEC exemptive rules. In the typical pattern, the SEC grants individual exemptive orders to specific fund firms. If these exemptions are successful and similar orders are sought by other firms, the SEC codifies the terms of the orders in a rule of general application. Subsequent chapters discuss specific SEC exemptive rules, notably those relating to variable annuities (chapter 3) and money market funds (chapter 4).

The exemptive process has greatly expanded the work of fund independent directors. Mutual fund firms often make director oversight a condition in their requests for exemptive orders. Typically SEC exemptive rules permit transactions provided a number of conditions are met, including review and approval by a majority of the independent directors. As the SEC has adopted more exemptive rules to accommodate industry change and innovation, directors' workload has increased correspondingly.

Moreover, as beneficial as the exemptive process has been, it can be misused to in effect rewrite the Investment Company Act. Jaretzki warned, "There exists at times a temptation, in granting exemptions, to impose restrictions deemed wise by the agency but not warranted by the terms of the Act."[30] The SEC's 2000 and 2003 amendments of various exemptive rules to require funds relying on those rules to have boards with high percentages of independent directors and independent chairpersons illustrate the danger. Fortunately, this has not been a common problem.

In sum, the drafters of the Investment Company Act had two principal goals—to prevent a recurrence of the abuses of the 1920s, and to permit investment companies to operate and innovate in the interest of investors. Thus, the most important sections of the act are those aimed at preventing a reappearance of the major abuses of the 1920s—excessive leveraging through borrowing (section 18) and dumping (sections 17(a) and 10(f))—and those permitting change and innovation (section 6(c) and exemptive provisions in other sections).

The 1940 act established a unique system of independent fund directors, but the system was quite limited. Only forty percent of fund directors had to be independent of management. Directors were not given any discretion in key areas addressed by the act. For example, directors cannot permit the fund to engage in borrowing beyond that permitted by the act, and cannot authorize the fund to buy securities from its adviser. The act gave directors only four duties—approving the advisory contract; approving the underwriting contract; approving the fund's accountant; and valuing portfolio securities that do not have readily available market quotations. None of the numerous articles written about the act in 1940 and 1941 focused on provisions dealing with directors. As discussed in chapter 9, the system of independent directors has been greatly enhanced over the last seventy years and today is a key component in the mutual fund industry.

Many observers have remarked on how successful the 1940 act has been. Sometimes veneration of the act can go a bit too far. In the early 1980s, the American Law Institute sponsored a project headed by Louis Loss of Harvard Law School to codify all of the federal securities laws into a single integrated statute. This led to a series of meetings focusing on the 1940 act among Loss and his colleagues, the SEC staff, and the Investment Company Institute's staff. At one of the meetings, we discussed section 12(d)(2), which provides that an investment company may not own more than 10 percent of the stock of an insurance company unless it owns 25 percent or more. None of us had a clue as to the reason for this provision. I was assigned to call Charles Jackson Jr., who had been an associate at Gaston, Snow, the law firm that represented the mutual fund industry during the drafting of the 1940 act, who was now retired. I called

Jackson and explained that the institute was part of a group reviewing the proposed Federal Securities Code, and I was calling specifically about section 12(d)(2). Jackson said something like, "I'm glad you are looking into that section. I was there when it was put in the 1940 act. I never could figure what it was all about. I'm curious what you find." I reported his reaction to the working group. David Silver, the institute's president, and I, its general counsel, argued that the Federal Securities Code should not contain this provision because no one knew its purpose. A member of the SEC staff admitted that this was true, but stated that for that very reason it would be a mistake to delete the section, saying something along the lines of "Maybe section 12(d)(2) is in the 1940 act for a very good reason that we simply don't know. Therefore we can't get rid of it." (The code project ended for a variety of unrelated reasons, and this mysterious section is still in the 1940 act.)

Formation of a Trade Association

In 1928 investment company executives in New York began meeting to discuss common issues. One writer urged the industry to form a trade association but noted, "On numerous occasions, effort has been made to form an association of investment trusts, yet always without success," possibly due to "the diversity of types [of investment companies]."[31]

The problem was more than diversity. As previously noted, there was a fierce rivalry between mutual funds located in Boston and closed-end funds headquartered in New York. Bad feelings between the groups increased in 1936, when the Revenue Act granted conduit tax treatment to mutual funds but not closed-end funds.

As the SEC prepared its study of the industry and legislation, a *Wall Street Journal* editorial urged investment companies to form an association to work on the bill, as well as to have a "continuing function when the regulation is put into effect." However, even when the proposed legislation was introduced in

Congress, observers doubted that the industry would be able to present a united front. *Business Week* observed, "Basic is the fact that open-end and closed-end trusts have anything but identical interests....In fact, they went to Washington in two groups and stopped at different hotels. They were represented by different lawyers and retained special public relations counsel."[32]

The threats and opportunities presented by federal legislation finally caused closed-end funds and mutual funds to put aside their long-standing differences. The two groups formed a joint task force that hammered out the final 1940 act with the SEC. The 1940 act authorized the SEC to adopt numerous rules and forms. A mutual fund publication has observed that under these circumstances, "the SEC felt a need existed for...[a trade] organization to serve as a continuing liaison between it and the investment company industry." At the SEC-industry dinner celebrating enactment of the act, David Schenker put the matter less elegantly: "You must form your own organization or we shall pick you apart, bone by bone."[33]

Closed-end funds and mutual funds heeded the SEC's suggestion and Schenker's warning, and formed a temporary industry association, the National Committee of Investment Companies, that commenced operations on October 1, 1940. A year later, it became a permanent trade association, the National Association of Investment Companies. In 1961, membership was expanded from closed-end funds and mutual funds to include the funds' investment advisers and principal underwriters, and the group's name was changed to the Investment Company Institute. In 1985, membership was expanded to include sponsors of fixed-unit investment trusts. Most recently, exchange-traded funds have become members.

From the outset, the association had as its principal mission assisting SEC officials in the effective regulation of the investment company industry. In September 1941, Walter Morgan of Wellington asked the first head of the association, Paul Bartholet, why he had been willing to accept the position. Bartholet replied:

> In my judgment the regulatory act can ultimately be a
> constructive force in the improvement and development

of the growth of the business, rather than a detriment. This assumes, however, that there is an honest and wholehearted attempt on the part of the industry to co-operate with the government in the administration of the statute. My desire to prove to myself that this could be done had a great deal to do with my taking on the job last Fall.[34]

The following year, Bartholet delivered an address in which he praised the Investment Company Act and its administration by the SEC:

> We believe that the Act has prevented the recurrence of abuses. It has discouraged irresponsible elements from entering the investment company field. It has confirmed sound fiduciary standards of conduct for those already in the field. Moreover, the very existence of this Federal regulation has stood as a warning to would-be wrongdoers.
>
> I can say without hesitation that investment company managers have been surprised that a regulatory measure so far-reaching could be administered, especially in its early stages, with so little friction, so few hardships and so little expense.
>
> We have been fortunate, to be sure, having as administrators Commissioners and staff members who are familiar with our business and have an intimate knowledge of the legislative history and objectives of the Act.

Bartholet went on to set forth his general views regarding government regulation. "Those of us to whom regulation applies must consider it not only a privilege but an important duty to help make it work. It is here to stay. We had better adjust ourselves accordingly. Let those who complain about the ruinous effects of regulation and its arbitrary and biased administration look instead for its advantages, seek to capitalize on its benefits, and try to cure its defects."[35]

In his 1942 address, Bartholet stressed the need for every managed investment company to participate in the industry's trade association so that the association could "speak with one voice" on behalf of the entire industry.

If the regulator is to do the best practicable job, he should
not be compelled, in rule making, to deal individually with
every company affected. Nor should he be called upon
to arbitrate conflicting points of view which exist in the
business. Composition of these differences is properly the
responsibility of the business itself. It is essential, therefore,
that business set up machinery to coordinate its divergent
needs, to win agreement when conflict exists, and to make
available to the administering authority, in organized form,
the technical knowledge and practical experience of the
business.[36]

When the association began in the early 1940s, members of the
executive committee implored investment companies around the
country to join what they called the "church."[37] The goal of universal membership has continued over the decades. (chapter 13
discusses the subsequent history of the association.)

Snapshot of the Industry in 1940

At the congressional hearings on the 1940 act, Mahlon E. Traylor,
president of Massachusetts Distributors, presented a list of
mutual funds as of December 31, 1939, showing eighty-seven
funds. The four largest ones were the three original funds
(Massachusetts Investors Trust, State Street Research, and
Incorporated Investors) and Dividend Shares, one of the funds
launched by Calvin Bullock. The vast majority of mutual funds
invested exclusively in stocks. Most invested in various types
of stocks, though there were some specialty funds, such as
Chemical Fund and Century Shares Trust, a fund that invested
in common stock of banks and insurance companies. There were
a few balanced funds that invested in a mix of stocks and bonds,
including Wellington Fund; Scudder, Stevens & Clark Fund; and
Bullock Fund. There also were a few bond funds, including four
of the ten Keystone Custodian Funds. Money market, international, tax-exempt, and index funds were not yet in existence.[38]

Most sponsors only managed a single fund. But there were a few, such as Calvin Bullock and Eaton & Howard, that managed several funds. The first family of funds was Keystone Custodian Funds, with four funds investing in different grades of bonds, two preferred stock funds, and four funds investing in different grades of common stock.

Fund sponsors typically were firms that only managed mutual funds and a few investment counseling firms and small broker-dealers. Commercial banks, national broker-dealers, insurance companies, and foreign conglomerates were not involved in the fund business. Fund groups with their own sales forces, such as Investors Diversified Services and Waddell & Reed, had not yet come into existence. There were a few no-load funds sponsored by investment counseling firms (such as Scudder, Stevens & Clark and Loomis, Sayles), formed to provide investment counseling services to small accounts owned by relatives and friends of clients.[39] No-load fund assets and sales were minuscule compared to load funds.

There is no evidence of sales by banks, insurance agents, or financial planners. Variable annuities, Keogh plans, individual retirement accounts (IRAs), and 401(k) plans had not yet been invented.

In sum, in 1940 mutual funds were heavily concentrated in equities, generally managed by small specialized firms, and sold almost entirely with front-end sales loads by broker-dealers. Mutual funds at this time were still viewed as the stepchild of the investment company industry. Observers continued to focus on closed-end funds. For example, the foreword of the first edition of the investment company industry's statistical bible, Arthur Wiesenberger's *Investment Companies and Their Securities,* stated:

> This book is intended to be a general compendium of information about the leading "closed-end" investment companies for the many thousands of stockholders and investment dealers interested in their securities. Some additional comparative data is included on the leading

mutual funds or "open-end" investment companies but we
have not attempted as detailed an analysis as in the case of
the "closed-end" investment companies.[40]

Importance of Early Events

Although no one could have realized it at the time, the events
of the 1920s and 1930s laid the foundation for mutual funds'
future success. The mutual fund structure that was created in
1924 avoided the premium-discount phenomenon and the use
of extreme leverage that characterized closed-end funds. The
Securities Exchange Act of 1934 created an agency of government, the SEC, whose sole responsibility was regulating the
securities markets, including mutual funds, in the interest of
investors. The Revenue Act of 1936 provided mutual funds
with favorable tax treatment and mandated that they follow the
first rule of prudent investing—diversification. The Investment
Company Act outlawed the major abuses of the 1920s while
providing mechanisms for innovation. These securities and tax
laws (as amended in 1942) applied to closed-end funds as well
as to mutual funds, but the 1940 act also codified into law mutual funds' unique attributes of daily redemptions and sales
at current net asset value and no leverage through issuance of
senior securities, attributes that in coming years were to make
mutual funds far more attractive to investors than closed-end
funds. In short, by 1940 the entire foundation for mutual funds'
success had been put in place. All that was needed was a period
of prosperity and rising stock prices.

3

Early Development

The greatest insurance against Socialism or Communism lies in having every income-earner [receive]...diversification and professional supervision. This...can be attained safely only through the mutual investment companies.

    —O. Glenn Saxon, Professor of Economics, Yale University

The first thirty years of the modern mutual fund industry, 1940 to 1970, witnessed an extremely strong stock market and a corresponding boom in mutual funds because they were heavily concentrated in stocks. The fund industry's success attracted the attention of competitors, and insurance companies became the first "outsiders" to enter the fund business. The industry's growth also led the Securities and Exchange Commission (SEC) to seek and obtain legislation addressing mutual fund sales charges and management fees.

Growth 1940–1960

At the final congressional hearing on the Investment Company Act, SEC Commissioner Robert F. Healy expressed his "belief...

that under this regulation [investment companies] will have a very fine future, a very promising future."[1]

Healy could not have been more prescient as far as mutual funds were concerned. In the two decades following enactment of the 1940 act, shareholder accounts went from 296,000 to 4.9 million, the number of funds grew from 68 to 161, and assets increased from $450 million to $17 billion. In 1944, for the first time, mutual fund assets exceeded those of closed-end funds, a situation that has prevailed ever since.[2]

Government officials, industry executives, and the media marveled at mutual funds' strong growth. In 1949, SEC Commissioner Harry A. McDonald observed, "Mutual funds are probably...one of the fastest growing businesses in this country." In 1959, industry leader Hugh Bullock stated, "Public acceptance of investment companies has been spectacular." That same year, a cover story on mutual funds in *Time* declared, "The funds have become the fastest-growing...phenomenon of the U.S. financial world."[3]

The mutual fund industry's success was not due to the introduction of new types of funds, new ways to distribute fund shares, or innovations in shareholder services but rather to a strong stock market and public confidence in the funds. From the beginning of 1941 through 1960, large company stocks had an average annual return of 14.8 percent, and small company stocks 18.9 percent, a great environment for an industry that was over 90 percent concentrated in equities. Observers also credited the industry's success to public confidence in mutual funds engendered by strict Investment Company Act regulation. In 1945, Paul Bartholet, first head of the industry trade association, stated that this regulation "through its psychological effects on both the companies and on the investing public...[has] established a new basis of confidence." That same year, Hugh Bullock declared, "There is no question but that the popularity of investment company securities has increased because of this series of [SEC] regulations."[4] The industry's success was evidenced by the growth of the nation's early mutual funds, the creation of additional funds by the early fund sponsors, and the entry of new firms into the business.

The three original funds experienced strong growth from 1940 to 1958. Massachusetts Investors Trust went from $123 million to $1.4 billion, State Street from $39 million to $199 million, and Incorporated Investors from $49 million to $307 million. Other early funds also did well. Calvin Bullock's Dividend Shares grew from $46 million to $267 million, and Affiliated Fund went from $23 million to $511 million.[5]

In 1940 most fund sponsors managed only one fund, typically a conservative stock fund. By 1958 many of these firms had brought out additional funds, such as bond funds, balanced funds, international funds, and specialty funds. Although single-fund organizations were the norm in 1940, by 1958 they had become the exception. For example, of the five early funds just discussed, by 1958 all but State Street had one or more "sister" funds.[6]

The two decades after 1940 witnessed the entry of many new firms into the mutual fund industry, a number of which were to become major players, such as Dreyfus, Franklin, Neuberger & Berman, and T. Rowe Price. Most notable was the entrance of groups that had their own sales forces. Before their arrival, fund shares typically were sold to investors by independent broker-dealer firms that had no affiliation with fund sponsors. The first of the integrated firms was Investors Syndicate (later known as Investors Diversified Services or IDS), which had been established in 1894 to distribute face amount certificates (installment notes) to investors. The 1940 act required registration of these certificates as investment companies. IDS began to consider entry into the mutual fund business in 1932 and brought out its first mutual fund in 1940.[7] A second major integrated firm was the United Funds, later known as Waddell & Reed. IDS and Waddell & Reed soon became two of the most successful firms in the industry, as evidenced by the fact that in 1960, the $2.1 billion in industry sales was divided as follows: independent dealers (65%), integrated sales forces including IDS and Waddell & Reed (29%), and no-load funds (6%).[8]

At year end 1958, the five largest funds were four of the early funds (MIT, Wellington, Fundamental Investors, and Affiliated

Fund) and one IDS fund, Investors Mutual. Similarly, at year end 1958, the five largest mutual fund complexes were three of the early fund groups (MIT and related funds, Wellington, and Hugh W. Long), IDS, and Waddell & Reed.[9]

Many observers hailed mutual funds' success in democratizing finance. The 1959 *Time* cover story praised funds for having: "taken the specialized world of Wall Street and put it within reach of every man with enough money to buy a fund share....The shares are bought by maids and wealthy dowagers, by doctors and factory workers, by labor unions and clergymen. No amount is too large...or too small....Ten years ago, most people had never heard of mutual funds; now, the term is a household word."[10] But success produced its own problems.

The fund industry had grown tremendously from 1940 to 1960 in terms of shareholders, funds, and assets, but in 1960 the industry was still heavily concentrated in equities, which accounted for over 90 percent of fund assets. This extreme concentration worked well during periods of rising stock prices, such as the 1940s and 1950s. But it could backfire badly if there were a sustained bear market in equities. Over ninety per cent of mutual fund sales continued to be made by salesmen, either independent broker-dealers or captive sales forces. As fund sales and assets increased, SEC officials expressed concern over high pressure sales practices, such as suggesting "that an investment in mutual fund shares is as safe as government bonds or a savings account," and "switching" an investor "from one fund to another in order to earn sales commissions."[11]

The success of the mutual fund industry drew the attention of competitors, notably insurance companies and banks. During the period 1940 to 1965, both insurance company and bank assets almost quadrupled, but these growth rates were nothing compared to the thirty-eight-fold increase in mutual fund assets. The 1959 *Time* cover story declared, "The funds have made life rougher for the banks and insurance companies by quadrupling their share of the savings dollar since 1948 (to 5.3% today)."[12]

The banking industry's response was to seek to offer commingled managing agency accounts, the economic equivalent of mutual funds, that they hoped would be free from SEC regulation. (The story of the banks' decades-long efforts to enter the mutual fund business is set forth in chapter 7.)

The insurance industry initially took a different approach than banks and did all it could to disparage mutual funds. *Forbes* reported, "For years the insurance industry has been telling anyone who would listen what a wretched idea it was to put money into mutual funds. Far better, they cautioned, to put it in safer, sane insurance whose values went only up, though perhaps slowly."[13] Insurance agents were armed with brochures to help them respond to clients' inquiries about mutual funds, with an emphasis on the negative aspects. Some companies used rougher tactics. *Time* reported that "some insurance companies now threaten to fire any man found selling mutual funds on the side."[14] Some of the insurance industry's response to mutual funds bordered on hysteria. The executive vice president and chairman of National Life Insurance authored a brochure, *Life Insurance versus the Ups and Downs of Mutual Funds*, that contained statements such as "From their very inception, investment companies lent themselves to exploitation," and "the Investment Company Act of 1940…did not contain the control features of the original bill, and instead became merely a disclosure measure."[15]

Entry of Insurance Companies

Insurance companies, which historically only offered products that paid fixed returns, sought to develop products that could keep up with inflation. As mutual fund growth continued unabated, many insurance companies stopped disparaging them and jumped on the bandwagon. These companies entered the fund business in three ways: by bringing out a new product, the variable annuity, that they hoped would be free from SEC regulation; by acquiring existing mutual fund firms; and by creating their own mutual funds.

The first way that insurance companies entered the mutual fund business was through the creation of a new product that

combined features of insurance and mutual funds, the variable annuity. Traditional fixed annuities typically promise the
purchaser that a specific sum will be paid every year for the
remainder of his or her life, or for a term certain (e.g., ten years).
In contrast, payments from variable annuities are based on the
investment results of the portfolio underlying the annuities. The
first variable annuity was developed by Teachers Insurance and
Annuity Association (TIAA), a nonprofit organization providing
retirement benefits in the form of fixed annuities to university
professors. In 1952, due to concern over the impact of inflation on
such fixed retirement payments, TIAA created the first variable
annuity fund, the College Retirement Equities Fund (CREF).[16]

CREF's success spurred commercial insurance companies
to enter the field. A new insurance company, Variable Annuity
Life Insurance, was incorporated in the District of Columbia.
Legislation was introduced in New Jersey authorizing a giant
insurance company, Prudential Life Insurance, to offer variable
annuities. Two battles broke out in the New Jersey legislature.
First, a number of insurance companies led by Metropolitan Life
opposed the legislation on the grounds that the essence of insurance
was a fixed guarantee. Second, the securities industry, including
the Investment Bankers Association, the National Association of
Investment Companies, and the National Association of Securities
Dealers, opposed the legislation on the grounds that the insurance industry would have tax and other advantages and that
variable annuities as insurance products would be exempt from
regulation under the federal securities laws.[17]

After years of controversy, the New Jersey legislation was
enacted. Prudential joined VALIC and other companies in offering variable annuities to the general public. There was litigation,
and a series of judicial decisions held that variable annuities were
securities subject to registration under the Securities Act of 1933
and that the pools of assets (called separate accounts) underlying
variable annuities were required to register as investment companies under the Investment Company Act of 1940.[18]

The second and easiest way for an insurance company to
gain entry into the mutual fund business was to acquire an

established fund firm. There were many immediate benefits—the fund business was up and running on day one, personnel had been trained, registrations under the federal securities laws were in place, the funds had well-documented performance records to use with salesmen and investors, and, perhaps most important, there was no need to change the culture of the acquired firm and its employees—they were already in the mutual fund business. On the other hand, an acquisition of a fund firm did nothing to move the insurance company itself into the fund business. Indeed, in many cases insurance companies simply became absentee owners of mutual fund companies, with few if any relationships and synergies between the insurance company parent and the fund company subsidiary. There was a wave of acquisitions in the late 1960s, including American General's acquisition of Channing; New England Life's acquisition of Loomis, Sayles; and Washington National's acquisition of Anchor. In 1970, *Business Week* reported that thirty-four insurance companies had purchased fund firms, and John C. Bogle, then president of Wellington, concluded that the acquired funds amounted to "some 12 per cent of [mutual fund] industry assets."[19]

Other insurance companies decided to enter the mutual fund industry by creating their own funds. This was the route taken by Connecticut General, John Hancock, and Mutual of Omaha (New England Life both purchased an existing fund group and started its own mutual funds). The advantage of this method was that the insurance company could put its own stamp on the mutual fund business. The disadvantages were the enormous effort, resources, and time required to build a new business from scratch. It therefore was not surprising that by 1970, these new insurance company–run funds accounted for only about 3 percent of total mutual fund assets.[20]

In 1969 *Forbes* wrote, "Mutual Funds, that sexy young girl, is marrying Life Insurance, a staid gentleman," and asked, "Will the marriage be a happy one?"[21] At first, the marriage was rocky, marked by angry disputes before state legislatures and federal judges. When these initial arguments were resolved, the insurance industry hit other roadblocks.

First, insurance companies had the misfortune to enter the mutual fund business just when the 1960s bull market was ending. *Forbes* noted: "Hardly was the trend well underway, when the stock market broke badly this year. Hardly had the insurance companies introduced their salesmen and customers to the delights of common-stock ownership, when the salesmen and customers began to learn the bitter taste of bear meat, which tastes very different than the bull meat they had expected."[22]

Second, insurance agents were put off by the relatively small commissions they could earn from selling mutual funds. *Business Week* reported, " 'An agent for us,' says Kelly [director of sales] of Nationwide, 'gets 55% of the first-year premium on a life insurance policy, but with mutual funds, the commission is just 3 1/4%. A guy has to adjust his thinking about the commission he gets.' "[23]

More generally, insurance agents lacked both confidence and experience selling investment products without guaranteed returns. A senior vice president of Prudential wrote, "The experienced life insurance salesman...hesitates in approaching a client to display what he considers to be a lesser degree of professionalism in this new and somewhat complex field of equities." *Forbes* reported, "Says John Hancock vice president of marketing Winthrop C. Giles: 'Life insurance agents didn't know how to ask for big sums of money.' "[24]

After reviewing these and other problems, *Forbes* went on: "Poor timing. Bad preparation. Disappointing results. Is, then, this strange mating headed for the divorce courts?" *Forbes* and leading insurance company executives, however, correctly concluded that the marriage would endure and improve.[25] The insurance industry has become a major player in the mutual fund business. By 2006 insurance companies (domestic and foreign) accounted for 22 percent of total mutual fund assets, consisting of $1.3 trillion in variable annuities and $1 trillion in conventional funds.[26] Insurance companies generally have fared better in the fund business than other outside industries, notably broker-dealers and banks. This is due to the fact that insurance companies have a unique product, the variable annuity, and also have acquired a number of large fund organizations, such as Alliance Bernstein, Massachusetts Financial Services, Oppenheimer, PIMCO, and Putnam.

The worst fears of the traditional mutual fund industry over the entry of insurance companies into the fund business— that it would be overwhelmed by powerful and unregulated competitors with salesmen in every town and hamlet in the country—never came close to being realized. Moreover, many insurance companies retained investment advisers to mutual funds to manage the insurance companies' separate accounts and mutual funds. Such "subadvising," a partnership between the insurance company that administers the fund and the adviser who makes portfolio decisions, has become a big business. An estimated one-third of variable annuity assets are subadvised.[27] On the regulatory front, although issues have occurred with respect to variable annuity sales practices, managers of insurance company funds have not otherwise been involved in an unusually high level of regulatory problems.

Continued Growth: The Go-Go Years

The fund industry's strong growth from 1940 to 1960 continued during the 1960s. The number of shareholder accounts more than doubled, the number of funds grew from 161 in 1960 to 361 in 1970, and assets climbed from $17 billion in 1960 to $48 billion in 1970. Almost all of the growth was accounted for by equity funds, which held 94 percent of industry assets in both 1960 and 1970.[28] Not only did the mutual fund industry remain extremely concentrated in equities, it moved from offering conservative stock funds to sponsoring far more aggressive growth funds, the most speculative of which were called "go-go" funds because they engaged in rapid in-and-out trading of large blocks of growth stocks.[29]

Several writers regard Fidelity Capital Fund, managed by Gerald Tsai, as the first of the aggressive growth funds. It was followed by others. In her book on Fidelity, Diana Henriques noted, "By the end of 1964, there were twenty large aggressive growth funds, with assets exceeding $100 million, that were endeavoring to catch Fidelity."[30] The largest was the Dreyfus Fund, run by Howard Stein. Others included Massachusetts Investors Growth Stock Fund, Putnam Growth Fund, Channing Growth Fund, Enterprise Fund run by Fred Carr, Security Equity Fund run by Fred Alger, and Fidelity Trend Fund. As John Brooks noted, during the boom years of the mid-1960s these funds racked up astonishing results: "Wiesenberger Reports announced that for the year [1965], twenty-nine leading 'performance' funds had averaged a net-asset-value rise of just over 40 percent, while the laggard Dow industrial average, made up not of swingers, like Polaroid and Xerox but of old-line blue chips like AT&T, General Electric, General Motors, and Texaco, had risen only 15 percent."[31]

The mutual fund and brokerage industries aggressively promoted go-go funds to investors. Brooks stated, "Here, then, was a new form of investment in which it appeared that by picking your fund at random you could still make 40 percent on your money in a year's time."[32] There were those like Warren Buffett, who warned that the speculative go-go boom would be followed by a bust.[33] But these warnings, like those in England in the late 1880s and the United States in the late 1920s, were ignored. Investors, brokers, and the mutual fund industry were to pay a heavy price for the go-go phenomenon when the bull market of the 1960s was succeeded by a prolonged bear market.

As fund sales and assets increased during the 1950s and 60s, SEC officials became increasingly concerned with sales practices. In 1952, SEC Chairman Donald Cook singled out salesmen who divided "almost contemporaneous sales to the same customer for the sole purpose of keeping each individual sale below the point at which reduced commission rates would be available." In 1957, SEC Commissioner Andrew Orrick listed complaints the SEC had received about salesmen who allegedly told investors "they could always receive back in full the amount of money to purchase shares," "no sales commission would be charged," and "the investment was guaranteed to grow and would produce increased income." In 1963, Allan F. Conwill, Director of the SEC Division of Corporate Regulation (the division then responsible for fund regulation), expressed dismay that "it is often said that mutual fund shares are 'sold, not bought,'" and criticized "emotional" selling, "hard sell" tactics, and the making of "extravagant claims."[34] Conwill particularly singled out questionable sales of contractual plans, arrangements under which investors agreed to purchase fund shares over a number of years, with sales charges concentrated in the early years:

> A complaint too often encountered is the sale of contractual plans without sufficient or, indeed, any explanation of the heavy front-end loading charges. Some purchasers, including a 72-year old widow, claim not only to have been unaware that as much as 50% of their first year's payments disappear into sales load but they also profess to have understood that theirs was a single purchase and not a contractual plan providing for ten annual payments, each equal to the amount of their single purchase.

Conwill's focus on contractual plans was important since in the 1960s these arrangements played a major role in the fund industry. The SEC reported, "At the end of 1965 the shares of more than 60 mutual funds, including some—but by no means all—of the oldest and largest in the country, could be purchased through contractual plans," and that in mid-1966, over 9 percent of fund assets consisted of contractual plan assets and over one-fourth of fund shareholders were contractual planholders.[35]

The Creation of Vanguard

Through an odd chain of events, the mutual fund industry's attraction to go-go funds led to the creation of the Vanguard Group, a large organization that is unusual in that the *funds* own their investment manager and distributor, rather than the usual pattern of funds contracting with an external manager and distributor.[36]

In 1928, Walter L. Morgan formed Wellington Fund, the nation's first balanced (stock and bond) fund. The fund was managed in the typical way, by an outside investment advisory firm owned by Morgan, Wellington Management. Jack Bogle joined Wellington in 1951 and helped form the group's second fund, a conservative common stock Windsor Fund. However, during the bull market of the 1960s, Bogle became convinced that Wellington had to join the go-go race:

> Bogle believed that the company needed something new to boost its assets—and there was no question in his mind what that something was. High performance ("go-go") funds had taken hold in the industry, climbing from 21 percent of new sales in 1955 to more than 40 percent in 1964 and 64 percent in 1966. Bogle knew, however, that growing a performance fund in-house would not be easy, as the experience in building Windsor Fund had proved.
>
> From Bogle's vantage point, one viable alternative was to buy the adviser to an already existing fund and merge it into Wellington Management Company.[37]

The decision was made to merge Wellington Management with a Boston investment counseling firm, Thorndike, Doran, Paine & Lewis, because Thorndike managed an extremely "hot" go-go fund, the Ivest Fund.

After the merger, there was a falling out between Bogle and the Boston partners, who gave him the choice of leaving Wellington or assuming a purely administrative role. Bogle countered by urging the fund directors to have the funds acquire Wellington Management. The two sides viewed this proposal in very different lights. The Boston partners "saw Bogle's mutualization as nothing more than a clever, last-minute tactic designed to salvage a job for himself." Bogle countered that he had raised the mutualization issue several years before, including in a profile in *Institutional Investor*.[38]

Whatever Bogle's motivation, the dispute led the funds to form and own a new company, Vanguard. At first, Vanguard only performed administrative functions for the funds. Later, it assumed the distribution function on a no-load basis, with the funds bearing distribution expenses. Finally, Vanguard became the investment manager of money market and bond funds, while continuing to employ Wellington and other outside firms to manage equity funds. Thus, ironically, Vanguard, well known today as the inventor of index mutual funds, had its origins in the desire to have a go-go fund. Moreover, because the funds owned their manager-distributor, there was no external adviser or underwriter to pay distribution costs. So Vanguard, famous for its low costs, was the first fund group to obtain an SEC order permitting funds to pay for the distribution of their own shares, a forerunner of rule 12b-1 (discussed in chapter 5).

The Investment Company Amendments Act: The Attempt at Rate Regulation

The success of the mutual fund industry in the postwar period raised concerns over the funds' sheer size. In 1949, one writer referred to the fear that mutual funds "are becoming a dominating and potentially dangerous voice in corporate management affairs through their large acquisitions of the voting stock of many companies." In 1959, *Time* reported, "Many critics charge that the funds, along with other institutional buyers, have needled the roaring bull market to artificial highs, that their constant buying, chiefly of blue chips, has helped create the present shortage of stocks."[39]

The mutual fund industry's strong growth also reignited SEC concerns over fund size. David Silver, former president of the Investment Company Institute, recalled that there was "this residual fear in Washington that again coming out of the Great Crash that if the mutual fund industry ever unwound for any reason it would lead to calamities in the marketplace as funds dumped their securities on the market to meet redemptions." For example, in 1952, SEC Chairman Donald C. Cook worried that "an attempt to liquidate on any substantial scale would result in a disastrous price decline or in the necessity for suspending the redemption privilege," and stated that the SEC was giving serious thought to undertaking a study of fund size.[40]

In 1958, the SEC used the authority granted to it by section 14(b) of the Investment Company Act to study the effects of increased size of investment companies.

The SEC's focus quickly shifted from issues raised by increased size to fees and charges paid by mutual funds and their shareholders. This focus stood in sharp contrast to the experience in 1940 when the drafters of the Investment Company Act largely steered away from rate regulation. Thus, the 1940 act did not address the level of management fees paid by funds or the level of sales loads paid by investors. The only rate regulation in the 1940 act related to contractual plans (arrangements under which investors agree to purchase fund shares over time) and provided that total sales loads in a contractual plan could not exceed 9 percent.

The shift in the SEC's focus toward rate regulation was reflected in a series of studies. In 1958 the SEC used its authority under section 14(b) to commission the Wharton School of Finance and Commerce to prepare a report regarding the effects of mutual fund size. Subsequently, the SEC asked Wharton to also address the activities of fund advisers, matters that admittedly had nothing to do with fund size. In 1962, the SEC published Wharton's *Study of Mutual Funds*. The Wharton Study found that "the main problems affecting mutual funds do not seem to relate to the size of individual funds or companies.... The more important current problems appear to be those which involve potential conflicts of interest between fund management and shareowners, the possible absence of arm's-length bargaining between fund management and investment advisers."[41]

In 1963, the SEC published the *Report of the Special Study of Securities Markets*, a report to the commission from a quasi-independent group within the agency, that dealt with securities markets for all types of securities, not just mutual fund shares. Portions of the special study addressed mutual fund sales and distribution practices, particularly contractual plans, where the Investment Company Act permitted up to half of the first twelve monthly payments to be deducted to pay the front-end sales load.[42]

These two reports to the SEC formed the basis for the com-
mission's own 1966 report, *Public Policy Implications of Investment
Company Growth*, which called for amendments to the Investment
Company Act in three economic areas:

- Management Fees. The SEC maintained that in most cases,
  investment advisers to mutual funds were not sharing economies of scale with their funds (i.e., although an adviser's
  expenses declined as fund assets increased, fee rates did not)
  and that existing restraints on management compensation,
  such as disclosure of fees, approval of advisory contracts by
  shareholders and unaffiliated fund directors, and litigation,
  were not effective. Therefore the SEC proposed that the act
  be amended to require that management compensation must
  be "reasonable," and provide that the SEC or a fund shareholder could sue in federal court to enforce this standard.

- Sales Loads. The SEC argued that the difference between the
  typical mutual fund sales load of 8.5 percent and the cost of
  investing in other securities was "unjustified," and recommended that the act be amended to limit mutual fund sales
  loads to 5 percent of the net amount invested in the fund.

- Contractual Plans. The SEC maintained that the front-end
  sales load was disadvantageous to the many investors who
  did not complete their plans, and recommended that the act
  prohibit future sales of contractual plans on a front-end load
  basis.[43]

The SEC's proposals for rate regulation of management fees,
sales loads, and contractual plans were incorporated in legislation that was introduced in both houses of Congress on May 1,
1967. Although some in the mutual fund, contractual plan, and
brokerage industries wanted to fight the SEC's proposals tooth
and nail, wiser heads concluded that "There was absolutely no
long-term solution to the SEC's legislative program except the
enactment of a legislative program. It would not go away and
that all that could happen over time was the erosion of public
confidence in the industry and then simply through the passage of time there would be some event or some scandal or

something which would provide the engine of more punitive legislation."[44]

There ensued an extended two-track approach: public congressional hearings and behind-the-scenes discussions aimed at reaching compromises agreeable to all parties, including the SEC, the National Association of Securities Dealers (NASD), mutual fund firms, sponsors of contractual plans, and the broker-dealer community. Early on, agreements were reached on sales loads (replacing the SEC's proposed 5 percent limit with NASD rule making) and contractual plans (permitting front-end loads but at a lower level). It took far longer to reach agreement on fund management fees. Finally, a compromise was reached on this issue, with the SEC's proposed reasonableness test replaced with a fiduciary duty standard.

In December 1970, over three and a half years after the SEC's original bill had been introduced, the Investment Company Amendments Act of 1970 was enacted into law. The act amended the Investment Company Act to address all three economic issues raised by the SEC—management fees, sales loads, and contractual plans—but in quite different ways than the SEC initially had proposed.

- Management Fees. New section 36(b) of the 1940 act imposed a specific fiduciary duty on investment company advisers with respect to compensation they receive from the funds and provided that an action for breach of fiduciary duty could be brought by the SEC or by a shareholder on behalf of the fund.

- Sales Loads. Section 22(b) of the 1940 act authorized the self-regulatory organization for broker-dealers, the NASD, to adopt rules designed to prevent "an excessive sales load" but "allow for reasonable compensation for sales personnel, broker-dealers, and underwriters, and for reasonable sales loads to investors." (In 1975, the NASD adopted a rule permitting a maximum sales load of 8.5 percent, which had to be reduced by specified percentages if certain rights, such as volume discounts, rights of accumulation, and dividend reinvestment in additional shares without loads, were not provided.)

- Contractual Plans. Section 27 of the 1940 act permitted two types of contractual plans. The first alternative retained the maximum 50 percent front-end sales load but provided the investor with certain rights on early surrender. The second alternative provided for more spread-out sales loads over time.

There were many differences between the Investment Company Act of 1940 and the 1970 amendments. The 1940 act focused on fiduciary standards, whereas the amendments sought to impose rate regulation. The original act with changes was strongly supported by the industry; the industry reluctantly went along with the 1970 amendments even as modified. The 1940 act was signed into law within six months after introduction of the original bill; the 1970 amendments took over three and a half years from start to finish.

Most important, the 1940 act had a major impact on the then-dominant closed-end funds, for example, sharply curtailing their use of leverage and prohibiting fund advisers from selling securities to their funds. In contrast, the 1970 amendments had little impact on the now-dominant mutual funds. A leading law review article noted, "Passage of the 1970 Amendments was not heralded as an event that would radically alter the structure or practices of the investment company industry."[45] The amendments regarding management fees spawned numerous lawsuits, but these suits have had little success. (On the other hand, breakpoints on fee rates as fund assets increase have become more common.) As discussed in chapter 12, although the Supreme Court recently rendered a decision on management fees, litigation is likely to continue. NASD's sales charge rule simply codified general industry practice. Total costs borne by fund shareholders have declined precipitously in recent years, but this appears to be largely the result of the replacement of sales loads with rule 12b-1 fees and shareholder movement to lower cost funds, rather than a consequence of the 1970 amendments.[46] The one area where the amendments clearly had a major impact is contractual plans. Following enactment of the amendments, most plan sponsors left the business.

The Investment Company Act had been greeted by numerous articles singing its praises. In contrast, very little was written about the 1970 amendments, and much of it was critical.[47] Perhaps most telling is the fact that whereas the Investment Company Act generally ended controversy about the areas it addressed, the issues covered by the 1970 amendments have continued to be matters of debate to this day. For example, the SEC staff's 1992 report, *Protecting Investors: A Half Century of Investment Company Regulation,* proposed new approaches to both of the major issues addressed by the amendments—management fees and sales loads. Regarding management fees, the report recommended that the SEC propose amending the 1940 act to permit a new type of mutual fund, a unified fee investment company (UIFC). A UFIC would have a single fixed fee that could not be "unconscionable or grossly excessive," and that would not require shareholder or director approval. As to sales loads, the report recommended that the commission propose amending section 22(d) to repeal the requirement that fund sponsors determine the prices at which retail dealers sell fund shares to investors.[48]

The leading historian of the SEC, Joel Seligman, attributes the failure of the 1970 amendments to the fact that the commission did not undertake rigorous economic analysis and instead relied on legalistic solutions.[49] My own conclusion is quite different. I believe that the difference in results between the Investment Company Act of 1940 and the 1970 amendments is due to the fact that whereas the drafters of the original act focused on fiduciary standards and eschewed economic regulation, in 1970 the SEC sought to impose rate regulation. In a competitive, ever-changing industry like U.S. mutual funds, such an approach is virtually certain to fail. The debate over whether the 1970 amendments did not go far enough in imposing rate regulation or went too far continues to this day.

Other Aspects of the 1970 Amendments

There were other, noneconomic provisions in the 1970 amendments that proved far more important than was realized at the time.

In the 1950s, banks created collective investment funds for sale to corporate employers to fund their defined benefit retirement plans. The SEC took the position that these funds did not have to register under the federal securities laws on the theory that they were being sold on a one-on-one basis to sophisticated corporations. Similarly, insurance companies developed separate accounts to fund variable annuities for corporate retirement plans, and the SEC adopted rules exempting them from regulation. The 1970 amendments codified these exemptions as amendments to the federal securities laws.[50]

Subsequent events totally undermined the rationale for these exemptions. Since 1970, there has been a dramatic shift away from defined benefit plans, where the employer makes investment decisions and bears the investment risk, to 401(k) and other defined contribution plans, where employees make their own investment decisions and bear the investment risk.[51] Employees in these plans generally are responsible for determining the investment of their accounts, typically from a menu of options provided by their employers. Yet as a result of the 1970 amendments, employees whose options include bank collective funds and variable annuities are denied the protections afforded to other investors by federal securities laws. The Investment Company Institute has urged the enactment of legislation to undo the damage done by the 1970 amendments by requiring bank collective funds and insurance company separate accounts offered to defined contribution plans to register under the federal securities laws. In 1992, the SEC staff recommended that the commission seek legislation requiring registration under the 1933 act.[52]

Unfortunately, the major gap in investor protection that was codified into law by the 1970 amendments remains uncorrected. Ironically, some sponsors of these exempt funds argue that they are preferable to and cheaper than mutual funds because "they don't have to send out prospectuses or quarterly shareholder reports."[53] Thus, the *lack* of investor protection has become part of the sales pitch for these unregulated funds.

There is an even greater irony. Basic mutual fund attributes, such as SEC-mandated disclosures and daily net asset values, have proven to be extremely popular with defined contribution plan sponsors and participants. This has helped mutual funds gain an increasing share of the defined contribution market. On the flip side, bank collective funds and insurance company separate accounts, with only voluntary disclosures and periodic computation of prices, have steadily lost market share. Thus, by resisting SEC regulation, bank and insurance company lobbyists painted their clients into a competitive corner. To break out, many banks and insurance companies have voluntarily forgone the exemptions provided by the 1970 amendments and registered their collective funds and separate accounts as mutual funds subject to full SEC regulation. But this took time, and mutual funds used this time to gain market share.[54]

The 1970 amendments addressed another problem—fund insiders trading in securities that are owned by the fund or that the fund is considering acquiring or selling. New section 17(j) of the Investment Company Act granted the SEC authority to adopt rules in this area, including requiring funds, their advisers, and underwriters to adopt codes of ethics addressing personal investing. One of the first projects that I worked on when I joined the Investment Company Institute in 1971 was drafting a model code of ethics that has become the industry standard. As discussed in chapter 9, in 1994 the institute's board of governors endorsed the *Report of the Advisory Group on Personal Investing*, which called on funds to adopt a series of additional measures.[55]

These legal and voluntary measures go well beyond requirements applicable to employees of other asset managers, including pension plans, banks, insurance companies, commodity pool operators, and hedge fund advisers. However, neither the 1970 amendments, the SEC's implementing rule, the industry's codes of ethics, nor the institute's 1994 report dealt with fund insiders trading in the fund's own shares, a problem that no one foresaw until the 2003 revelations of trading scandals discussed in chapter 11.

Thus, just as the economic aspects of the 1970 amendments dealing with management fees and sales loads proved failures, other sections—those exempting bank and insurance funds, and insider trading provisions—also fell short. In sum, whereas the 1940 act was a great success, the 1970 amendments were not.

The lengthy legislative process that led to the 1970 amendments put extreme pressure on the Investment Company Institute, as the association sought to hold the fund industry together in the face of intense Congressional and media scrutiny. I joined the institute the year after the amendments were enacted, and I remember the institute's president, Bob Augenblick, telling me that Congressional reconsideration of the Investment Company Act could both produce odd results and fragment the industry. Bob also told me that each week during the legislative process the institute convened a meeting of the many lawyers who represented different industry segments. At one meeting, Bob realized that a particular attendee was representing two clients that had diametrically opposing views on the same issue. Bob asked the attorney if he didn't have a conflict of interest. The attorney replied: "I don't have a conflict of interest. My clients do."

A major benefit of the process that led to the 1970 amendments was the good will it produced between the SEC and members of Congress and industry representatives. The industry had ample reason to oppose the legislation, but instead it sought resolution of the various issues through reasonable compromise. The good will engendered by this process paid off in spades a few years later. In 1972 the Second Circuit Court of Appeals held that an investment adviser to a mutual fund breached its fiduciary duty by profiting from its recommendation of a new adviser.[56] The decision cast doubt on an adviser's ability to sell its business for a profit. The Investment Company Institute sought remedial legislation that was supported by the SEC and the U.S. Department of Justice. As part of the Securities Act Amendments Act of 1975, Congress added new section 15(f) to the Investment Company Act, which permits a fund adviser to profit from the sale of its business provided specific conditions are met. I believe that the smooth resolution of this matter was the direct result of the industry's cooperative attitude during consideration of the 1970 amendments.

Snapshot of the Industry in 1970

In 1970, following enactment of the amendments to the 1940 act, there were 361 funds with over 10 million shareholder accounts. Industry assets stood at a record $48 billion.[57]

Fund families had become increasingly common and larger. By 1970, Keystone had ten funds, Fidelity nine, Waddell & Reed eight, Putnam seven, IDS six, and Franklin five. The five largest funds were two of the early funds (MIT and Affiliated Fund), two IDS funds (Investors Mutual and Investors Stock Fund), and the Dreyfus Fund. The five largest groups were two of the early fund groups (MIT and Fidelity), the two major direct sales force groups (IDS and Waddell & Reed), and Dreyfus.[58] Sales continued to be dominated by broker-dealers (73 percent) and direct sales forces (16 percent), with no-load funds accounting for only 11 percent of sales.[59]

Two facts deserve special mention. First, by 1970, insurance companies managed a significant share (in the 15 percent range) of total mutual fund assets. This was the first time another industry had entered the mutual fund business on a wholesale basis.

Second, the main drivers of mutual funds' extraordinary success from 1940 to 1970 were the equity markets, with large cap stocks returning an average of 12.5 percent a year and small cap stocks 17.1 percent.[60] This was an ideal environment for the mutual fund industry which had over 90 of its assets in equities. There was no apparent need for the industry to develop new products, new distribution systems, or new investor services. The industry's almost total reliance on one product, stock funds, and one distribution system, broker-dealers, was about to undergo a severe test.

4

Responding to the Bear Market:
Money Market Funds

I sometimes even think that there is a certain advantage in
difficulties.

—Oliver Wendell Holmes

Just as three decades of a strong stock market, from 1940
to 1970, spurred mutual fund growth, the prolonged
bear market of the 1970s devastated mutual funds. Fund
assets plummeted due to falling portfolio values and net
redemptions of fund shares. The 1970s were also a terrible time for consumers, who paid high interest rates
on their borrowings but were limited by federal law to
receiving low interest rates on their savings. The mutual
fund industry turned lemons into lemonade by sponsoring money market funds, which earned high short-term
rates that were passed on to shareholders. Money market
funds enjoyed spectacular success and revolutionized the
fund industry and the entire American financial system.

The 1940s, 1950s, and 1960s had been great times to be in the
stock market and mutual funds, which were heavily concentrated in equities. Shareholder accounts increased from fewer

than 300,000 in 1940 to almost 11 million in 1972. Assets grew from $450 million in 1940 to a record $60 billion in 1972.[1]

All of this changed when the economy soured, stagflation took hold, and a prolonged bear market began. An Investment Company Institute research paper stated: "The 1970s were a period of stagnation in the stock market: the S&P index reached a record high in December 1968, pushed briefly above the level in late 1972 and early 1973, but did not return to it until late 1979. The compound rate of increase in the S&P index between the cyclical peaks in December 1968 and November 1980 was only 2.1 percent."[2]

This shift in the market had a devastating impact on stock mutual funds. Equity fund assets fell from $56 billion in 1972 to $31 billion in 1974, due to a combination of falling stock prices and net redemptions. First, *Business Week* reported, "Stock prices plunged in 1969 and 1970 and the mutual funds came down with them. In fact, the funds came down faster. Where 84% of the funds outran the Dow in 1968, only 9% did in 1970."[3] Second, broker-dealers, the mainstay of the fund distribution system, turned from selling equity funds to selling hard assets, which offered investors the chance for protection against infla-tion, such as oil and gas limited partnerships and commod-ity funds. As a result of the fall-off in fund sales, for the first time in history, equity funds had net redemptions, month after month, year after year.[4]

It appeared to some that the mutual fund industry might go out of existence. A recent history of Franklin Resources notes, "As equity mutual fund redemption rates reached alarming lev-els, some observers began wondering if the industry was due to disappear altogether." Indeed, in 1973 Donald Pitti, president of Weisenberger Services, predicted that "the fund industry as we know it is likely to disappear."[5]

I do not recall anyone in the industry panicking or giving up on mutual funds, but no one was happy. I particularly remem-ber four incidents. First, the Investment Company Institute's Board of Governors normally held its January meeting at a sunny vacation resort in the Caribbean or Hawaii. But Charlie

Johnson, CEO of Franklin Resources, recalls that in 1973, "they had it in Williamsburg [Virginia]," so people could drive and save the cost of airfare. "It rained, and it was just miserable, and everybody was down in the dumps."[6] Second, one fund executive urged the Investment Company Institute to move from publishing industry statistics on a monthly basis to quarterly to reduce the number of negative press stories on net redemptions. Everyone else in the industry opposed this proposal, and fortunately it died.

Third, at another meeting of the institute's board of governors in the early 1970s, the governors went around the table, with each one expressing his views on the state of the industry and what the industry should tell investors. Charles F. Eaton Jr., who had formed the first Eaton & Howard Fund in 1931 at the bottom of the Depression and was known for his dry New England wit, offered advice, "Well, fellows, when you come right down to it, mutual funds offer the public only two things: first, diversification of investments and second, professional management. When times are difficult, as they are today, we should stress diversification." Fourth, Charles W. Schaeffer, one of the founders of T. Rowe Price and chairman of the institute in 1974–75, was convinced that mutual funds had a great future. When industry assets had fallen from $60 billion to $45 billion, he stated, "I'm not looking to go back up to $60 billion. I'm thinking of $100 billion. I'm very optimistic about the industry because it's no longer just growth-oriented but now has a full product mix."[7]

Indeed, as will be discussed in chapter 5, the industry's main reaction to the prolonged bear market was to develop new types of funds that had been under consideration for years, such as tax-exempt funds and index funds, and assist the Securities and Exchange Commission (SEC) in permitting new ways to distribute fund shares, such as advertising and the use of fund assets to pay for distribution. By far the most effective measure in helping the mutual fund industry respond to the bear market was the creation of a totally new type of mutual fund—a development that revolutionized both the fund industry and the entire American financial system.

Money Market Funds

For more than two decades after World War II, inflation had
been virtually nonexistent. The late 1960s ushered in the highest
inflation in generations due to President Lyndon Johnson's decision to finance the war in Vietnam and new domestic programs
through massive deficit spending. Joseph Nocera reported: "In
1967, the cost of living, as measured by the Consumer Price
Index, rose 3 percent. The following year the CPI rose another
4.7 percent. And on it went: 6.2 percent in 1969; 5.6 percent
in 1970....In 1974, as a result of the Arab oil embargo, the
Consumer Price Index rose an almost unthinkable 12 percent."[8]
Consumer borrowing costs on homes, automobiles, and other
purchases shot up as interest rates soared.

On the investment side, institutions and wealthy individuals were able to earn high market rates of interest by purchasing
Treasury bills in amounts of $10,000 or higher and bank cer-
tificates of deposit in excess of $100,000. But the overwhelming
majority of Americans, who were paying record rates of interest
on their borrowings, were limited to earning less than 5 percent
on their savings. This was because most people saved by means
of passbook saving accounts, and federal banking Regulation
Q imposed interest rate ceilings of 4.5 percent on bank and
4.75 percent on savings and loan (S&L) passbook accounts.
(Subsequently the ceilings were increased to 5.25 and 5.5 percent).
Banks and S&Ls certainly had a great deal: they borrowed
money from millions of consumers at 4.5–4.75 percent interest
and then loaned it out at double-digit rates of return. It was a
rotten deal for most Americans: they paid 10 percent or more
on their borrowings but earned less than 5 percent on their
savings.

In hindsight, it is not surprising that a number of individuals had the same idea: create a mutual fund that would invest
in Treasury bills, jumbo certificates of deposit (CDs), and other
short-term instruments; earn high interest on those instruments;
and pay out that interest less expenses to fund shareholders.
What is somewhat surprising is that the idea for money market

funds did not originate with people in the mutual fund industry. The first such fund, the Reserve Fund, was started in New York in September 1972 by two former employees of TIAA-CREF, Henry Brown and Bruce Bent. A few weeks later, across the country in San Jose, California, a former Merrill Lynch broker, James Benham, started the Capital Preservation Fund. There were favorable stories in the media about these funds, and money began flowing to them.[9]

Seeing the success of the first money market funds, traditional mutual fund groups brought out their own funds. In early 1974 Dreyfus launched the Dreyfus Liquid Assets Fund, accompanied by a massive advertising campaign. Fidelity countered with Fidelity Daily Income Trust, the first money fund to offer redeemability through check writing. The funds were smash hits and aggressive rivals.[10] (To those with a historical memory, the Dreyfus/New York–Fidelity/Boston competition was reminiscent of the closed-end/New York–mutual fund/ Boston rivalry of the 1920s.)

Initially, most fund firms viewed money funds as temporary mechanisms ("reserve" funds or "cash management" funds) to capture money that was fleeing the stock market. When an investor called to redeem equity fund shares, a service representative would ask if he wanted to place the proceeds in the firm's money market fund pending the investor's return to the stock market. Some fund groups came to view money funds quite differently. Howard Stein, the head of Dreyfus, was a bear on the stock market, and I sensed early on that he saw money market funds as a long-term product for retail investors. A number of groups like AIM brought out money funds designed to help large institutions manage their cash more efficiently, whether the stock market was up or down. Federated developed programs whereby small bank trust departments could sweep clients' dividends and interest into its money funds on a daily basis. Securities firms swept customers' cash balances into the firms' money funds. Merrill Lynch developed the Cash Management Account that combined aspects of a money fund with check writing, a sweep account, and a credit/debit card for its brokerage customers. In short, a product that originally was seen as a temporary holding tank for cash until the stock market righted itself soon took on a wide number of permanent uses.

Money market fund assets increased at a rapid pace, growing from less than $2 billion in 1974 to $11 billion in 1978 to $76 billion in 1980. In that year, money fund assets exceeded those of all other mutual funds combined. In 1997, money fund assets crossed the $1 trillion mark, and by 2007 exceeded $3 trillion.[11]

Money market funds totally changed the fund industry. Before the advent of money funds, the industry consisted almost entirely of equity funds. Money funds ended this overdependence on equities. In addition, they introduced millions of Americans to investing through mutual funds. They started out in money funds, and when the stock and bond markets finally improved, they moved to mutual funds investing in those markets. In 1982 the Investment Company Institute's president, David Silver, reported on a survey, "It is clear that money market funds have the youngest, best educated group of customers of any financial institution." He went on to predict, correctly, "These young, intelligent and increasingly affluent shareholders will be a major source of business for years to come."[12] Money funds also revolutionized the banking and S&L industries by leading to the end of interest rate controls on deposits.

Issues under the Securities Laws

Money funds raised unique issues under the securities laws. Different funds with similar portfolios and expenses quoted different yields because they used different formulas. The formulas were all legitimate, but there was a need to agree on a single method so investors could compare funds. The institute convened a meeting of the major money funds to agree on a single formula to be recommended to the SEC as the standard method for computing yields. At the first meeting, there was an angry disagreement as to the proper formula, with Dreyfus leading one camp and Fidelity the other. Dave Silver and I urged attendees to calm down, return to their offices, discuss the issue with their colleagues, and reconvene at the institute. We met two weeks later to learn that as we had suggested, both Dreyfus and Fidelity had thought the matter over, but now Dreyfus supported Fidelity's initial position and Fidelity backed Dreyfus's original formula. Both sides were dug in and refused to budge. For the only time in my experience, the institute provided the SEC with two alternatives.[13]

Under the Securities Act of 1933, issuers of securities, including mutual funds, pay the SEC registration fees based on the amount of securities proposed to be sold. This system had always been unfair to mutual funds because the fee was based on gross sales with no credit for redemptions. The creation of money market funds, where investors moved money in and out on a rapid basis, magnified the inequity. For example, for the twelve months ending September 30, 1975, money funds had sales of $7.7 billion and paid registration fees of over $1.5 million. The funds had redemptions of $5.6 billion; had fees been based on *net* sales ($2.1 billion), they would have amounted to only $431,000. The institute raised this inequity with the SEC, and in 1977 the commission adopted a rule permitting mutual funds to pay SEC registration fees based on net sales.[14] The change has saved mutual funds and their shareholders hundreds of millions of dollars.

The defining characteristic of a mutual fund is that its shares are redeemable—on any business day an investor can tender shares to the fund and receive a price based on the current value of the fund's portfolio. In addition, most funds continuously issue new shares to investors, again at a price based on the portfolio's current value. Therefore, each day a mutual fund must value its portfolio securities by reference to the current market prices for those securities, and then must price its own shares for purposes of redemptions and sales. Thus, the price of a typical mutual fund share goes up or down each day as the value of the fund's portfolio changes. Sponsors of money funds learned that many shareholders wanted to invest in funds that had a constant share value. For example, Federated Investors, which specialized in sponsoring money funds for use by bank trust departments, found that "Trustees could not put their clients' money in any investment that had a fluctuating net asset value, no matter how high the returns might be, for fear of losing the money through a sudden market change."[15]

Therefore, to maintain a constant $1 per share net asset value, some money funds added or subtracted any realized or unrealized gains and losses on their portfolio securities from their daily dividends. Federated and other funds used another approach and valued portfolio securities according to a procedure known as amortized cost valuation. Under amortized cost, a debt instrument is assumed to increase in value on a straight-line basis until maturity. Thus if an instrument is purchased at $90 today and will come due in ten days at $100, its amortized cost value tomorrow will be $91, the next day $92, and so on. Still other fund groups (including Merrill Lynch) made use of a procedure known as penny rounding, whereby the current net asset value per share is rounded to the nearest cent based on a share value of $1.

In 1977, the SEC issued a release prohibiting the use of amortized cost valuation for securities with more than sixty days to maturity. Several money funds sought SEC exemptive orders permitting them to use amortized cost or penny rounding. The SEC staff opposed these applications, a public hearing was held, and the commission granted the orders subject to numerous conditions, notably that the portfolio consist of high-quality, short-duration investments. Other funds obtained similar exemptive relief, and eventually the SEC codified the standards for use of amortized cost and penny rounding by all money market funds in rule 2a-7.[16] The rule has been amended a number of times over the years, and today it forms the basis for the more than $3 trillion invested in money market funds.

Issues under the Banking Laws

Because money market funds presented severe competition to banks and S&L associations, they quickly drew the attention of federal bank regulators, who proposed a number of actions to impede money fund growth.[17]

In 1976, the Federal Reserve Board, the Federal Deposit Insurance Corporation, and the Federal Home Loan Bank Board proposed prohibiting sale of large-scale ($100,000 and up) CDs to money market funds. The proposal was vigorously opposed by the institute, consumer groups, leading members of the Senate and House banking committees, a number of large banks, and the American Bankers Association and was withdrawn. The comptroller of the currency initially took the position that bank trust departments were prohibited from investing in money market funds. The institute and individual fund organizations discussed this matter with the comptroller, who reversed his position. Bank trust departments have become major investors in money funds. Similarly, the National Credit Union Administration initially took the position that federally regulated credit unions could not invest in money funds, but subsequently changed its position.

Banks launched their own efforts to restrict money market funds. In October 1979, the Bowery Savings Bank wrote to federal and state regulators asserting that money funds' check-writing privileges violated banking law. The U.S. Department of Justice swiftly rejected this assertion. Other banks urged laws imposing interest rate ceilings, similar to Regulation Q, on money funds.

The banks' most common call was for legislation imposing reserve requirements on money funds that offered check writing. The fund industry's response was that studies by several Federal Reserve banks and the institute demonstrated that fund shareholders rarely drew checks, so money funds resembled bank savings accounts, which were not subject to reserve requirements, as opposed to bank checking accounts, which did have such requirements. However, every time Dave Silver and I met with Federal Reserve Board Chairman Paul Volcker, he told us that his wife, a bookkeeper for a small company in New York, paid bills by checks drawn on Dreyfus Liquid Assets Fund. We often worried that public policy might be driven by Mrs. Volcker's personal experience rather than by careful economic studies.

Dave and I began thinking of the institute's response should the banking and S&L industries launch an all-out drive for legislation imposing interest rate ceilings or reserve requirements on money funds. During this time, my wife and I lived in downtown Washington, DC, and Dave often would give me a lift in the evenings when he drove home to the suburbs. We spent the time discussing the situation and kicked around the idea of an ad aimed at money fund shareholders, urging them to write to their senators and representatives in Congress. We toyed with the headline: "To America's Money Market Fund Shareholders: Don't Let Them Take it Away."

In January 1980, the Subcommittee of Financial Institutions of the Senate Banking Committee held oversight hearings on money funds. The SEC's testimony emphasized the significant legal and practical distinctions between money funds and banks, stated that existing regulation successfully protects fund shareholders, and noted that fund growth had not resulted in substantial regulatory problems. The tenor of the testimony of all four bank regulatory agencies was that money fund growth underscored the need to lift regulatory restrictions on banks rather than imposing new restrictions on money funds. In particular as to reserves, Fed Governor Charles Partee stated that money funds did not then pose a critical problem for monetary control purposes, but that if these funds over time began to exhibit more clearly the characteristics of bank transaction (checking) accounts, the possibility of extending reserve requirements might be reconsidered.[18]

Based on the regulators' testimony and money funds' popularity with the public, it appeared that, absent a crisis, money funds had a good chance of avoiding punitive legislation. But a crisis hit.

On March 14, 1980, the Carter administration sought to dampen inflation through the imposition of credit controls. One control required every money fund to maintain a non–interest-bearing deposit with the Federal Reserve equal to 15 percent of the increase in the fund's assets over their March 14 level. The credit controls, including the money fund provisions, were extremely cumbersome and difficult to administer and ultimately failed in their goal of curtailing inflation. The only good thing about them was that they were temporary. Just as they were being imposed, there were press reports that the banking and S&L industries, who normally fought with one another, were about to join together in a major effort to have permanent restrictions placed on money funds. We anticipated the start of a major congressional battle.[19]

State Battles

In late March 1980, a reporter in Nashville called the Investment Company Institute with questions about an amendment that had been offered to a bill in the Tennessee legislature. We obtained a copy of the amendment and found that it would prohibit the offer and sale of shares of money market funds in the state. The battle had begun—in state capitals rather than in Congress.

Money market funds faced an extremely difficult situation in the states. Banks and S&Ls had offices and employees in every city and town and usually had well-connected lobbyists in state capitals. In contrast, in most states there were no mutual fund firms. Even in states such as California, Massachusetts, and New York, where there were a number of fund firms, they had relatively few offices and employees. Mutual fund firms tended not to be politically active. Money funds had only one thing going for them: there were thousands of satisfied shareholders in every state. If the institute could learn of anti–money fund proposals in time to alert and mobilize fund shareholders, we might be able to end-run the normal state political process and defeat anti–money fund legislation.

Tennessee presented the first case. The banks and S&Ls were politically powerful: the amendment had been drafted by a lobbyist for the Tennessee Savings and Loan League and had been offered by a state senator who was a banker from Chattanooga. No money market fund firms were located in Tennessee. But some 33,000 Tennesseans owned money funds. Dave and I drafted an ad along the lines we had discussed on our car rides together, with the headline: "To Tennessee's Money Market Fund Shareholders: Don't Let Them Take it Away." Institute staff flew to Tennessee to place the ad in newspapers in cities around the state. We contacted money funds and brokerage firms so that they could alert their Tennessee shareholders and customers to the amendment. We waited to see what would happen.

All hell broke loose. Angry fund shareholders contacted their state legislators to urge defeat of the amendment. The state insurance commissioner (who also regulated securities) slammed the proposal. The Tennessee press had a field day and particularly enjoyed pointing out that the sponsor was a banker. The sponsor withdrew the amendment.

In the course of the next two years, legislation to outlaw or restrict money funds was introduced in Alaska, Arkansas, Connecticut, Georgia, Iowa, Kansas, Kentucky, Louisiana, Maryland, Massachusetts, Nebraska, New Jersey, New York, North Carolina, North Dakota, Ohio, Oklahoma, Oregon, Rhode Island, Texas, Utah, and Washington.[20] The anti–money fund proposals took a number of forms. Some, like the amendment in Tennessee, would have explicitly prohibited the offer and sale of money fund shares in the state. Others would have imposed on the fund reserve, community reinvestment, or other requirements based on the value of fund shares sold in the state. Such a requirement would impact the fund as a whole and thus its shareholders in *all* states. Therefore, if a particular state were to enact such a requirement, money funds would have to cease offering shares in that state so as not to harm shareholders in other states.

The institute's first task was to create a surveillance system to identify anti–money fund proposals in states. There were no nationwide or even single-state monitoring services to which to subscribe. Bills and amendments did not have clear titles, such as "A Bill to Prohibit the Sale of Money Market Funds." Proposals could be quietly slipped in with little or no notice. We needed someone on the ground in each state capital who would constantly be on the alert. We built a fifty-state surveillance

to tennessee's money market fund shareholders:

Money market funds now give all Americans the chance to do what previously only the wealthy could do: earn the highest available rates of return on their savings. The funds afford those with moderate incomes the badly-needed opportunity to cope with inflation—and they do so by making investments that are generally agreed to be among the safest available.

Residents of Tennessee have put some $600 million in these mutual funds— which invest mainly in short-term money market securities of the federal government, blue-chip corporations and leading banks. The funds presently are returning about 15 per cent at minimal risk.

Now powerful interests want to take it away. The excerpt from the newspaper article reprinted at the right exposes the nationwide plan of bank and savings and loan groups to stifle money market funds.

In Tennessee the attack is under way. An amendment has been offered in the Senate to Bill 1925, which would, in the guise of increasing protection, totally prevent residents of Tennessee from buying money market funds. If the amendment passes Tennesseans will be the only people in the United States unable to get the high rates being paid by these funds. Some protection!

Do Tennesseans have to be protected against earning high rates of return on their money? What do United States government agencies think about money market funds?

Five regulatory bodies of the federal government testified at U.S. Congressional hearings in January 1980 and made the following comments.

"Money market funds also offer the small investor what institutional investors with their greater resources have always had: convenient and efficient access to the large denomination instruments of the money market and their current high yields . . . In the words of former SEC Chairman Ray Garrett, 'No issuer of securities is subject to more detailed regulation than mutual funds.'"
Commissioner Irving S. Pollack,
U.S. Securities and Exchange
Commission

"For investors with limited resources, the funds are a convenient substitute for investing directly in the money market . . . Diversification in such market instrument would otherwise be beyond the means or expertise of most households."
Governor J. Charles Partee,
Federal Reserve System Board
of Governors

"It is my understanding that to date the SEC has closely followed the growth and operation of the money market funds and that they are being run on a sound basis and there is a minimum of risk to the investor . . ."
Lawrence Connell,
Chairman of the National Credit
Union Administration

"Money market funds are a device by which savers pool their money together so that they can obtain a return on their funds close to the yields available on large money market instruments."
Jay Janis, Chairman of the
Federal Home Loan Bank Board

We believe that the proper way to solve the problems faced by competitors of money market funds is to eliminate rules and laws which prevent them from paying market rates of return and from competing with each other—not to enter pacts to restrain money market funds.
We believe that Americans who want to have the opportunity to combat inflation should not have the door slammed in their face by envious competitors.
And we believe the citizens of Tennessee will agree with us.

The Washington Post Tuesday, March 11, 1980

Banks, S&Ls Unite to Stop Money Market Funds Rise

By Merrill Brown
Washington Post Staff Writer

RICHMOND, March 10—Leaders of two of the nation's largest financial lobbying groups disclosed today that they had opened negotiations designed to develop legislation to stem the flow of consumer dollars from banks and savings and loans to money market funds.

These negotiations were revealed by C. C. Hope Jr., president of the American Bankers Association, and by Edwin B. Brooks, president of the United States League of Savings Associations.

Bankers view the talks between the groups as unique because the two are frequently both commercial competitors and political rivals on issues facing the financial industry.

"This is the first time we've decided to move together on legislation."
Hope said in an interview. "The S&Ls, the credit unions, the savings banks and the banks are all regulated industries. Now we have coming at us from all sides unregulated people."

The two association executives were among about 175 participants at the opening session of a two-day conference here on banking in the 1980s sponsored by Virginia Commonwealth University.

The program today featured speeches by banking executives and focused on the difficult times they face. Much of the discussion covered the loss of savings dollars from banks and S&Ls to money market mutual funds, which are virtually unregulated.

Money market mutual funds invest in securities that are sensitive to short-term interest rates.

Sales volume of these investment funds, which can offer savers interest rates now approximating 13 percent—more than double what most conventional banking institutions offer—has skyrocketed from about $2 billion a year and a half ago to about $60 billion today. Just last month money market funds grew by $11 billion, Hope said.

"It's imperative that we get a handle on this." Hope declared. These funds have no "insurance, no race ceilings, no early-withdrawal regulations, no peripheral benefits and no social requirements," he argued.

"If we are to be realistic, the regulated industries need to make certain that we work together with the Congress to level out the playing field," he said. . .

don't let them take it away.

Published by the Investment Company Institute, the national association of mutual funds, 1775 K Street, N.W., Washington, D.C. 20006.

Figure 4.1. Tennessee advertisement. Courtesy of the Investment Company Institute.

system of lobbyists, mutual fund employees, brokers, and consumer groups. At times, state securities officials or newspaper reporters would alert us. Our surveillance system was cobbled together. But it worked.

Once we learned of legislation in a particular state, one of us would immediately go there to meet in person with the sponsor to urge him to withdraw the proposal. Arkansas was a typical case. We received a call from our person on the ground in Little Rock that a legislator was about to introduce an anti–money market fund bill. I grabbed my overnight bag (which I kept in the office for these types of emergencies) and went to the airport to get a flight. While I was en route, Dave was to retain a lobbyist who was to meet me at 8 A.M. the next morning in the lobby of "the best hotel in town." I managed to get a flight to Little Rock, but when the plane was about to land it was diverted to another city due to weather conditions. As I stood in line to rent a car, I overheard the man in front of me say that he was driving to Little Rock. I offered to pay his rental fees if he gave me a ride, and off we went. We drove for a while and I asked my companion where he lived. "Arkansas," he replied. We drove on, and I asked what he did for a living. "Farmer." I explained that I was going to Little Rock on a legislative matter. He said that in addition to being a farmer he was a member of the legislature. "What luck," I thought. He asked me if I knew anything about Arkansas politics, and I said, "Not much." He said something like, "There are only three Republicans in the legislature. I'm one of them. So I can't help you." We arrived in Little Rock in the middle of the night, I got a hotel room, and at 8 A.M. I met the lobbyist Dave had retained, as well as an executive from Merrill Lynch. We went to the capitol building and met with the legislator who had introduced the bill to explain its likely impact. He decided to withdraw it. We were similarly successful in North Carolina and Washington.

In other states, there was no time for meetings because the sponsors attempted to rush the legislation through as quickly and stealthily as possible. For example, in Kansas a bill that had passed the state Senate was amended on the House floor to place reserve requirements on money funds. Thus there were no hearings on the bill. In these situations, the institute could not run newspaper ads in time. So we engaged in the tactic, highly unusual at that time, of running radio ads, typically during rush-hour drive times, urging money fund shareholders to contact their legislators to demand a hearing. In some cases, local radio announcers and disc jockeys fell in love with the issue and on their own urged listeners to contact their state legislators.

We were able to obtain hearings in several states. In these cases, we worked with state officials to arrange for witnesses, including consumer groups, law professors, economists, and, if they existed, local funds. Some hearings were chaired by the very legislators who had introduced the anti–money fund legislation and became quite contentious. At the hearing in Texas, the chairman of the committee went into a tirade about fund lobbyists in Washington pushing buttons to directly contact millions of fund shareholders around the nation. I was sitting in the hearing room, lost my temper, demanded to be sworn in as a witness, and found myself in a heated exchange with the chairman, while representatives of Texas broker-dealers and mutual funds in the audience looked on in utter horror. The high point of the hearing occurred when one of our witnesses, a law professor from the University of Texas, said, "Mr. Chairman, I went back in my records and saw that twenty years ago you took my Corporations Course. Today I understand why I gave you a D." After we won, a lobbyist for the Texas S&L associations told the institute's press spokesman, Reg Green, "You didn't fight fair. You had a legislative issue, but you went to the people."

On several occasions we faced battles in two or three states at the same time, and we had to enlist the services of every professional at the institute. For example, we put Bill Tartikoff, our tax and pension attorney, in charge of the hearing in North Dakota. Bill was nervous, and I assured him that he couldn't lose because accompanying him would be an executive of the

Mutual of Omaha funds who was from North Dakota origi- nally, had written the state university's fight song, and must be an expert attorney on fund law because I had seen him at meetings of the institute's SEC Rules Committee. About 3 A.M. Washington time, I was awakened by a panicked phone call from Bill, who was calling from a bar in Bismarck to tell me that his "expert" was not an attorney but a salesman who liked to attend institute committee meetings. But Bill and our "expert" were successful. In fact, after each state hearing, the legislation died.

The toughest battle was in Utah.[21] The state had not had a new banking law in decades, and the anti–money fund provi- sion was tied to a much-needed modernization bill. The Utah banks were extremely powerful. Before we learned of the pro- posed legislation, they had succeeded in portraying the fight as the people of Utah against Merrill Lynch. Dave Silver went to Utah to try to take the spotlight off Merrill and shift the percep- tion of the fight to the people of Utah versus the bankers. The Utah Senate passed the bill, and everyone expected the House would do the same. A few days before the House vote, our Utah lawyers advised us to cease our efforts because our only hope was that the bankers would turn off House members by press- ing too hard.

On the evening of March 10, 1981, Steve Paggioli, an insti- tute attorney, and I sat in the House gallery to watch the vote on an electronic scoreboard. The banks were ahead, when sud- denly, a number of votes switched our way and money funds were ahead thirty-nine to thirty-six. The speaker banged his gavel and announced that voting was over and money funds had won. It turned out that under the rules of the Utah House, a legislator must vote in favor of a measure to seek to recall it. Our opponents had failed to coordinate among themselves. By error, *four* of them had switched to our side to be able to seek a recall. They demanded a recall, only to be reminded that the rules provided that in the last three days of a session, a two- thirds vote was needed for a recall. Money funds had won, due to a parliamentary blunder by their opponents. The House gallery broke into absolute pandemonium, similar to the end of an exciting sports event. I fought my way to a telephone, called Dave, and told him the unexpected good news.

Money funds' only legislative defeat was in Rhode Island, where we did not learn of the legislation until it had passed one house and was being voted on by the other. After the bill passed the second house, there were mounting protests from fund shareholders and concern expressed in the media. Fund industry representatives met with Governor John Garrahy, who vetoed the legislation.

The last major state battle was Kentucky. Dave went to Frankfort, ran into the sponsor of the bill in the hallway, and asked, "Do you realize that your bill would wipe out money market funds?" He replied, "I certainly hope so." I went to Kentucky to relieve Dave and prepare our witnesses for a hearing. For once, I had a local fund representative, an executive from Hillard-Lyons, a Kentucky securities firm that sponsored a money fund. This backfired when our opponent, the committee chairman, announced with his voice rising: "Mr. Fink's next witness is Mr. Smith, from *Louisville*." It suddenly dawned on me that to most members of the Kentucky legislature, Louisville was akin to New York City, Paris, and Sodom and Gomorrah. Somehow, we made it through the hearing and defeated the bill. It turned out that our opponent had a sense of humor. After we had defeated his bill, Senate Bill 306, he introduced a resolution providing "it is the desire of the Senate that the number SB 306, as a legislative number, be hereby retired, never to be used again—on any piece of legislation."

Looking back today, it may seem as though the state money fund battles, with the final score something like twenty-three to nothing, must have been walks in the park. I assure you, they were not. There were many gut-wrenching moments and a number of close calls. In the end, money market funds and their defenders changed history. Money funds provided millions of average investors with market rates of return similar to those earned by wealthy investors and institutions. They led to the removal of interest rate ceilings on bank and S&L deposits. They provided the mutual fund industry with millions of new shareholders, many of whom went on to invest in stock and bond funds. Money funds were clearly the most important product innovation in the history of the mutual fund industry.

5

Other Responses to the Bear Market

Nine tenths of wisdom is being wise on time.
—Theodore Roosevelt

Well before the start of the prolonged bear market of
the 1970s, people in the mutual fund industry, at the
Securities and Exchange Commission (SEC), in academia,
and elsewhere thought about the creation of new types
of mutual funds and new ways to distribute fund shares
to investors. But these ideas did not get off the ground.
The fund industry was doing so well with its traditional
product, equity funds, and its traditional distribution
system, broker-dealers, that no one sought to create new
types of funds and distribution systems. The bear market changed everything. Clearly, it was time to put these
ideas into practice.

Tax-Exempt Funds

For many years, mutual fund companies had thought of creating
funds that would invest in tax-exempt state and municipal bonds

and pass the interest on to fund shareholders (minus expenses) in the form of tax-exempt dividends. This would provide investors with a number of advantages: the investor could invest in a fund with smaller amounts than the usual $10,000 minimum required to buy municipal bonds directly; by purchasing fund shares, the investor would obtain diversification and professional management; the investor could see the fund's price in the newspaper every day, whereas prices on the vast majority of tax-exempt bonds were not reported; and the fund would be fully subject to the investor protections afforded by the federal securities laws, whereas municipal bonds were exempt from SEC regulation. In addition, states and municipalities would have a new market for their obligations. There was just one small problem: federal income tax law prevented the creation of tax-exempt mutual funds. Specifically, because the law treated mutual funds (whether organized as corporations or business trusts) as corporations, *all* dividends paid by a mutual fund, even those derived from tax-exempt interest, were subject to federal income tax.

Interestingly, the first call for legislation to permit mutual funds to pass through tax-exempt interest to fund shareholders did not emanate from the fund industry but from President Dwight D. Eisenhower in his economic report to Congress in January 1955. Thereafter, the Investment Company Institute drafted legislation, bills were introduced in Congress, and hearings were held in 1958, but the legislation was not enacted into law. Edwin S. Cohen, the institute's outside tax counsel, suspected that key members of Congress, specifically Wilbur Mills, chairman of the House Ways and Means Committee, were not favorably disposed toward tax-exempt interest and were concerned that enactment of the proposal would increase the number of voters who would oppose limiting or eliminating the exemption.[1]

In the history of the mutual fund industry published in 1960, Hugh Bullock reported, "Best opinion is that...[legislation] will come in due course."[2] In this case, "due course" took sixteen years.

During the 1960s, the mutual fund industry was focused on the strong bull market in equities; no one gave much thought to reviving the municipal bond fund initiative. But in the early 1970s, with the onset of the bear market, the industry's attention shifted to the development of nonequity products. In particular, due to prevailing high interest rates, the industry was attracted to the creation of funds investing in long-term debt instruments, including tax-exempt funds. Kemper created the first municipal bond fund in the form of a Nebraska limited partnership. Fidelity followed with the first no-load municipal bond fund in the same format. The Kemper and Fidelity funds were able to pass tax-exempt interest on to their shareholders but were incredibly complex to administer. Many in the mutual fund industry returned to the idea of legislation that would permit the creation of tax-exempt funds in the traditional corporate form. I remember in particular that Howard Stein, the head of Dreyfus, was extremely pessimistic about prospects for the stock market, was focused on money market and bond funds, and very much wanted legislation permitting the creation of tax-exempt funds.[3]

At the same time, external events made enactment of legislation more likely. New York City was in difficult financial shape, there was increasing concern over the financial condition of America's cities, and there was general recognition that state and local governments would have to increase their spending and hence their borrowing. Traditionally the largest purchasers of municipal securities, banks were decreasing their purchases because they had found more profitable ways to invest. More individuals were entering high income tax brackets, thus making tax-exempt obligations attractive to them.

So the Investment Company Institute's president, Bob Augenblick, dusted off the 1958 proposal. Augenblick assembled a team consisting of himself, Ed Cohen, and Ramsay Potts, the institute's legislative counsel. They were assisted by Donald Petrie, an attorney and investment banker retained by Dreyfus. The legislation was supported by the Municipal Finance Officers Association; the National Governors Conference; the National Association of Counties; the Conference of Mayors; the American Federation of State, County and Municipal Employees; and the

Council of State Housing Authorities. The Treasury Department did not object to the proposal but did not sponsor it because it was seeking other changes related to tax-exempt interest. The Senate Finance Committee reported out a tax reform bill that did not include the municipal bond fund provision. On the Senate floor, Senator Charles Percy of Illinois, who was not a member of the Finance Committee, offered an amendment incorporating the institute's proposal, which was accepted by Finance Committee Chairman Russell Long. The Senate-House Conference adopted the proposal, which was enacted as part of the Tax Reform Act of 1976.

The 1976 legislation had a greater positive impact than any of us had imagined. As we expected, the fund industry brought out funds that permitted investors to own portfolios consisting of tax-exempt securities issued by states and municipalities from across the nation. At year end 2008, these "national" municipal funds had assets of $202 billion. In addition, the industry developed two other products we had not anticipated. First are funds that invest exclusively in tax-exempt securities issued by entities in a *single* state, so that fund dividends are exempt from both federal and state income tax. At year end 2008, single-state municipal funds had assets of $134 billion. Second are money market funds that invest in short-term tax-exempt instruments. The first of these tax-exempt money market funds was offered by Fidelity in 1980. At year end 2008, these funds had assets of $491 billion.[4] The development of these latter funds gave rise to a new problem that necessitated additional legislation, which in turn required a third piece of legislation.[5]

Index Funds

Just as the idea for tax-exempt funds had been discussed for years, academic researchers had long maintained that investors would reduce risk and generally obtain better returns by investing in the market as a whole, rather than selecting individual securities. William F. Sharpe, who went on to receive the Nobel Prize in Economic Science, authored a leading paper in 1961.

He was recently quoted as saying, "The most efficient thing to do is hold the market portfolio....The idea was that your combination of risky securities ought to be 'the market'—everything that's out there."[6]

Institutional money managers were the first to put these academic concepts into practice. In 1971, Wells Fargo Bank created an indexed portfolio for Samsonite's pension fund account. The portfolio, which held equal dollar amounts of each of the roughly 1,500 stocks listed on the New York Stock Exchange, proved unwieldy to manage. It later became part of the bank's commingled trust account that tracked the Standard & Poor's (S&P) 500 index, weighted according to each security's outstanding capitalization. Later that same year, Batterymarch Financial Services, an institutional money management firm, decided to pursue index investing, although it did not obtain its first client until 1974. In 1974, the American National Bank in Chicago formed a common trust fund that invested in the S&P 500 index.[7]

In 1973, Burton G. Malkiel of Princeton University, in his book *A Random Walk Down Wall Street,* called for the creation of an indexed mutual fund. In 1974, Paul A. Samuelson of the Massachusetts Institute of Technology and a Nobel laureate in economics, suggested that CREF or the American Economic Association create an indexed vehicle. In 1975, Charles D. Ellis, president of Greenwich Associates, a pension consulting firm, argued, "If you can't beat the market, you should certainly consider joining it. An index fund is one way." That same year, *Fortune* associate editor A. F. Ehbar urged the creation of "a mutual fund with low expenses and management fees, about the same degree as the market as a whole, and a policy of always being invested."[8]

Against this background in 1976, Vanguard, under Jack Bogle's leadership, created the first indexed mutual fund, First Index Investment Trust, now named the Vanguard 500 Index Fund. The initial underwriting for the fund produced only $11.4 million, less than one-tenth the assets that Vanguard hoped to attract. Over time, this first indexed mutual fund proved to be extremely popular, and today it is one of the largest mutual funds.[9] In subsequent years, Vanguard brought out additional index funds and currently offers domestic stock index funds, international stock index funds, and bond index funds. A number of other mutual fund firms have sponsored index funds.At year end 2008, index funds had assets of approximately $604 billion, 10 percent of total stock and bond fund assets.[10]

Proponents of indexing remain adamant in their belief that it is the best way to invest. As is often the case with true believers, they are sharply divided on the proper way to accomplish their goal. First, there is a running debate between those who favor indexing via the use of indexed mutual funds and those who favor it through the use of exchange-traded funds, a new type of investment company whose shares trade in the secondary market. Second, proponents of indexing are split on the proper way to index. Burton Malkiel and Jack Bogle continue to vigorously support indexing based on capitalization. In the other camp, Professors Jeremy Siegel, Eugene Fama, and Kenneth French advocate "fundamental" indexing, in which components are weighted according to such factors as sales, earnings, book values, and dividends. Both sides in this debate point to history to support their claims. Proponents of traditional capitalization indexing stress its thirty-year track record. Proponents of fundamental indexing point out that it has outperformed traditional indexing in recent years.[11] Index funds are here to stay, but it is not clear which particular type of indexing will prevail.

Advertising

Today's newspaper and magazine readers, as well as television viewers, are accustomed to seeing advertisements for mutual funds. Fund ads, including those presenting a fund's past performance, are common and do not seem unusual. But for most of mutual funds' history, it was illegal for funds to advertise. This was not the result of any scandal or any congressional or SEC policy decision. Instead, it was due to a strict interpretation given to the first of the federal securities laws, the Securities Act of 1933, a statute that is ill-designed for mutual funds.

The 1933 act was enacted to regulate offerings of new securities by operating companies. Section 5 makes it illegal for a company seeking to sell its securities to investors to transmit any advertisement or other communication offering such securities unless the communication meets the requirements of a full statutory prospectus or is preceded or accompanied by the full prospectus. There is a limited statutory exception for a tombstone advertisement, which is not considered to be an offer for securities because it can only identify the securities, their price, who will execute orders, and from whom a full prospectus can be obtained. (In 1954 Congress granted the SEC authority to permit additional information in tombstones and the use of prospectuses that omit or summarize information in the full prospectus.)[12]

Section 5's restrictions do not impose undue burdens on most corporations. They only issue new securities occasionally; even during an offering they are free to advertise their products. But a literal reading of section 5 has a devastating impact on marketing by mutual funds. Mutual funds issue new shares on a continuous basis, so are always subject to the strictures of section 5. Moreover, a fund's only product is its shares, and under a strict reading of section 5, these shares can never be advertised. A syndicated financial columnist put it well:

> None of these restrictions, ironically, were ever intended by the SEC to be a harrassment [sic] to the mutual fund industry. They were originally designed to regulate the securities offerings of industrial issuers who were hitting the market once and, it was felt, had to be restrained from going overboard in their promises to would-be-investors. What this didn't take into account was the fact that mutual funds have nothing to sell but shares in themselves, and that this is a continuous process—not a one-shot sales effort. And the result, predictably, has been to cut off, almost entirely, any really effective mutual fund advertising.[13]

In the early 1970s, the SEC was concerned that the industry was dominated by load funds sold by broker-dealers, and in 1972 the commission held hearings on fund distribution. The SEC sought to encourage alternative, less costly methods of distribution and create a "demand pull" for fund shares that would permit them to be sold with no load or at low loads. In the release announcing the hearings, the SEC flagged the mutual fund advertising problem: "Advertising, an effective and a relatively low-cost method of conveying information to prospective purchasers, has been confined to a minimal role in the marketing of investment company securities. Restrictions on advertising have made it difficult for the mutual fund industry to tell its story through the mass media."[14]

The SEC, with strong industry support, attempted to ameliorate the situation by successively expanding the tombstone rule for mutual funds. But each step of the way the commission expressed concern that permitting a fund tombstone to contain too much information would result in the impermissible offer of securities through an advertisement.

First, in 1972, the SEC permitted a fund tombstone to contain a general description of an investment company, including its general attributes, method of operation, and services offered, provided the description was not inconsistent with the fund running the ad. After the SEC acted, Chairman William J. Casey warned the industry:

> It is...a basic principle of the Securities Act of 1933 that securities which are being distributed pursuant to registration under that Act shall not, in effect, be "pre-sold" by advertising before the investor even has an opportunity to see the prospectus....In view of the special problems of the mutual fund industry, we have undertaken to relax to some degree the traditional interpretations with respect to the advertising of registered securities....We probably have not gone as far in this respect as you would like— indeed, perhaps not as far as we would like—but there are limits upon the extent to which we can tamper with this important principle under the Securities Act in the mutual fund area without gravely compromising it as to registered securities in general.[15]

Second, in 1974, the SEC expanded the rule by allowing additional items, such as a description of the fund's objectives and policies, identification of the principal officers, the year of the fund's and adviser's organization or the period of their existence, and the aggregate asset value of the fund (or all funds under common management). Following adoption of these amendments, a senior SEC staff official stated that inclusion of performance figures "has always been prohibited, on the theory that it would amount to selling securities through an advertisement."[16] In 1975, the SEC further broadened the tombstone rule to permit "descriptive material relating to economic conditions, or to retirement plans or other goals to which an investment in the company could be directed, *but not directly or indirectly relating to past performance or implying achievement of investment objectives.*"[17]

Despite these repeated expansions of the fund tombstone rule, everyone involved—industry officials, media representatives, SEC commissioners, and SEC staff—felt frustrated that strict application of the 1933 act was preventing mutual funds from engaging in meaningful advertising, particularly prohibiting them from presenting the item investors most wanted to see—a fund's past investment performance. A number of new approaches were suggested. SEC Chairman Casey and Commissioner Roberta S. Karmel raised the possibility of seeking legislation to amend the 1933 act to address the unique situation of mutual fund advertising.[18] The Investment Company Institute suggested that the SEC adopt a general mutual fund advertising code to replace the expanded tombstone and other fund advertising rules.[19]

The tension between funds' desire to advertise and strict application of the 1933 act further increased when the Supreme Court decided a series of cases making it clear that the protections of the First Amendment extend to commercial speech. I recall Dave Silver asking if I had read the cases. I had only read stories about them. Dave asked how, in light of the cases, could the SEC prevent mutual funds from advertising. I replied something like, "Come on, Dave, there is the Securities Act of 1933." He responded, "Matt, which do you think takes precedence, the Securities Act of 1933 or the First Amendment to the Constitution?" As a result of Dave's insight, the institute retained David L. Ratner of Cornell Law School to analyze the applicability of these cases to fund advertising. Ratner concluded, "The recent decisions mandate a completely new look at the overall scheme of regulation of mutual fund advertising." The institute submitted his analysis to the SEC, and Commissioner Karmel stated that "the recent awareness that advertising is entitled to some constitutional protection under the First Amendment should influence the Commission's rulemaking."[20]

The logjam was broken when a senior SEC staff official, Stanley Judd, suggested a new regulatory approach to his boss, the associate director of the SEC Division of Investment Management, Joel Goldberg. Judd pointed out that in 1954, Congress had given the SEC authority to permit a prospectus that omits information in the full statutory prospectus, and suggested that such an "omitting prospectus" could take the form of an advertisement. This led the SEC in June 1977 to propose rule 434d, which would have permitted a fund to run an ad (technically a summary prospectus) containing *any* information (including the fund's performance), the substance of which is in the fund's regular prospectus. The proposal would have limited an ad to 600 words and required that it appear in a newspaper or magazine of general circulation (not on radio or television). The Investment Company Institute and other industry commentators objected to these restrictions and expressed concern that mutual funds would be reluctant to run these types of ads because they would be subject to strict prospectus liability under the 1933 act. In August 1979, the SEC adopted rule 434d (subsequently renumbered rule 482) with two significant changes from the original proposal: first, the final rule deleted the proposed 600-word limitation; second, it deleted the proposed ban on radio and TV ads.[21]

The rule has proved to be of major benefit to funds that market directly to the public and to investors. Between 1980 and 2001, the percent of equity fund sales due to no-load funds and no-load share classes rose from 34 to 58 percent, and the percent of no-load bond fund sales rose from 47 to 64 percent.[22] Many factors contributed to the increased popularity of no-load funds, including the growth of 401(k) plans, investors' increased use of financial planners who recommend no-load funds, and the decision by several major fund groups (Dreyfus, Fidelity, Vanguard) to move from broker-dealer distribution to direct marketing. I have no doubt that advertising pursuant to rule 482 has provided a major boost to the no-load segment of the industry. Moreover, the popularity of these funds placed competitive pressures on the entire industry, helping produce a sharp decline in fees and expenses, particularly in the area of distribution costs.

Rule 12b-1

No aspect of mutual fund operations has been more debated than the practice of funds paying for the distribution of their own shares to investors. For many years, the SEC took the position that this practice was prohibited by the Investment Company Act. The distribution of fund shares was paid for in two other ways. In the case of load funds, investors paid sales charges when purchasing shares. In the case of no-load funds, fund advisers paid for advertising and other marketing activities. In 1980, a confluence of factors led the SEC to adopt rule 12b-1, which permits funds themselves to pay for distribution. Today the vast majority of funds have 12b-1 plans, which are primarily used to compensate financial advisers for the sale of fund shares and the provision of ongoing services to shareholders. The rule contains a number of safeguards, and others have been added. Even so, rule 12b-1 remains enveloped in controversy.

The Investment Company Act contains provisions addressing the costs of distributing fund shares in different situations. Section 10 deals with no-load funds, section 22 with load funds, and section 27 with contractual plans. Section 12(b) addresses a fourth situation, where the fund itself acts as the distributor of its shares, and provides that it is unlawful for a mutual fund to "act as a distributor of securities of which it is the issuer, except through an underwriter, in contravention of such rules and regulations as the Commission may prescribe." The legislative history indicates that the section was intended to protect mutual funds "against excessive sales, promotion expenses, and so forth." Similarly, Alfred Jaretzki Jr., one of the industry participants who helped draft the 1940 act, explained, "Apparently the Commission was particularly fearful of the possibility that open-end investment companies in their formative stages might be made to shoulder the unprofitable burden of selling and distributing their shares during this period of heavy expense and small return, building up the investment company for the benefit of some controlling person."[23]

On its face, section 12(b) bars a fund from acting as distributor of its shares only "in contravention of [SEC] rules," and the SEC had never adopted rules. Still the SEC took the position that it was unlawful for a fund to bear distribution expenses, stating, "The cost of selling and purchasing mutual fund shares should be borne by the investors who purchase them and thus presumably receive the benefits of the investment, and not, even in part, by the existing shareholders of the fund who often receive little or no benefit from the sale of new shares. To impose a portion of the selling cost upon the existing shareholders of the fund may violate principles of fairness which are at least implicit in the Investment Company Act."[24]

In the late 1970s, the SEC to begin to rethink its position. The Vanguard funds were in the process of acquiring ownership of their investment manager and distributor. This internalization meant there would not be the usual outside third party to bear distribution costs. For this reason and because the funds were no-load, the only potential source of financing fund distribution was the funds themselves. Therefore, the Vanguard Group sought and obtained SEC exemptive orders permitting the funds to bear distribution expenses. At around the same time, the SEC staff was faced with a request from an adviser-distributor to a newly formed money market fund to reallocate 50 percent of its advisory fee to dealers who sold fund shares, a practice that is tantamount to using fund assets to pay for distribution.[25] Another adviser designed an arrangement whereby its fund would pay two separate fees: a 0.25 percent fee for investment management and a separate 0.25 percent fee for distribution, an explicit use of fund assets for distribution.

These developments led the SEC to hold two public hearings on the issue of funds bearing distribution expenses. As stated in an SEC release, some industry participants "supported use of fund assets for distribution by arguing that net redemptions may harm fund performance by reducing the adviser's flexibility in managing the fund's portfolio. Others have contended that use of fund assets for distribution could lead to economies of scale or net savings."[26]

On October 28, 1980, the SEC adopted rule 12b-1. The rule makes it unlawful for a mutual fund to act as a distributor of its shares unless it adopts a written distribution plan. A fund is considered to be acting as a distributor if it finances any activity designed to result in the sale of its shares, including advertising and compensation of sales personnel. The plan must be adopted and renewed annually by the fund's directors, including a majority of independent directors. Although the rule does not set forth factors the directors should consider, the SEC's release that accompanied the rule lists nine factors that normally would be relevant, including the nature and causes of the "problems or circumstances" that make the plan appropriate and the way the plan would be expected to address them.[27]

It was anticipated by the SEC and the industry that 12b-1 plans in the 0.25 percent or lower range would be used by no-load groups to supplement their marketing activities and by load funds to supplement their front-end sales charges. The first distribution plans were of the type envisioned when the commission adopted the rule. That is, the plans typically provided for payments of 0.25 percent or less of average annual fund assets to fund advisers and underwriters for advertising, printing and mailing of sales literature, and printing and mailing of prospectuses to nonshareholders.[28]

An entirely new type of 12b-1 plan was conceived of by Gary Strum, an attorney with E. F. Hutton. Strum was aware that variable annuities often used a system whereby investors purchased the product without paying front-end sales charges. Instead, the insurance company paid sales personnel up-front commissions and over time recovered those payments through annual "mortality and expense" charges assessed against the fund. If an investor redeemed before a stated period of time, he or she paid a contingent deferred sales load (CDSL). Strum was the first to realize that the CDSL structure could be adapted to conventional mutual funds, with a 12b-1 fee substituting for variable annuities' mortality and expense charges. In 1982, a mutual fund, E. F. Hutton Investment Series, received an SEC exemptive order permitting imposition of CDSLs, and an entirely new type of 12b-1 plan, the "spread load" plan, was born.[29]

Spread load plans soon became common. Fund sponsors also developed other types of 12b-1 plans, and pursuant to SEC exemptive orders (subsequently codified into an SEC rule), many funds began offering different classes of shares with different types of 12b-1 plans, typically as follows:

- Class A shares have a traditional front-end sales charge at the time of purchase plus an annual 12b-1 fee of 0.25 percent.

- Class B shares have a spread load. The investor does not pay a front-end sales charge. The class pays an annual 12b-1 fee of 1.00 percent, and an investor pays a CDSL on a redemption within five or six years. The CDSL decreases each year and reaches zero after six or seven years. At that point, B shares usually convert to A shares.

- Class C shares have a level load. The investor does not pay a front-end sales charge, the class pays an annual 12b-1 fee of 1.00 percent, and the investor pays a CDSL on shares redeemed within the first year. C shares, unlike B shares, do not convert to A shares.

Class A shares are an example of the kind of 12b-1 plans that the SEC and the industry had anticipated: the 0.25 percent 12b-1 fee is designed to supplement the front end sales charge. In contrast, Class B and C shares have a totally different purpose: the 1.00 percent 12b-1 fee allows individual shareholders to pay sales loads over time and is a substitute for a front-end load.

There are other types of 12b-1 plans. For example, many funds use 12b-1 plans to pay brokers, pension fund administrators, and fund supermarkets that distribute fund shares for shareholder record-keeping services customarily provided by the fund's transfer agent. In these situations a 12b-1 plan helps insulate the fund from the assertion that the record-keeping fee is inflated to award these parties for distributing fund shares.

A study conducted by the Investment Company Institute indicated that in 2004, 92 percent of 12b-1 fees went to compensate financial advisers and other intermediaries for assisting investors in purchasing fund shares (40 percent) and for ongoing shareholder services (52 percent). Six percent went to fund underwriters, and only 2 percent went for promotion and advertising.[30]

Subsequent events regarding rule 12b-1 plans are discussed in chapter 9.

Snapshot of the Industry in 1980

In 1980, the mutual fund industry looked totally different than it had in 1940, 1950, 1960, and 1970. In every one of those years, over 90 percent of fund assets consisted of equity funds, with the small remainder in bond and income funds. The advent of money market funds changed everything. In 1979, for the first time, money fund assets ($46 billion) exceeded those of equity funds ($36 billion). By 1980, money market funds accounted for 57 percent of total industry assets, stock funds for 33 percent, and bond and income funds for 10 percent.[31]

The explosion in money market funds was reflected in the fact that in 1980 the five largest funds were this type of fund: Merrill Lynch Ready Assets Trust, Intercapital Liquid Asset Trust, Dreyfus Liquid Assets, Cash Reserve Management (Morgan Guarantee Trust), and Morgan Stanley Liquid Assets

Fund. This phenomenon was also reflected in the fact that the four largest groups (Merrill Lynch, Dreyfus, Fidelity, and Federated) were major sponsors of money funds. IDS, which had been the largest group in 1970, was now number five.[32]

In addition to the dominant story of money market funds, there were other trends.

Equity funds had had a rough time during the 1970s, but bond funds did well. Equity fund assets were *less* in 1980 ($44 billion) than they were a decade earlier ($45 billion). Bond and income funds in 1980 amounted to $14 billion, up more than five-fold from 1970. Thus, for the first time the fund industry offered a robust family of equity, bond, and money market funds.[33]

Direct marketed (no-load) funds were on the rise. In 1970, they accounted for only 11 percent of long-term fund sales. As broker-dealers stopped selling fund shares, several major fund groups that had traditionally sold through that channel switched to direct sales to investors on a no-load basis. The first to do so was the Vanguard Group in 1977. In response to Vanguard's action, Dreyfus ran an advertisement with the Dreyfus lion roaring "No Load? No Way!"[34] However, both Dreyfus and Fidelity soon moved to the no-load format. By 1980, no-load funds and no-load share classes accounted for over 30 percent of equity fund sales and over 40 percent of bond fund sales.[35]

Transformation of the Industry

From its start in 1924, the mutual fund industry relied almost exclusively on a single product, equity funds, and a single distribution system, broker-dealers. The severity and length of the 1970s bear market undermined this narrow strategy. The response to adversity was to create new types of funds and distribution systems, thus transforming the industry and positioning it for future growth. That growth was accelerated by two other developments—a revolution in the country's private retirement system and the reentry of securities firms and banks into the investment company business.

6

The Revolution in Retirement Plans

When the end of the world comes, I want to be living in retirement.

—Karl Kraus

Today it is quite natural to associate mutual funds with retirement plans. After all, mutual funds are the largest funding medium for 401(k) and other defined contribution plans as well as for individual retirement accounts (IRAs). Mutual funds constitute 23 percent of all U.S. retirement plan assets.[1] The close association between mutual funds and retirement plans is a relatively new phenomenon. For many years, the corporate retirement market was dominated by defined benefit plans, which did not invest to any significant degree in mutual fund shares. Management of the smaller universe of defined contribution plans was dominated by banks and insurance companies, which did not make use of mutual funds. The revolution in retirement plans began quietly in 1962 when Congress permitted self-employed individuals to establish retirement plans. It accelerated with the enactment of the Employee Retirement Income Security

Act of 1974, which created the first IRAs, and took a quantum leap forward in 1981 when Congress permitted all workers to have IRAs and the Internal Revenue Service adopted regulations laying the groundwork for 401(k) plans.

First Fund Involvement with Retirement Plans: Keogh Plans

The revolution in the relationship between mutual funds and retirement plans began in 1962 when Congress authorized self-employed individuals to establish retirement plans. These plans were commonly referred to as Keogh plans because Congressman Eugene J. Keogh, a Democrat from New York, led the long effort to enact legislation.

Before 1962, the federal income tax code only permitted employees to be covered by qualified pension plans; therefore, self-employed individuals were not able to obtain pension coverage. For over a decade, attorneys, physicians, architects, and other professionals lobbied for legislation permitting self-employed individuals to establish retirement plans similar to corporate plans. They were vigorously opposed during both the Eisenhower and Kennedy administrations by the Treasury Department, which raised a number of objections, notably the creation of a new "tax preference" or "subsidy" that would erode the tax base. Each year, Congressman Keogh introduced his bill, which always bore the number H.R. 10. The legislation passed the House a number of times but never made it through the Senate.

While professional associations and Treasury Department staff publicly battled over the issue, representatives of various segments of the financial industry, including banks, insurance companies, and mutual funds, met behind the scenes to work out legislative drafting problems and "to see to it that the legislation did not give one industry a competitive advantage over the others in furnishing investment opportunities for the self-employed."[2]

Finally, in 1962, in the face of continued Treasury opposition, Keogh and his allies succeeded in obtaining enactment of the Self-Employed Individuals Tax Retirement Act of 1962. The act

- permitted self-employed individuals to establish retirement plans;
- allowed a self-employed individual to contribute the lesser of $2,500 or 10 percent of self-employed income, but provided that only 50 percent of the contribution was deductible;
- required the self-employed individual to make contributions for employees with three years of service on a basis that was not discriminatory compared to his own contributions;
- permitted additional voluntary contributions that, though nondeductible, grew tax-free;
- prohibited the payment of benefits before age fifty-nine and a half; and
- required benefits to begin before age seventy and a half.

Although these and other requirements were far more restrictive than those imposed on corporate retirement plans, they did represent a beginning.

The 1962 act provided that funding of Keogh plans could be accomplished in a number of ways, including contributions to a bank-administered trust, purchase of annuity contracts, purchase of special government bonds, and contributions to bank custodial accounts invested solely in mutual fund shares. As one observer noted, this latter provision was based on the theory that if the trust agreement restricts investment to fund shares, the law "should require only that a bank be custodian of the securities in the trust under appropriate regulations of the secretary of the treasury. This proposal came from the National Association of Investment Companies [the predecessor of the Investment Company Institute]."[3] This was the first time the fund industry actively participated in the development of retirement plan legislation and the first time retirement legislation explicitly recognized mutual funds as an appropriate funding medium for retirement plans.

At first, there was relatively little interest in Keogh plans due to the complexity of the law and the severe limitation on deductible contributions. One mutual fund executive reported, "The original bill was so burdened by limitations and a history of opposition dating back over the several years of its development that there was little left to recommend it to the public when it finally passed."[4] But the self-employed were hopeful that over time Congress would expand the program so as to make Keogh plans comparable to corporate retirement plans.[5]

Their expectations were realized as Congress successively enhanced the program:

- In 1967, Congress eliminated the 50 percent limit on deductibility. A self-employed individual could now contribute and deduct the lesser of $2,500 or 10 percent of earned income.

- In 1974, the Employee Retirement Income Security Act (ERISA) increased the deductible limit to the lesser of $7,500 or 15 percent of earned income.

- In 1981, the limit was raised again, to the lesser of $15,000 or 15 percent of earned income.

- Finally, the Tax Equity and Fiscal Responsibility Act of 1982 granted full parity to Keogh and corporate plans—maximum contributions to both types of plans were set at the lesser of $30,000 or 25 percent of earned income.

Thus, the effort by the self-employed to obtain equal treatment that had begun in the early 1950s finally achieved total victory.

The reader may wonder about the process that produced the successive dollar limits on deductible contributions to Keogh plans, perhaps imagining that they resulted from careful analytical studies by economic experts or from shrewd political horse trading in Congress. In his autobiography, Edwin S. Cohen, who served as undersecretary of the Treasury for tax policy in the Nixon administration, recounted the story of how the 1974 limits on contributions to Keogh plans (and IRAs) were established. In November 1971, Peter Flanigan, a senior official in the White House, convened a meeting consisting of himself and top officials of the Treasury, Commerce, and Labor Departments and the Office of Management and Budget. Views differed sharply on the proposed IRA ceiling, and after bargaining the group voted: two in favor of a $2,000 limit and three in favor of $1,500. A similar split developed with respect to Keogh limits, with the vote two in favor of $5,000 and three for $7,500. Cohen reported: "As the meeting broke up, we all laughed at the way we had reached the decision, and agreed that it probably was of little moment because the Congress would doubtless reach a compromise at some different figures." Cohen was grilled about the proposed numbers when he testified before Congress, and he still assumed that Congress would establish its own limits. But when ERISA was enacted over two years later, Cohen, who had left government, found that "I had to smile when I saw the final figures in the new law: $1,500 for IRAs and $7,500 for the self-employed, just the figures we had reached by the 3-to-2 votes in Peter Flanigan's office."[6]

Keogh plans, including those funded with mutual funds, grew rapidly. In 1967, there were 20,000 mutual fund Keogh plans with $82 million in assets. By 1970, there were 122,000 fund plans with assets of $350 million. By 1980, there were 225,000 fund plans with assets of $3.8 billion. The government did not compile statistics categorizing Keogh plans by funding media. But in 1968 *Barron's* reported that "plans run by mutual funds and life insurance companies apparently are the most popular." In 1974, the Investment Company Institute estimated that mutual funds accounted for about one-third of all Keogh plans and concluded, "The mutual fund industry has been *the* most successful financial institution in promoting the sale of Keogh plans since the original Act was passed in 1962." Subsequently, the institute reported that at year end 1976 mutual funds accounted for "well over 40 percent of the Keogh total."[7]

Not only was the fund industry extremely successful in the Keogh market, but the industry's experience with these plans laid the groundwork for funds' future success in other retirement markets. For the first time, fund marketing departments had to learn how to appeal to employers to establish plans and fund them with mutual funds. Back offices had to develop ways to economically administer small accounts and contributions for a number of individuals in the same firm. Legal counsel had to master meshing the differing requirements of the securities laws and pension laws. The Investment Company Institute began dealing with federal pension officials on a regular basis and started developing a wish list for future retirement legislation. The industry's learning from the Keogh experience paid off in spades when Congress took up major pension legislation in the early 1970s.

Most important, the Keogh debate changed the way retirement plans are viewed by policy makers, a change that proved to be of immense benefit to mutual funds. Traditionally, retirement plans had been regarded as a way to help employers manage their workforces, for example, as a means by which employers could induce older, highly paid workers to retire, so they could be replaced with younger, lower-paid employees. In the Keogh debate, the Treasury Department categorized retirement plans an entirely different way—as a government "subsidy" or "tax preference" designed to provide income to retirees—and the self-employed argued that it was unfair for the government to provide this subsidy or tax preference to some retirees but not others. A leading historian of retirement plans observed, "Debate about the tax subsidy prompted a shift in thinking about pension plans. In the emerging view, pension plans were more than tools for meeting personnel needs. They were vehicles for government to channel income to the aged."[8] This shift in thinking led future Congresses to enact a series of laws designed to channel more income to the aged. Mutual funds were to become the favored investment vehicle for this huge flow of money.

Increased Fund Involvement with Retirement Plans: ERISA

In 1940, Senator Sheridan Downey, a Democrat from California, referred to enactment of the Investment Company Act as a "miracle." Surely an even greater miracle was passage of the 1974 pension reform law, the Employee Retirement Income Security Act, commonly known as ERISA. ERISA had everything going against it. Both business groups and organized labor vehemently opposed comprehensive pension reform legislation. In both houses of Congress, jurisdiction over retirement plans overlapped two committees—the Senate Labor and Finance Committees, and the House Labor and Ways and Means Committees—an almost certain recipe for legislative paralysis. I doubt if any observer in 1972 and 1973 bet on the enactment of ERISA. Yet this miracle occurred. It is beyond the scope of this book to explain how this happened. I do want to focus on the provisions of ERISA that most directly affected mutual funds.

It cannot be emphasized too strongly that the congressional draftsmen of ERISA were concerned almost exclusively with defined benefit (DB) plans—plans where employers promise specific benefits to employees, make the investment decisions, and bear the investment risk. DB plans were by far the dominant type and the source of the problems that led to the legislation. Defined contribution plans—plans where employees make their own investment decisions and bear the investment risk—were barely on policy makers' radar screens. Mutual funds had zero interest in DB plans because DB plans did not invest in funds to any significant extent. Mutual funds' interests were confined to specialized segments of the defined contribution market.

When congressional committees started considering pension reform legislation, Dave Silver, then the institute's general counsel, asked me to assemble a committee of institute members to develop the mutual fund industry's recommendations. At that time, very few people in the fund industry had expertise in retirement plans. I put together an ad hoc group of members, including Harry Lister of Calvin Bullock, Wayne Leizear of Chemical Fund, Royce Sanner of IDS, and Gary Strum of Lord, Abbett. Harry and Wayne were well versed in Keogh plans. Royce had experience with 403(b) plans, which at the time could be funded only with insurance annuities. Gary was a securities lawyer who wanted to learn about retirement plans.

The group developed a wish list that included expanding the contribution limits and technical amendments for Keogh plans, permitting section 403(b) plans to invest in fund shares in addition to annuities, and technical suggestions relating to the Nixon administration's idea of creating IRAs for workers who were not covered by employer plans.

Dave and I decided we should seek inclusion of these suggestions in proposed legislation at the earliest possible time. The institute testified on the early bills, and I immediately began meeting with members and staff of the four congressional committees. There were scores of lobbyists all over Capitol Hill focused on defined benefit plans. I seemed to be the only lobbyist interested in Keogh plans, 403(b) plans, and IRAs.

ERISA enacted the mutual fund industry's *entire* wish list and laid the foundation for funds' future explosive growth in the retirement market. Looking back now, I can identify the reasons for our success. We had a small, well-defined agenda. We were the only group concentrating on defined contribution plans, Keogh Plans, and IRAs, so we had no competition. In contrast, major participants in the pension world were slugging it out with one another over issues relating to defined benefit plans. We did not have to coordinate a team of actuaries, attorneys, and lobbyists. With coaching from Dave, *I* was the team. I would come to the office at 6 or 7 A.M. to draft testimony and talking points, and at 9 A.M. would go up to the Hill to lobby.

Keogh Plans

Mutual funds' expertise in the Keogh plan world gave the ad hoc committee insight into ways to improve the program, such as raising contribution limits to make them more comparable to those permitted for corporate plans, permitting qualified entities other than banks to serve as custodians, permitting cash basis taxpayers to make deductible contributions up to the time for filing their tax returns, and permitting owner-employees to withdraw voluntary nondeductible contributions prior to age fifty-nine and a half.[9]

We conveyed our suggestions to the Nixon administration's Treasury Department which was reviewing the taxation of retirement plans. The administration wanted to narrow the disparity between contributions that could be made to Keogh and corporate plans and also extend retirement plan coverage to the millions of Americans who were not covered by employer plans. The approach chosen would be to allow these workers to make tax-deductible contributions to a new vehicle, the IRA However, if the IRA contribution limit were set too high, there was the danger that self-employed individuals would adopt IRAs and terminate their Keogh plans (which covered both themselves *and* their employees). The administration ended up proposing raising the Keogh limit from $2,500 to $7,500 and imposing a $1,500 limit on IRAs. Congress adopted these dollar limits as well as the technical changes we recommended. The tripling of the contribution limit was a boon to Keogh plans and to mutual funds in which the plans invested. At year end 1974, Keogh plans had $1.1 billion invested in mutual funds. By 1980, despite the bear market, assets of fund Keogh plans had more than tripled to $3.8 billion.[10]

403(b) Plans

Prior to the enactment of ERISA, public school teachers and employees of nonprofit organizations, such as colleges and hospitals, could provide for their retirement through a unique portable system. Section 403(b) of the Internal Revenue Code in effect authorized an employee to reduce compensation and contribute the reduced amount to the plan, where it would grow tax-free until retirement. Section 403(b) had its own set of highly complicated rules on the level of contributions, which referred to a variety of factors, such as current compensation, the number of years employed, and contributions made in previous years. (My wife was covered by a section 403(b) plan, and in her first year of coverage, three experts she consulted arrived at three different exclusion amounts.) Most surprising was the fact that section 403(b) plans could invest only in insurance company annuities. The insurance industry had a statutory monopoly.

At the time ERISA was being formulated, the largest and best known no-load mutual fund was T. Rowe Price Growth Fund. T. Rowe Price regularly received letters and calls from professors and teachers around the country, complaining that they could not invest their 403(b) contributions in the fund. The institute's ad hoc task force on pension reform made amendment of section 403(b) to permit investment in fund shares a priority. I kept expecting to hear opposition from the insurance industry or calls from the banking and other financial industries to be included in any expansion. But there was no controversy, and ERISA amended section 403(b) to permit investment in mutual fund shares.

Section 403(b) plans have become a major market for mutual funds. By the first quarter of 2009, approximately $243 billion of 403(b) assets was invested in mutual funds.[11]

IRAs

The Nixon administration proposed the creation of IRAs as a way to provide retirement benefits for workers not covered by employer plans. Under its proposal, a noncovered worker could make a tax-deductible contribution of up to $1,500 a year to an IRA. The money would grow tax-free and would be taxable on withdrawal at retirement. The institute testified in strong support of the IRA proposal and offered suggestions to hold down the costs of these small accounts, notably by permitting entities other than banks to serve as IRA custodians. The administration also proposed that IRAs could be used to help in the portability of pension benefits, specifically proposing that a worker who left a job or retired be permitted to take a lump-sum distribution from the employer's plan and "roll it over" to an IRA on a tax-free basis. ERISA authorized a $1,500 deductible IRA for workers not covered by employer plans, provided for rollover IRAs, and permitted the use of nonbank custodians.

The deductible IRA got off to slow start. Contributions amounted to only $1.4 billion in 1975, growing to $4.8 billion in 1981. One reason was the low contribution limit. Another factor was that banks, thrifts, insurance companies, brokerage firms, and mutual funds had no easy way to mass market IRAs to the very disparate universe of workers not covered by employer retirement plans. Mutual funds garnered only a small share of the IRA market, constituting just 7 percent of IRA assets in 1981. The dominant IRA investments were bank and thrift deposits, with a 72 percent share.[12]

I recall that some in the fund industry were discouraged by the early results from IRAs. However, those who were familiar with the Keogh experience, where Congress repeatedly raised contribution limits and funds gained an increasing share, viewed the original IRA as just the beginning. They were proven correct. By the first quarter of 2009, IRA assets amounted to $3.4 trillion, 44 percent of which was invested in mutual funds.[13]

Fiduciary Provisions

There was another major issue. In 1972, Dave Silver handed me a copy of an early Senate version of ERISA, bill S. 3598. I noticed it contained provisions dealing with prohibited transactions involving "fiduciaries" of employee benefit plans. I became concerned that if a retirement plan invested in a mutual fund, this arguably could cause the fund, its adviser, or principal underwriter to become a fiduciary and could trigger the prohibited transaction rules in unintended ways. For example, if a plan purchased shares in a fund and the fund thus became a fiduciary, would the plan be prohibited from purchasing additional shares or redeeming shares? It seemed particularly odd to apply these prohibitions to mutual funds because they were already subject to extensive conflict of interest prohibitions under the Investment Company Act.

Dave shared my concern, and we considered the best way to address this problem. One approach would be to obtain a clarifying statement in the legislative history. A second would be to have a provision included in ERISA exempting purchases and redemptions of fund shares from the prohibited transaction restrictions. The third and broadest solution would be to provide that a mutual fund normally would not be a fiduciary in the first place. We selected this third approach, testified before Congress, and met with members and staffs of all four congressional committees in 1972, 1973, and 1974. We were successful. ERISA contained two provisions. First, section 3(21)(B) provided: "If any money or other property of an employee benefit plan is invested in securities issued by an investment company registered under the Investment Company Act of 1940, such investment shall not by itself cause such investment company or such investment company's investment adviser or principal underwriter to be deemed to be a fiduciary." Second, section 401(b)(1) provided: "In the case of a plan which invests in any security issued by an investment company registered under the Investment Company Act of 1940, the assets of such plan shall be deemed to include such security but shall not, solely by reason of such investment, be deemed to include any assets of such investment company."

The conference report accompanying ERISA explained the rationale for these provisions: "Since mutual funds are regulated by the Investment Company Act of 1940 and, since (under the Internal Revenue Code) mutual funds must be broadly held, it is not considered necessary to apply the fiduciary rules to mutual funds merely because plans invest in their shares." These provisions have kept the mutual fund industry free from the problems that have bedeviled banks, insurance companies, and other funding media for employee benefit plans subject to ERISA.

There was another provision in ERISA that proved to be of immense benefit to mutual funds. Section 404(c) provided that if, pursuant to Department of Labor regulations, a retirement plan provides individual accounts for employees and permits them to select their own investments from a broad range of alternatives, the employer will not be responsible for an employee's investment decisions. In 1976, the Investment Company Institute submitted to the Department of Labor extensive suggestions for regulations, covering such matters as what constitutes a broad range of investments, the type of control that each employee needs (including information on which to base investment decisions and the frequency of investment instructions), and the limited role of the employer.[14] The 404(c) regulations adopted by the Department of Labor were quite similar to the institute's suggestions and, as discussed shortly, have been critical to the fund industry's success in the defined contribution plan market.

In sum, although mutual funds were far from the center of the principal area addressed by ERISA (defined benefit plans), it is hard to overemphasize the importance of the 1974 pension reform law to mutual funds. ERISA

- tripled the amount of contributions that could made to Keogh plans, the one type of retirement plan where mutual funds had a sizable foothold;
- authorized mutual funds as an investment medium for 403(b) plans;
- permitted the establishment of IRAs, both to provide coverage for workers not covered by employer plans and to enhance portability; and

Figure 6.1. *Barron's,* June 22, 1992. Courtesy of Dow Jones & Company.

- set forth fiduciary standards that encouraged employers to establish participant-directed plans invested in mutual funds.

Those of us involved in enactment of these provisions had some sense at the time of how beneficial they would prove to be for mutual funds. What no one realized was that by imposing substantial costs and burdens on defined benefit plans, ERISA helped produce a huge shift from DB plans to defined contribution plans, where mutual funds have become the largest funding medium.

Universal IRAs

In the late 1970s Dave Silver, then president of the Investment Company Institute, became interested in the concept of a universal savings plan that would be available to all American workers. Such a plan would assist individuals in saving for their futures and provide the economy with needed capital. In particular, Dave became aware of a universal savings initiative that recently had been adopted in France. We contacted the French government for details, began looking at similar plans in other countries, and discussed the matter with the institute's executive committee. The committee instructed ICI staff and outside tax counsel Ed Cohen to devise a universal savings plan that provided both for the deductibility of contributions and tax-free build-up until withdrawal at retirement. Ed and ICI staff began drawing up the outlines for such a plan. In the middle of our deliberations, we realized that the guts of such a plan were already in existence: the Internal Revenue Code as amended by ERISA permitted any worker who was not "an active participant" in an employer's retirement plan to establish an IRA. If we simply deleted this limitation, voilà, we would have a *universal* savings plan.[15]

The next step was to find a member of Congress to act as sponsor of the legislation. Ed had developed a close relationship with Congressman Henson Moore, a Republican from Louisiana. Moore was enthusiastic about the idea and agreed to lead the effort. We began meeting with representatives of other financial industries that might have an interest in universal IRA legislation, including broker-dealers, banks, savings and loan associations, and insurance companies. Each of these industries had already developed its own initiative for tax reform and was unwilling to drop it in favor of the universal IRA. Ed then made a suggestion that was both simple and brilliant: ask each industry to make the universal IRA number two on its wish list, that is, to agree that if its own initiative failed, it would join us in advocating the universal IRA. This is precisely what occurred. For one reason or another, the various industry initiatives did not pan out. They joined the institute in calling for the universal IRA, which was enacted into law as part of the Economic Recovery Tax Act of 1981, permitting *any* worker to make a tax-deductible contribution of up to $2,000 a year to an IRA.[16]

The universal IRA was hugely successful. Financial institutions ran massive advertising campaigns, typically in the weeks before April 15, urging *all* Americans with earned income to "get a tax break by contributing to an IRA." Money poured in to IRAs. In 1982, contributions amounted to $28 billion, rising to $38 billion in 1985. Universal IRAs became popular among workers who needed them the most. The median income (expressed in 1984 dollars) for workers contributing to IRAs for the first time dropped from $41,000 in 1982 to $29,000 in 1986.[17]

In 1986, Congress decided to make dramatic reductions in income tax rates and pay for the resulting loss in tax revenue by eliminating or cutting back on various deductions. Deductions for IRA contributions were limited to individuals not covered by plans and individuals who were covered but whose income fell below specified levels. The universal IRA was gone. Under the complicated new eligibility rules, financial institutions no longer could mass-market IRAs. Due to the lack of marketing and confusion as to eligibility, many individuals who remained eligible to make deductible contributions stopped making them. Deductible contributions plummeted from $38 billion in 1986, the last year of the universal IRA, to $14 billion in 1987, the first year under the new rules. Deductible contributions continued to drift downward in subsequent years, amounting to only $9 billion in 2002.[18]

However, as Joseph Nocera observed, the universal IRA introduced millions of Americans to investing.

> In 1986, when Congress repealed some of the tax benefits attached to IRAs, more than $82 billion had come into mutual funds alone via IRAs or other retirement accounts. Fifteen million new IRA mutual fund accounts had been opened. At least as much money had arrived at brokerage firms the same way. Perhaps most important, IRA customers tended to be younger than those who didn't have IRAs, with a median household income of $51,000. Three quarters of them were married, a third held graduate degrees, and, best of all, they had "a greater tendency to accept a moderate amount of risk when investing," according to another of those ICI surveys. Although the mutual fund and brokerage industries complained loudly when IRAs lost some of their tax benefits, they had much to be thankful for by then. [Universal] IRAs had done their job.[19]

Over the ensuing years, Congress made a series of improvements to IRAs. In 1997, it raised the income level for deductibility by individuals covered by plans and created the Roth IRA, under which individuals below specified income levels can make nondeductible contributions to a new type of IRA where withdrawals are not subject to tax. In 2001, Congress increased IRA contribution limits and allowed older workers to make catch-up contributions. Despite these reforms, we are far from the universal IRA of 1981 through 1986. What was once simple for the average worker to comprehend is now a morass of rules, regulations, and exceptions. In 1982, the IRS publication explaining IRAs to taxpayers was twelve pages long. By 2005, the publication had grown to 104 pages.

Although the individual IRA has had its ups and downs, the rollover IRA, designed to permit workers to maintain retirement assets on job change or retirement, has enjoyed steady success. Studies indicate that the vast majority of individuals who receive distributions from employer plans at retirement roll them over into IRAs. Other studies indicate that on job change, larger distributions tend to get rolled over into IRAs, and small distributions tend to get cashed out. As a result of these trends, rollovers have moved steadily upward, growing from $114 billion in 1996 to $214 billion in 2004.[20]

The make-up of IRA investments has changed dramatically over time. In 1981, bank and thrift deposits accounted for 72 percent of IRA assets, with the remainder made up of brokerage accounts (12 percent), insurance annuities (9 percent), and mutual funds (7 percent). As noted by Nocera, "Over time, IRA money began gravitating away from banks and toward brokerage firms and mutual fund companies, drawn in part by the bull market and in part by a marketing blitz that dwarfed anything that had come before." By the first quarter of 2009, mutual funds accounted for 44 percent of IRA assets and brokerage accounts for 35 percent. Bank and S&L deposits had fallen to 12 percent, and insurance company annuities remained in the 9 percent range.[21]

401(k) Plans

All of the pieces of legislation I have discussed that created new types of retirement plans, including Keogh plans in 1962, IRAs in 1974, and universal IRAs in 1981, were intentionally designed to encourage individual saving for retirement. In contrast, the 1978 legislation providing for the establishment of 401(k) plans was intended to settle a technical tax issue. Yet the 1978 legislation produced a sea change in retirement plans that has been of immense benefit to mutual funds.

The technical issue arose with respect to a particular type of defined contribution plan—a cash or deferred profit-sharing plan, an arrangement under which an employee can choose to take a bonus in stock or have it invested in the plan. The first cash or deferred profit-sharing plans were created by three

New York City banks in 1953. The Internal Revenue Service (IRS) expressed concern that that the plans were discriminatory because it believed that lower-paid employees would take cash and be subject to current tax, whereas the higher-paid would have the amounts deferred and grow tax-free. Ed Cohen, tax counsel to Irving Trust, was successful in obtaining an IRS ruling under which a plan would qualify for favorable tax treatment if a majority of the employees electing deferral were in the bottom two-thirds of the payroll. After this favorable ruling, other New York City banks and several corporations adopted similar plans.[22]

The IRS then raised a second issue, that of "constructive receipt," that is, because the employee had the right to take the bonus in cash, she would be taxed as though she had received it, despite the fact that it actually had gone into the plan. This issue had its ups and downs for a number of years. In 1972, the IRS proposed regulations that raised the threat of constructive receipt treatment. In 1974, in ERISA Congress delayed implementation of the regulations with respect to plans already in existence. In 1978, Congress sought to resolve the controversy by adding sections 401(k) and 402(a)(8) to the Internal Revenue Code, which provided that if a plan met specified conditions, including nondiscrimination tests, a payment by an employer that the employee elects to defer would not be included in the employee's income. In 1981, the IRS adopted regulations implementing these statutory provisions and made it clear that they encompassed salary reductions as well as bonuses. The congressional committee reports for the 1978 legislation indicate that Congress acted because it was dissatisfied with the 1974 moratorium that discriminated against employers that had not yet established plans, and Congress did not realize that it was giving birth to 401(k) plans. As one expert stated, "Congress thought that it was simply resolving a conflict involving cash-deferred profit-sharing plans rather than setting the stage for the 401(k) savings plan that would drastically alter our national retirement system."[23]

The number of 401(k) plans skyrocketed from 30,000 in 1985 to 417,000 in 2005. During this same period, the number of participants in these plans grew from 10 million to 47 million. Assets increased from $144 billion in 1985 to over $2.3 trillion in the first quarter of 2009.[24] There has been a dramatic shift from defined benefit plans to 401(k) and other types of defined contribution plans. James Wooten has observed:

> When Congress passed ERISA, defined-benefit plans dominated the private pension system. As late as 1979, more than 80 percent of individuals who participated in a private retirement plan were in a defined-benefit plan. In the same year, private trusteed defined-benefit plans held assets valued at roughly two and one-half times the value of assets held by private trusteed defined-contribution plans. Less than two decades later, the make-up of the private pension system was greatly changed. By the mid 1990s more private-sector workers looked to a defined contribution plan as their primary retirement savings arrangement, and contributions to defined-contribution plans far outstripped contributions to defined-benefit plans.[25]

A number of explanations have been offered for the massive shift from defined benefit plans to 401(k) plans, including the change from manufacturing jobs (where DB plans are common) to service industries, a far more mobile workforce (DB plans work well for career employees but less so for those who frequently change employers), employees' desire for control over their retirement savings, and the burdens and costs that ERISA imposed on DB plans.[26] Whatever the reasons, the shift to 401(k) plans has been dramatic.

Initially, 401(k) plans offered only two investment options—a guaranteed investment contract provided by an insurance company and a single equity mutual fund or company stock.[27] Mutual fund firms entered the picture fairly quickly, in a massive way. Mutual funds had a number of things going for them.

First was the law. As previously discussed, the pension reform law, ERISA, provided that an investment by a plan in a mutual fund would not cause the fund to be a fiduciary. There were no similar provisions for bank collective funds and insurance company separate accounts. Two pension experts have noted:

> The mutual fund industry alone had been granted a total exemption from the fiduciary liability provisions of ERISA when it was enacted....The industry could therefore heavily promote the 404(c) regulations to expand its defined contribution business without assuming additional fiduciary liabilities. It took several years for banks and insurance companies to convert their traditional investment products into the technical legal form of a mutual fund and become competitive on this front.[28]

Second were Department of Labor regulations. As previously discussed, section 404(c) of ERISA provided that if, pursuant to regulations, a retirement plan offers an individual account for each employee and permits an employee to select her own investments from a broad range, the employer will not be responsible for the employee's investment decisions. The Department of Labor's regulations closely tracked mutual fund practices and provided funds with a fantastic marketing tool. The two experts observed:

> The mutual fund industry—for whom the 404(c) regulations were almost tailor made—was also influential in persuading employers to shift responsibility for investment choice to employees. The industry already had the product—a vast array of investment funds—necessary to satisfy the broad range of alternatives requirement of the 404(c) regulations. It already had the technology—daily transfers, voice (and now Internet) initiated transactions—necessary to satisfy the frequency of investment instructions requirement. And it already had the disclosure material—prospectuses prepared under Securities and Exchange Commission (SEC) requirements—necessary to satisfy the sufficient information requirement. It also had a bundled product of investment options, record-keeping services, and prototype plans to offer just as employers were beginning to lessen their administrative burden through outsourcing.[29]

Third, mutual fund share prices appeared in the newspapers every day. David L. Wray, president of the Profit-Sharing/401(k) Council of America, observed:

> The problem [of]...trust was a huge issue. Employees, no matter how good you made these programs, if they didn't trust that this money was going to be properly managed for them, they would not participate. . . .
>
> The mutual fund program was very, very important to the growth of the 401(k) system because it played right into managing this trust issue. You had mutual funds, they were daily valued. They were listed in the *Wall Street Journal* or your local paper. You could have newspaper validation of the return. So if...you went to employees and said, you know, give us your money. We will put your money into our programs and manage it for you and you can trust us because we're using a mutual fund. And the mutual fund is right there in the newspaper and you can track that. Right along with what we're telling you, you can see that in the newspaper. So newspaper validation was a critical element and gave mutual funds a tremendous advantage over any other competitive investment alternative.[30]

Fourth, Wray believes there was the "Peter Lynch factor":

> Employees have always been very nervous about having this money invested for them or investing themselves....But in the mid-1980s we had an investment phenomenon. We had Peter Lynch [manager of Fidelity's Magellan Fund]. And he was in the paper every day. He was the guru. Fidelity Magellan was out performing everybody and it got [a] tremendous amount of press....Fidelity...recognized the business opportunity here and said you should put Fidelity Magellan into your 401(k) plan....Peter Lynch is validating the system because you're going to have your money invested with Peter Lynch. So I call it the Peter Lynch factor.[31]

These factors, and the record 1982–2000 bull market, resulted in mutual funds becoming by far the largest funding medium for 401(k) plans. In 1990, funds had a 9 percent market share; by 2000, it had grown to 48 percent; and by the first quarter of 2009, 401(k) plans had almost $1.1 trillion invested in mutual funds, a 48 percent market share.[32]

Impact of IRAs and Defined Contribution Plans on Mutual Funds

It is impossible to overestimate the importance of IRAs and defined contribution plans to the mutual fund industry. They have provided positive cash flows into mutual funds year after year. Moreover, investment flows from IRAs and defined contribution plans are much less volatile than those from nonretirement sources. IRAs and defined contribution plans have become linchpins of the mutual fund industry. By March 31, 2009, they accounted for 33 percent of mutual fund assets.[33]

7

Reentry of Securities Firms and Banks

History may not repeat itself, but it rhymes a lot.
—Attributed to Mark Twain

Securities firms and banks have had an on-again, off-again relationship with the investment company business. First, in the 1920s, they were major sponsors of closed-end funds. In 1928 one observer wrote, "About sixty per cent of the investment trusts are under the control of investment banking houses, and another ten percent are affiliated with banks and trust companies."[1] Second, following the 1929 crash, securities firms and banks exited the investment company business. Banking's exit was ratified in 1933 by the Glass-Steagall Act, which generally prohibited a firm from engaging in both banking and securities activities. Third, in the late 1970s, securities firms began sponsoring and underwriting mutual funds. Banks sought legislation that would permit them to engage in mutual fund and other securities activities but were blocked by the securities and mutual fund industries. Eventually, banks gained entry through a series of judicial decisions. Most recently, a number of securities

firms have exited the fund business, whereas banks continue to manage a substantial portion of fund assets.

Securities Firms

Securities firms were the largest sponsors of closed-end funds
during the bull market of the 1920s, but left the business following the 1929 crash. As mutual funds became increasingly
popular after World War II, some Wall Street investment banking firms, including Lazard Freres and Lehman Brothers, began
sponsoring mutual funds. In addition, a few national brokerage firms (called wirehouses because their local offices were
connected to New York headquarters by electronic wire) with
strong research and investment management departments, such
as Shearson Hamill and Smith Barney, brought out their own
mutual funds. However, the nation's largest national broker-
dealers, including Dean Witter, E. F. Hutton, Merrill Lynch,
Paine Webber, and Reynolds & Co., decided not to sponsor and
underwrite mutual funds. In fact, the country's largest securities
firm, Merrill Lynch, Pierce, Fenner & Smith, steadfastly refused
to create its own mutual funds or even sell funds managed by
other firms. The head of the firm, Charles Merrill, was totally
opposed to any involvement with mutual funds.

Merrill's biographer, Edwin J. Perkins, offered four reasons
for his position. First, in the late 1920s, Merrill had come close
to sponsoring a closed-end fund.

> Charlie probably thanked his lucky stars for his good tim-
> ing on that missed opportunity. If he had proceeded at
> a faster clip and actually sold fund shares to the general
> public, he might easily have been stigmatized in the 1930s
> as the irresponsible promoter of a closed-end mutual fund
> that produced tremendous losses for thousands of unso-
> phisticated investors. Having dodged a speeding bullet
> once with respect to the lure of mutual funds, Charlie was
> extremely careful not to put himself directly in the line of
> fire on a second occasion.

Second,

> He was concerned that if the funds became too popular, the demand for the transaction services routinely performed by brokerage firms would correspondingly diminish.....Mutual fund investors had the reputation of rarely reducing or shifting their assets to alternative investments....Brokerage would become a less remunerative occupation if the services performed became increasingly one-dimensional—arranging purchases of mutual fund shares and doing little else. From Charlie's perspective, the firm's endorsement of mutual funds would be the equivalent of advising all investors to adopt a rigid buy and hold policy. In that altered atmosphere, brokerage houses would steadily lose volume and might not generate sufficient revenues to stay afloat.

Third,

> Charlie likewise believed that the individual investor could achieve all the benefits usually associated with mutual funds by working closely with Merrill Lynch brokers to build a personal portfolio designed to meet very specific needs.

Finally,

> Charlie was unwilling to concede that the managers of mutual funds had any better sources of timely financial information than the typical Merrill Lynch customer. By the 1950s the firm had assembled one of the best, if not the very best, staff of security analysts anywhere in the country. By discussing their specific financial goals with their regular broker and listening to sound advice, Merrill Lynch customers could successfully manage their own personalized portfolios.[2]

In the late 1960s, Merrill Lynch, then headed by Don Regan, decided to diversify its business away from securities brokerage and capital market activity. As part of this effort, in 1969 the company began distributing mutual funds sponsored by other firms. In addition, that same year it acquired Lionel D. Edie & Co., an investment management and consulting firm.[3] Edie had two small, no-load mutual funds. In 1973, Merrill Lynch underwrote a third Edie fund, this time one with a front-end sales charge. However, Edie was operated as an independent organization and was not integrated into Merrill Lynch. Merrill sold most of the Edie operation in 1976. The remnants of Edie were repackaged into Merrill Lynch Asset Management, which was fully integrated into Merrill Lynch, staffed by Merrill employees and headed by Arthur Zeikel, a noted expert on portfolio management who had worked at three mutual fund firms (Dreyfus, Standard & Poor's, and Oppenheimer).

Merrill proceeded to bring out a large number of money market, bond, and equity funds. By 1992, it was the nation's second largest mutual fund firm, exceeded only by Fidelity.[4] Merrill's entry into the fund business coincided with the explosion of money market funds. In particular, the company used its money funds for the investment of customers' cash balances and as the linchpin of its Cash Management Account, which combined aspects of a money fund, check writing, a sweep account, and a credit/debit card for its brokerage customers. In 1982, 95 percent of Merrill's fund assets consisted of money market funds. In the mid-1980s, when investors turned to bond funds, Merrill became a major player in that area as well. By 1996, 50 percent of the company's fund assets consisted of money funds, 22 percent of bond funds, and 10 percent of stock funds.[5]

Merrill's success led other national broker-dealers, including Dean Witter, Paine Webber, and Prudential, to enter the mutual fund business. By 1991, of the $1.1 trillion invested in mutual funds, one-fourth consisted of broker-dealer "in-house" funds, with heavy concentration in money market and bond funds.[6] By 1992, three of the ten largest fund groups were affiliated with brokerage firms.[7]

With the advent of the record bull market in the 1980s and investors' renewed preference for equity funds, broker-dealer in-house funds lost substantial market share to other mutual funds.

A number of reasons have been advanced for this trend: the inferior investment performance of many broker-dealer equity funds, the reluctance of securities firms to sell a rival broker's funds, and individual brokers' hesitancy to recommend in-house funds for fear that poor performance would result in customer dissatisfaction with the firm and the broker, whereas an unaffiliated fund's bad performance could be attributed to an outside fund organization. In addition, in recent years regulators have expressed concern over brokers preferring in-house products, thus increasing their reluctance to sell affiliated funds.

Securities firms have responded in a variety of ways:

- In 2000, Paine Webber gave up management of a number of its mutual funds and, like many insurance companies, turned to the use of subadvisers.[8]

- In 2005, Smith Barney (owned by Citigroup) swapped management of its mutual funds with Legg Mason in exchange for Legg's brokers, thus getting Smith Barney out of the mutual fund business and Legg Mason out of the brokerage business.

- In 2006, Merrill Lynch transferred management of its mutual funds to BlackRock, a money management–mutual fund firm, in exchange for almost half of BlackRock's outstanding shares.

Industry observers believe that similar transactions involving mutual fund divisions of other leading broker-dealers are likely to occur. After decades of talk about "financial supermarkets" and the beneficial synergies between banking, securities underwriting and brokerage, insurance, and mutual fund management, the current focus is on the avoidance of conflicts of interest and the advantages of specialization to customers and the firm. As a result of the trend away from in-house funds and these types of transactions, broker-dealers' share of mutual fund assets has plummeted from 25 percent in 1991 to just 6 percent in 2006.[9]

It remains to be seen how permanent this low level will be. It should be remembered that after the calamitous events of the

1920s, securities firms exited the investment company business, only to reenter in the 1970s. Securities firms remain the major distribution system for mutual funds managed by other firms and thus are extremely familiar with the product. I suspect that in a few years, securities firms that have left the mutual fund business will decide to reenter. On the other hand, it will be difficult to distinguish between securities firms and banks. Several major securities firms, such as Merrill Lynch and A.G. Edwards, have been acquired by banks. Others, such as Goldman Sachs and Morgan Stanley, have become bank holding companies.

Banks

One observer of the 1920s reported: "The new era banker felt he must rescue the people by encouraging them to come to the bank for investment advice. The small investor was told that he should share the opportunity to grow rich with America, by putting his money in investment trusts. In order to facilitate this new service many large banks organized investment trusts of their own."[10] In 1930, John T. Flynn wrote: "Investment trust affiliates of banks are well known. The National City, the Chatham-Phenix, the Chase, the Chemical, many if not most of the banks have them. They are always organized by the bank and are directed for all practical purposes by the bank....people who buy stock in them as a rule depend upon this alliance as the basis of their confidence in the investment trust."[11]

Following the 1929 crash and the onset of the Great Depression, commercial banks left the securities business, including the sponsorship of closed-end funds. In 1933, due to abuses that had taken place in connection with bank securities activities, Congress enacted the Glass-Steagall Act, which was designed to generally separate commercial banking and securities activities. In effect, Glass-Steagall ratified banks' exit from the securities business.

After World War II and the return of prosperity, large banks sought to reenter various aspects of the securities business, including the sponsorship and underwriting of mutual funds, the underwriting of municipal revenue bonds, and dealing in commercial paper. The banks pursued two routes to overcome barriers created by the Glass-Steagall Act—legislation and actions by federal bank regulators. Actions taken by regulators in turn produced years of litigation. From the mid-1960s through the 1990s, there was often concurrent activity in all three arenas: Congress, the banking agencies, and the courts. In fact, it was not unusual for there to be simultaneous activity before several Senate and House committees, several banking agencies, and several courts.

The bank–mutual fund story is lengthy and complex.[12] Beginning in the 1920s, banks formed common trust funds for commingling trust accounts already managed by the bank. In 1940, Congress exempted common trust funds from registration under the Investment Company Act. Banks also managed nontrust money on an individual basis in the form of managing agency accounts. In 1962, the comptroller of the currency authorized banks to pool managing agency accounts, thus permitting them to operate the economic equivalent of mutual funds. The comptroller took the position that commingled managing agency accounts were common trust funds, and therefore, "the SEC has no business in this area." However, in 1965, First National City Bank (now Citibank) conceded SEC jurisdiction by filing an application for an order exempting its commingled account from provisions of the Investment Company Act. The Investment Company Institute sued the comptroller, alleging that his regulation violated the Glass-Steagall Act. The district court held in favor of the institute. The banking industry then obtained an amendment to the pending Investment Company Act legislation to authorize commingled accounts subject to limited Securities and Exchange Commission (SEC) regulation. According to one writer, "There is some suggestion that the SEC may have agreed not to object to the banking industry's proposed provisions if it, in turn, would back the proposed reforms to the mutual fund industry."[13] Next, the court of appeals for the District of Columbia reversed the district court's decision and held that the comptroller's regulation did not violate Glass-Steagall. The Senate-House conferees on the 1940 legislation deleted the provisions relating to commingled accounts, leaving the decision to the Supreme Court. In 1971, the Supreme Court held in *Investment Company Institute v. Camp*[14] that the comptroller's regulation violated the Glass-Steagall Act.

Thus, banks failed in their initial attempts, in both the courts and Congress, to gain entry into the mutual fund business.

Almost every year during the 1970s, 1980s, and 1990s, legislation was introduced in Congress to grant banks mutual fund and other securities powers. The legislation was supported by banks and the comptroller and was opposed by the securities and mutual fund industries. Countless hearings were held before Senate and House committees, but legislation was not enacted. During this same period, the banking industry pressed on at the second front—the bank regulatory agencies. Although it took years, the banks' efforts with regulators met with success. In the mutual fund area, the Federal Reserve Board adopted regulations permitting bank holding companies to serve as investment advisers to closed-end funds. The institute challenged the board's action, and in 1981, the Supreme Court upheld the Fed's regulations. This decision led a number of bank holding companies to begin serving as investment advisers to both closed-end funds *and* mutual funds. Over time, through this and other decisions, banks obtained almost complete entry into the mutual fund business. Under these rulings, banking organizations could manage mutual funds and sell their shares to the public. The only missing power was the ability of a banking organization to serve as principal underwriter for a mutual fund. Banks solved this problem by having their funds retain independent third parties to serve as underwriters.

In 1999, with the Gramm-Leach-Bliley Act, Congress granted banks full entry into the securities business generally and the mutual fund industry in particular. The law permitted banking firms to advise and underwrite mutual funds and to sell the funds' shares to the public. Just as in 1933, when the Glass-Steagall

Act ratified banks' exit from the securities business, in 1999, the Gramm-Leach-Bliley Act ratified banks' reentry.

Banks, like insurance companies before them, pursued a number of different routes to enter the mutual fund business. Many started their own mutual funds. Others acquired existing mutual fund organizations, a notable example being Mellon Bank's acquisition of Dreyfus. Still others, like Citigroup, acquired securities firms that had mutual fund divisions. In addition, many banks converted their common trust funds and collective investment funds for retirement plans into mutual funds. At mid-year 2007, mutual funds affiliated with U.S. and foreign banks had assets of approximately \$1.9 trillion, constituting 17 percent of total industry assets.[15] Many of these assets were due to banks' acquisitions of independent fund firms, conversion of bank common and collective funds into mutual funds, and banks otherwise using their mutual funds as investment vehicles for trust and agency accounts they managed.

In recent years, a number of banks have merged, thus combining their fund operations. Other banks have exited the mutual fund business by selling their mutual fund subsidiaries to independent fund firms such as Federated, securities firms such as Goldman Sachs, and large banks, such as Bank of America, J.P. Morgan Chase, Wachovia, and Wells Fargo. It is unclear whether these trends will continue. My hunch is that more small and mid-size banks will leave the fund business, and large players will remain. One thing is clear: banks have not done nearly as well in the mutual fund business as bankers had hoped and traditional mutual fund firms had feared. I believe that that there would have been a far different result had the banking industry won the *Camp* case and entered the fund industry in 1971, a time when the fund industry was minuscule compared to the banking industry.

Bank-sponsored mutual funds have encountered more than their share of regulatory and enforcement problems, leading some observers to raise the possibility of reinstating Glass-Steagall prohibitions on bank mutual fund activities.[16] I seriously doubt this will occur.

Impact of Securities Firm and Bank Entry

The reentry of securities firms and banks into the investment company business in the 1970s and 1980s expanded the mutual fund industry in new ways. Securities firms and banks used their mutual funds not only as stand-alone investment vehicles but also as part of their securities and banking services. Thus, securities firms swept customers' cash balances into their mutual funds, and banks used their mutual funds for trust and managing agency clients. Though neither industry has had remarkable success in the retail mutual fund market, securities firms and banks have contributed to the overall growth of the fund industry and to increased public acceptance of mutual funds.

8

Responding to Fund Growth: Calls for New Types of Regulation

The world advances, and in time outgrows the laws
That in our fathers' time were best.

— James Russell Lowell

The eighteen-year bull market of 1982 to 2000, combined with new fund products and distribution systems and legislation providing incentives for individual retirement savings, propelled mutual funds into becoming the largest financial industry in the world, surpassing U.S. banking institutions. These developments led to proposals to subject mutual funds to bank-type regulation and move from direct regulation of mutual funds by the Securities and Exchange Commission (SEC) to self-regulation by the mutual fund industry itself. Fortunately for both mutual fund shareholders and the fund industry, neither type of proposal was adopted.

The Bull Market and the Explosive Growth of Mutual Funds

In 1982, inflation and interest rates peaked and began their long declines, sparking a huge rally in the equity and bond markets. The rally was given a major boost by the tax reductions in the Economic Recovery Act of 1981. From 1982 to 2000, although there were some sharp downturns, the markets trended upward.

Mutual funds enjoyed explosive growth. From 1982 to 2000, the number of households owning fund shares soared from less than 10 million to 47 million, the number of funds grew from 857 to 8,155, and fund assets increased from $297 billion to over $6.9 trillion. All industry segments boomed. Equity fund assets went from $54 billion to $3.9 trillion, bond funds from $23 billion to $811 billion, and money market funds from $220 billion to $1.8 trillion. Mutual funds became the largest financial industry in the world.[1]

Many factors contributed to the extraordinary growth of mutual funds, including the industry's development in the 1970s of new types of funds and new ways to distribute fund shares, discussed in chapters 4 and 5; consumers' movement from tangible assets to financial assets and from direct ownership of securities to ownership via funds; and a boom in individual saving for retirement. However, the key driver of mutual funds' spectacular growth was a bull market of unprecedented scale and duration.

The average annual return on the S&P 500 Stock Price Index from August 1982 to March 2000 was an astounding 19.7 percent, as the price earnings multiple on the index almost quadrupled, going from 7.5 to 29.4. Equity fund assets increased year after year, due to a combination of portfolio appreciation and net sales. Bond prices moved sharply higher in the mid-1980s and early 1990s as inflation slowed and interest rates fell. From the middle of 1984 to early 1987, net flows into bond funds were about six times the amount of total bond fund assets at the beginning of the period. Whereas bond funds always had been the stepchild of the mutual fund industry, by 1985 bond fund

Figure 8.1. Copyright 1989 *The Oregonian*. All rights reserved. Reprinted with permission.

assets exceeded those of equity funds, a situation that prevailed through 1990. For much of this period, yields on money market funds were greater than those on savings deposits, leading both consumers and businesses to shift from deposits to money funds.[2]

Returns on financial assets far exceeded those on hard assets. For example, during the 1990s, the average annual return on the S&P Index was 18 percent, whereas the median sales price of existing single-family housing rose at only a 4 percent annual rate. Not surprisingly, households shifted from owning real estate and other hard assets to financial assets. In 1990, almost 40 percent of household assets consisted of real estate and other tangible assets, but by 2000 the share had fallen to less than 30 percent. Conversely, discretionary financial assets rose from 34 percent of household assets to 44 percent.[3]

As consumers moved to financial assets, they increasingly favored ownership through mutual funds, rather than direct ownership of equities and bonds. At the end of 1989, mutual funds accounted for 12 percent of household discretionary financial assets. Ten years later, the percentage had more than doubled to 28 percent. This trend applied to all asset categories. In 1990, equity mutual funds accounted for 10 percent of equities owned by households; ten years later, this figure had tripled to 30 percent. In 1990, bond funds accounted for 17 percent of bonds held by households; ten years later, the percentage had increased to 26 percent. In 1990, money market funds accounted for 11 percent of short-term assets owned by households; ten years later, the percentage had climbed to 19 percent.[4]

The 1980s and 1990s witnessed a continuation of the shift from defined benefit (DB) retirement plans to 401(k) and other defined contribution (DC) plans. In 1980, 30 million employees were covered by DB plans versus 19 million in DC plans. By 2000, DC plans had 51 million participants versus 22 million in DB plans. Mutual funds gained an ever-increasing share of 401(k) and other DC plan assets, growing from 8 percent in 1989 to 45 percent in 2000.[5]

Individuals also increased their saving for retirement through investment in individual retirement accounts (IRAs). In 1982, IRAs had assets of $68 billion, with only 9 percent invested in mutual fund shares. By 2001, IRAs had assets of $2.6 trillion, with 44 percent invested in fund shares.[6]

Three new types of funds introduced during the bear market of the 1970s took off in the 1980s and 1990s. Money market funds, introduced in 1972, had assets of $220 billion in 1982, $498 billion in 1990, and $1.8 trillion in 2000. Municipal bond funds, introduced in 1976, had assets of $21 billion in 1984, $120 billion in 1990, and $395 billion in 2000. Index funds, also introduced in 1976, had assets of $3 billion in 1990 and $389 billion in 2000.[7]

Two new methods of distributing fund shares introduced in the 1970s became increasingly popular during the 1980s and 1990s. In 1979, the SEC adopted Rule 434d, which authorized mutual funds, for the first time since 1933, to run meaningful advertisements. Advertising and other factors, such as investors' increased use of financial planners and the growth of 401(k) plans, boosted no-load sales. Between 1980 and 2001, the share of equity fund sales due to no-load funds and no-load share classes grew from 34 to 58 percent, and the share of no-load sales of bond funds and share classes increased from 47 to 64 percent. In 1980, the SEC adopted rule 12b-1, which authorized mutual funds, for the first time since 1940, to pay for the distribution of their shares. During the 1980s and 1990s, practically all load funds adopted 12b-1 plans and offered investors a number of share classes, each with a different method of paying for distribution.[8]

Increased Media Coverage

The record bull market and expanded investor demand for financial assets led to a tremendous increase in media coverage of the financial markets in general and mutual funds in particular. Increased coverage in turn fueled retail demand for financial assets and influenced investor behavior. In 1992, in the midpoint of the bull market, SEC staff noted that in the case of mutual funds, "Specialized newsletters are published by a host of organizations, and many financial and general interest publications provide extensive coverage and analysis of mutual funds, including periodic rankings of performance and fund expense ratios. As a result of these changes, funds that have low expenses have enjoyed substantial growth."[9]

Morningstar was perhaps the best-known newsletter specializing in mutual funds. It was particularly known for its rankings of funds based on their past investment performance and its awarding of four or five stars to top-performing funds. Though *Morningstar* maintained that its stars were not intended to be buy and sell recommendations, many investors viewed them that way. In addition, many fund advisers compensated portfolio managers based on *Morningstar* and other rankings, and ran advertisements boasting of their funds' four and five stars.

Money was an example of a personal finance magazine that ran numerous articles on mutual funds. *Money* was relentlessly upbeat and had cover headlines such as "How to Turn

$50,000 into $250,000 in Just Five Years" and "How to Start Investing...And Do It Right." *Money's* competitors were similar. *Smart Money* used the headline "The One Stock You Should Buy Now."[10] It often occurred to me that if a mutual fund firm ever dared to use these types of headlines, it would be castigated in the media and might face regulatory action. General business publications, such as *Business Week* and *Forbes,* began devoting more attention to personal finance and mutual funds. The *Wall Street Journal* started running a "Fund Column" every day. The *New York Times* and other papers periodically published special sections devoted exclusively to mutual funds.

For decades, the mutual fund industry had sought to obtain more press coverage. Every two years, when the Investment Company Institute selected a new chairman, the Public Relations Department would arrange a "chairman's tour" with media outlets across the country designed to drum up press stories. Any major newspaper or magazine story on mutual funds, pro or con, would receive wide circulation within the industry. By the early 1990s, the fund industry, due its size and visibility, found itself in a totally different situation. There was heavy media coverage every day. The few reporters with experience covering mutual funds suddenly were outnumbered by rookies. Editors and reporters were particularly fascinated by the industry's claim that it had avoided major scandal. Each wanted to be the first to uncover and expose a critical flaw. The media's overall tone became more skeptical and far more critical. In 1994, I asked a veteran fund reporter, Tom Petruno of the *Los Angeles Times*, why news coverage of the fund industry had become so harsh and intense. He replied, "Matt, I can tell you in three words—two trillion dollars."

I believed that greatly increased media coverage would affect the way policy makers dealt with the fund industry. It was unclear exactly how this would evidence itself, but the institute tried to get ready. The PR Department shifted from seeking more press coverage of mutual funds to dealing with the media on a daily basis concerning regulatory, legislative, and economic issues. Similarly, the Research Department moved from undertaking marketing studies to working on public policy issues, such as shareholder behavior in market breaks and trends in fund expenses. The institute also decided that it had to do all it could to prevent a scandal that could touch off a media frenzy that in turn could help produce unwise government action. I also had been impressed by a number of independent fund directors who were committed to serving as "watchdogs" looking out for the best interests of fund shareholders. It struck me that if the institute could help educate independent directors generally, they could serve as a backstop to SEC oversight of the fund industry. Therefore, in 1994 the institute formed the Director Services Committee (now the Independent Directors Council) to oversee a series of programs and services for fund directors, including an annual conference, workshops, and a regular newsletter. At the same time, the institute's governing body, the Board of Governors, was expanded to include independent directors. Meanwhile, the institute repeatedly urged Congress to provide the SEC with increased staff and resources to police the fund industry.

The phenomenal rate of growth and change experienced by the fund industry during the 1982–2000 bull market led regulators, the industry, and others to seek changes in fund regulation designed to meet new conditions. Some proposals called for a sea change in fund regulation, such as subjecting mutual funds to bank-type regulation and moving from the historic system of SEC regulation to a system of industry self-regulation.

Proposals to Impose Bank-Type Regulation

Historically, banks have been regarded as special because they play quasi-governmental roles in our economy: they issue transaction accounts, they are the back-up source of liquidity for other institutions, and they are the transmission belt for monetary policy. Therefore, government traditionally has placed unique restrictions on banks and has granted them unique privileges. For example, banks are required to maintain reserves on their transaction (checking) accounts, are prohibited from engaging in risky nonbanking activities, have their core liabilities (deposits) insured by the federal government, and can borrow from the Federal Reserve System.[11]

Banking regulation, with its focus on the safety and soundness of banking institutions, is very different than securities regulation, which is centered on investor protection. Former SEC Chairman William Cary testified, "The great objectives of banking regulation are controls over the flow of credit in the monetary system, the maintenance of an effective banking structure, and the protection of depositors. These objectives neither utilize the same tools nor achieve the same ends as investor protection."[12]

However, as mutual funds gained an ever-increasing share of the nation's savings and banks' share declined, there were proposals to impose bank-type regulation on mutual funds.

As discussed in chapter 4, in the early 1980s, banks and S&Ls called for the imposition of reserve requirements on money market funds, based on the fact that the funds offered investors the ability to redeem shares through check writing. (Banking regulations impose reserve requirements on bank checking accounts, but not on bank savings accounts.) However, the Federal Reserve Board never called for such legislation, presumably because studies indicated investors were not using money funds as checking accounts. Whereas bank customers typically drew many small checks on their checking accounts, fund shareholders drew only a few large checks on their funds. There also were efforts in a number of states to impose reserve requirements on money funds, and thus to drive the funds out of the state, but all were defeated due to the outcry from fund shareholders. (As discussed in chapter 12, in 2008, Reserve Primary Fund became the first major money market fund to break a dollar a share, leading the Treasury Department to offer insurance to all money funds. As a result, there were calls to regulate money funds as "near banks.")

A second type of proposal to impose bank-type regulation emanated from Henry Kaufman, a well-respected Wall Street economist often referred to as "Dr. Doom." In a 1994 speech to the directors of the Federal Reserve Bank of Kansas City, Kaufman resurrected the run-on-the-bank concern that the SEC had raised during the congressional hearings that led to the Investment Company Act:

> Mutual funds have mushroomed and now substitute for traditional bank deposits....The average investor in equity mutual funds has never experienced a prolonged bear market. Neither has the average investor in fixed-income mutual funds....It is a potentially grievous error to assume that individual investors will always be slow to react to sudden, highly visible setbacks in stock prices, bond prices, or both....The technology is in place for a cascade of selling by investors in mutual funds.

Kaufman's proposed solution was to subject mutual funds to requirements borrowed from banking regulation:

> The time has come when we have to be concerned not only with the issues of fraud and abuse, which is the conventional focus of the SEC, and consider the systemic implications of the explosion of mutual funds....I propose that investors in bond and stock mutual funds be required to give 60 or 90 days' withdrawal notice. This condition would be roughly analogous to the long-standing requirement that applies to Certificates of Deposit and time deposits at banks and thrifts.[13]

The Investment Company Institute and the Federal Reserve Bank of New York published studies demonstrating that in all of the market breaks since World War II, fund shareholders had never panicked and redeemed en masse. Kaufman's proposal did not gain traction. However, it still sits in policy makers' medicine cabinet and is likely to be brought out in the case of a new financial panic.[14]

A third proposal was to extend community reinvestment requirements imposed on banks to mutual funds. (The Community Reinvestment Act [CRA] requires that banks make

loans in their local communities.) Calls to impose CRA requirements on mutual funds came from community activists; bank
regulators, such as Frank N. Newman, undersecretary of the
Treasury for domestic finance in the Clinton administration;
and bankers, such as Richard M. Rosenberg, chairman and
CEO of Bank of America. The press was quick to point out
that the bankers' goal in urging expansion of CRA was not
to help local communities but to obtain a reduction in obligations imposed on banks. One banking publication stated, "there
is serious doubt as to whether the banking industry is really
interested in the notion or whether it is using the...argument
as a weapon in its front-burner efforts to convince Congress to
amend CRA to make it less burdensome on banks."[15]

Whatever the banks' motivation, the reasons for imposing
the CRA on banks are not apposite to mutual funds. In 1993,
acting SEC chair Mary Schapiro told Treasury Undersecretary
Newman in no uncertain terms:

> Funds are not community lending institutions, and are not
> chartered to serve the needs and convenience of the com-
> munity. Moreover, funds have shareholders nationwide
> and rarely serve a particular community or location. In
> addition, funds do not receive the benefits associated with
> federal charters. The Investment Company Act requires
> that investment companies be managed in the sole interests
> of their shareholders. Imposing community reinvestment
> requirements on funds, similar to those imposed under
> the CRA would require fund directors and managers to
> take into account factors other than the interests of their
> shareholders, which would be fundamentally incompatible
> with the requirements of the Investment Company Act.[16]

However, proposals to extend the CRA to mutual funds continue
to be offered, albeit at a lower level of intensity. For example,
legislation has been introduced to extend the CRA to those
mutual funds and other entities that are part of bank holding
companies, based on the theory that the federal safety net for
banks benefits all parts of the holding company.[17] I am confident

that if such legislation is ever enacted, it will only be a matter of time before the CRA is extended to all mutual funds.

A fourth type of proposal to impose bank-type regulation was contained in legislation introduced in Congress in the wake of the 2003 late trading and market timing scandals. Banking regulation often requires a banking institution to obtain approval from a bank regulator before engaging in a new activity. Legislation introduced by Senator Peter Fitzgerald of Illinois would have required a mutual fund to obtain SEC approval before imposing a new fee, presumably for a new service. As discussed in chapter 11, fortunately the SEC took a large number of regulatory actions in response to the scandals, and the bill never moved in Congress.

In the first edition, I wrote, "As this book goes to press, there are relatively few calls to impose bank-type regulation on mutual funds. In the event of a crisis, I am certain policy makers will reach inside the medicine cabinet and find these prescriptions. One can only hope that they will never be administered." Unfortunately, this is precisely what may occur.

In response to the 2008 financial crisis, Congress enacted the Dodd-Frank Wall Street Reform and Consumer Protection Act, which provides that if a council of regulators determines that a financial entity poses risk to the financial system, the Federal Reserve Board, as agent for the council, can impose prudential standards on the entity, such as capital requirements, leverage limits, and limits on concentrations of risk. Unfortunately, the legislative language is broad enough to encompass mutual funds. Given the fact that the council is dominated by bank regulators who historically have been hostile to mutual funds, particularly money market funds, there is a danger that the council will impose prudential standards on funds.

Proposals for Self-Regulation

From the time of the enactment of the Securities Exchange Act of 1934, mutual funds have been subject to direct regulation by the SEC. The commission adopts regulations governing funds, conducts inspections of fund organizations, and brings enforcement actions. In contrast, broker-dealers, municipal securities dealers, futures professionals, and accountants have functioned under systems of statutorily authorized self-regulation, whereby quasi-private industry groups regulate their members, subject to SEC oversight.

Over the years, suggestions have been made to create various systems of self-regulation for mutual funds. In a 1962 address to the Investment Company Institute, SEC Commissioner Jack Whitney stated that the SEC and the industry's "parallel tasks would be much simpler if the Institute or its predecessor had been occupying a status loosely comparable to that of the NASD," the self-regulatory organization for broker-dealers.[18] In 1963, the SEC and the industry discussed a self-inspection program involving independent auditors. This led to the development of a new SEC annual report, form N-1R, for investment companies. In 1969, in light of increased SEC concern over fund management fees and sales charges, the Investment Company Institute proposed creation of a self-regulatory organization (SRO) with authority to regulate these areas. The proposal was opposed by the SEC and was not enacted.

As mutual funds experienced explosive growth in the 1980s and 1990s, proposals were repeatedly made to move funds to a form of self-regulation centered on inspections. These proposals emanated not from the fund industry but from the SEC, which was concerned that it did not have sufficient staff and resources to adequately examine mutual funds. I and many others have been skeptical about the wisdom of developing an organization requiring mutual funds to assume significant responsibility for regulating themselves. I believe that government regulation has proven to be more effective in protecting investors than self-regulation. Self-regulation may work where industry participants regularly deal with one another, as in the brokerage industry. But mutual fund firms do not deal with one another. For these reasons, and because an SRO inevitably would result in needless duplication and costs, the fund industry has been lukewarm to suggestions to create a self-regulatory system and instead has consistently urged that the SEC be provided with adequate staff and resources to continue to directly regulate, inspect, and police the industry.

In 1983, the SEC issued a concept release concerning the creation of one or more SROs to inspect mutual funds. In its comment letter, the Investment Company Institute stated that except in extraordinary circumstances, a fund that participates in an SRO should not also be subject to inspections by the SEC; absent compelling circumstances, a fund that satisfies remedial requirements imposed by the SRO should not be subject to an SEC enforcement action; and a fund's SEC registration fees should be reduced by the amount of fees it pays to the SRO. The SEC did not pursue the matter.[19]

In 1993, SEC Chairman Arthur Levitt delivered a speech in which he renewed the issue of self-regulation of the fund industry.[20] In 2003, in what seems to be part of a ten-year cycle, the SEC again raised the idea of creating an inspection-only SRO for mutual funds. The commission has not followed up on the idea, possibly due to adopting rules mandating the establishment of compliance systems at the individual fund level, discussed in chapter 9.

More recently, Joel Seligman, now president of the University of Rochester, suggested the creation of a full-blown investment company SRO, with the power to register mutual funds and other investment companies, establish standards of practice, conduct inspections, and investigate and discipline members.[21] Many of the problem areas he cites as justifying the creation of an SRO, such as late trading, directed brokerage, volume discounts on sales loads, and revenue sharing with broker-dealers, are already regulated by the existing SRO for securities broker-dealers, the Financial Industry Regulatory Authority (FINRA) (formerly known as the National Association of Securities Dealers, NASD). Because these problems developed despite being subject to a system of self-regulation, it is unclear how creation of another SRO would help. More generally, Seligman argues that a mutual fund SRO is needed because of the SEC's lack of resources and the fact that "investment company regulation is technical, not a field of expertise for the typical Commissioner, and, as a historical matter, rarely has seemed as urgent as activities the SEC has treated as its core functions, such as the mandatory disclosure system, stock market and broker-dealer oversight, and enforcement."[22] I submit that given the importance of mutual funds to some 88 million Americans, fund regulation *must* be one of the SEC's "core functions." If, for some reason, the SEC cannot order its priorities in this way, it would be preferable to create a new federal agency to regulate mutual funds, rather than turning over regulation to industry participants. In his landmark work, *The Administrative Process*, former SEC Chairman James Landis argued against assigning regulatory responsibility to larger governmental entities and in favor of the creation of a number of small government agencies because "number affords assurance of expertise in the performance of duties and results in a desirable focusing of responsibility."[23] (As discussed in chapter 1, these were some of the reasons Congress did not assign securities regulation to the Federal Trade Commission, but instead created the SEC in 1934.) If, in fact, the SEC's responsibilities are overly broad now, it is time to shift some of them to small new agencies of government.

Proposals to move the mutual fund industry to a system of self-regulation—be it a full-blown SRO or an inspection-only SRO—are bound to be revived in the event of a future crisis involving mutual funds. I believe it would be preferable to increase the SEC's resources or create a new specialized agency of government to regulate mutual funds, rather than move to a system of self-regulation.

During the 1990s, in addition to the debate regarding self-regulation for mutual funds and their advisers, there was a separate debate regarding how best to regulate the tens of thousands of investment advisers to clients other than investment companies, such as investment advisers to retirement plans, endowments, and wealthy individuals. Proposals ranged from creating a new SRO for nonfund advisers, to having the NASD regulate them in addition to broker-dealers, to exempting small nonfund advisers from SEC regulation, to providing the SEC with increased funding so it could better regulate them. I had the shortest congressional meeting of my career when I saw Senator Phil Gramm, a Republican from Texas and chairman of the Senate Banking Committee, to urge that Congress provide the SEC with additional funding to regulate nonfund advisers. After the usual introductions, I began my presentation with something like: "Mr. Chairman, although I'm of two minds about—" Senator Gramm stood up, interrupted me, and said, "Mr. Fink. I'm not of two minds. I wouldn't give the SEC under [Chairman] Richard Breeden one red cent." The meeting was over. Later that day, I dropped the Senator a thank-you note for the shortest and most candid meeting I ever had on Capitol Hill. (I subsequently recalled that the Senator's wife, Wendy Gramm, had been chair of the Commodity Futures Trading Commission, and that she and SEC Chairman Breeden had had bitter fights over regulatory jurisdiction.) The investment adviser issue continues to be the subject of debate.

Significance of the Regulatory Debates

Fortunately for mutual fund shareholders, the fund industry, and the nation's economy, policy makers have not decided to move mutual funds to a system of bank-type regulation or to authorize the fund industry to regulate itself. However, the debates regarding these issues demonstrated the greatly expanded role that mutual funds had assumed in the nation's economic life and underscored the need to see to it that traditional systems of fund regulation were modernized and strengthened to meet new conditions.

9

Modernizing SEC Regulation

Social necessities...are always more or less in advance of
Law....The greater or less happiness of a people depends on
the degree of promptitude with which the gulf is narrowed.
—Sir Henry Maine

The explosive growth of and dramatic changes in the
mutual fund industry during the 1980s and 1990s led
the Securities and Exchange Commission (SEC) and the
industry to seek to modernize SEC requirements in the
areas of disclosure, substantive regulation of fund activities, and fund compliance with law and regulation.
Disclosure requirements relating to fund prospectuses,
shareholder reports, advertisements, and newsletters
were updated (although disclosure of "shelf space" went
unaddressed). Similarly, a number of SEC substantive
rules and industry best practices in areas such as permissible investments by money market funds, 12b-1 plans,
personal investing by fund managers, and the independence and effectiveness of fund directors were improved
(although hedge funds and asset–backed arrangements
were left unregulated). In the area of compliance, the

SEC did not adopt the industry's recommendation to require funds to establish formal compliance systems. Moreover, the SEC transferred oversight of its own inspections of mutual funds from the division responsible for fund regulation to a separate new unit, a step which many observers believe has harmed compliance.

Improving Disclosure

Prospectuses

A major tenet, perhaps *the* major tenet, of the federal securities laws is that an investor must be provided with complete and accurate information when purchasing a new issue of securities. This emphasis on disclosure has its origin in Justice Louis Brandeis's famous observation, "Sunlight is said to be the best of disinfectants," and his admonition: "To be effective, knowledge of the facts must be actually brought home to the investor, and this can best be done by requiring the facts to be stated in good, large type in every notice, circular, letter and advertisement inviting the investor to purchase. Compliance with this requirement should also be obligatory and not something which the investor could waive."[1] The Securities Act of 1933 implemented Brandeis's concept by requiring that the prospectus for a new issue of securities set forth every material fact regarding the securities and the issuer and by imposing strict liability for failure to do so.

The difficulty is that by requiring a prospectus to contain every fact that might be material to at least some investors, the law virtually guarantees that a prospectus will be incomprehensible to most investors. This is not a problem for the overwhelming majority of American corporations—they rarely issue new securities, and when they do, their prospectuses are designed for market professionals, not ordinary investors. One observer quipped, "I imagine that the same number of people have read one of those things through as have read and finished Edmund Spenser's *Faerie Queene*."[2]

In contrast to most American corporations, mutual funds continuously offer new shares, so they must continuously provide current prospectuses, and these go to millions of ordinary investors. Furthermore, whereas other corporations can market their products and services without supplying prospectuses, mutual funds must furnish prospectuses to their customers, investors. Thus, the problem of the unreadable prospectus is acute for mutual funds. For years the SEC and the fund industry have struggled to create a short, readable mutual fund prospectus. Figure 9.1 is the cover page of an industry proposal designed to simplify fund prospectuses. There is nothing startling about the proposal—except that it is dated December 22, 1943. On repeated occasions, the SEC, with strong industry support, has amended its rules and forms to encourage the creation of a reader-friendly prospectus. Each time the reform works for a while, and then "disclosure creep" sets in. SEC examiners decide that a particular area of current regulatory concern merits more discussion, industry lawyers seek to protect their clients from liability by adding qualifications and caveats, the SEC determines that all prospectuses should cover a totally new item, and so on. A short time after each wave of prospectus reform, we end up back where we started. The short, readable prospectus has been transformed into a lengthy legalistic document.

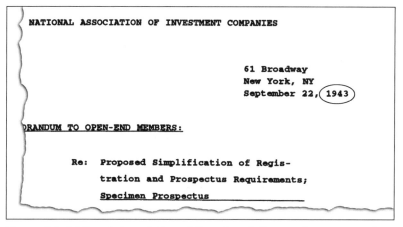

Figure 9.1. National Association of Investment Companies memorandum re prospectus simplification, September 22, 1943 (year circled for clarity).

In 1983, at the start of the bull market, the SEC introduced a novel, far-reaching reform by adopting a two-part disclosure format under which a mutual fund may furnish to investors a simplified prospectus setting forth essential information and may place more detailed information in a "statement of additional information" that an investor can obtain on request. Initially, this reform was a success, and fund prospectuses became shorter, simpler, and easier to read. In 1988, the SEC further improved the simplified prospectus by requiring inclusion of a uniform fee table showing all fees paid by the investor and the fund, plus a hypothetical example, thereby enabling investors to estimate costs and easily compare costs among different funds. (One of my regrets is that as general counsel of the Investment Company Institute, I approved a comment letter criticizing the SEC's proposed fee table, which, with modifications, was a giant step forward.)[3]

By the mid-1990s, disclosure creep once again had taken its toll, making the simplified prospectus a good deal less simple. The development of multiclass funds exacerbated the problem because the prospectus had to discuss each class. So the SEC, under Chairman Arthur Levitt's leadership, undertook another round of reform. Whereas the 1983 reform had taken a top-down approach of splitting the document in two, the simplified prospectus and the statement of additional information, the 1998 reform took a bottom-up approach of making the prospectus more understandable through the use of "plain English" and other devices.[4] The 1998 reform helped, but predictably it was followed by disclosure creep.

In November 2007, the SEC initiated yet another major attempt at prospectus reform.[5] It appears that due to the commission's imaginative reliance on technology, this attempt has a better chance of success than its many predecessors. Under the SEC's reform, key information is provided in a concise summary prospectus, and the full statutory prospectus is placed on a Web site. In its release, the SEC stated that use of this option would satisfy the prospectus delivery requirements of the Securities Act of 1933, and that the summary prospectus could "incorporate by reference" information in the full prospectus. I agree with the SEC's statement that these reforms "have the potential to revolutionize the provision of information to the millions of mutual fund investors who rely on mutual funds for their most basic financial needs." However, given the failure of so many previous efforts at prospectus reform and the likelihood that attorneys will test the legality of the SEC's new approach in court, I would not bank on the success of this revolution until all of the obstacles have been removed.

Shareholder Reports

The Investment Company Act requires mutual funds to provide annual and semi-annual reports to fund shareholders. For decades, the SEC required these reports to list *all* securities in the fund's portfolio as of a recent date. In the case of large funds, the lists ran for dozens of pages. The lists went unread by the vast majority of shareholders. Therefore, the industry repeatedly recommended that lists in shareholder reports be limited to the largest fifty or so holdings, with the entire portfolio available on request. At the other extreme, several advocacy groups filed petitions with the SEC urging that funds be required to disclose their entire portfolios on a monthly basis, arguing that this would help investors better monitor how funds were complying with their stated investment objectives and help deter portfolio manipulation. The industry countered that few shareholders wanted this information, and even under the current twice-a-year system, professional traders were using fund portfolio disclosures to "piggyback" and "front run" fund trades to the detriment of fund shareholders.[6]

The controversy between the industry and advocacy groups was mirrored in the media, with longtime fund experts opposing more frequent disclosure and the popular press supporting it. Jason Zweig, a well-known fund columnist at *Money,* wrote:

> If your fund starts telling everyone what it owns each month, Wall Street's sharp traders will be able to follow—far

better than they already can—what your fund is doing. These folks can profit by running ahead of a big fund, buying whatever the fund is buying and selling what it's selling. That maneuvering by outside speculators will drive up the price your fund pays for stocks—and drive down the price it gets when it sells. As a result, higher trading costs will eat away at your returns.[7]

On the other hand, *USA Today* ran an editorial in support of the petitions seeking monthly disclosure of entire fund portfolio holdings.[8]

In early 2004, the SEC adopted a reasonable middle ground: allowing funds to reduce disclosure in shareholder reports to the largest fifty holdings and securities accounting for more than 1 percent of fund assets and requiring funds to file their entire portfolios with the SEC within sixty days after the end of each quarter.[9] Thus, the SEC permitted reduction of the length of lists in shareholder reports, increased the frequency of disclosure from two to four times a year, and provided a sixty-day reporting delay to reduce the chances for predatory trading practices.

Advertisements

Mutual fund disclosure involves a good deal more than documents required by the securities laws, such as prospectuses and shareholder reports, and encompasses a wide range of other communications between funds and investors, including advertisements and fund company newsletters.

As discussed in chapter 5, for most of their history, mutual funds were prevented from engaging in effective advertising due to strict application of the Securities Act of 1933, which prohibits the written offer of a security unless it is preceded or accompanied by a prospectus. Not until 1979 and the SEC's adoption of rule 482 could mutual funds advertise in a meaningful way. But the rule did not set forth standards governing different types of advertisements because no one could know in advance the kinds of advertisements that would be used. Standards had to be developed over time.

When rule 482 was adopted, money market funds were experiencing explosive growth, with assets increasing from $11 billion in 1978 to $46 billion in 1979. Therefore, it is not surprising that the first issue under rule 482 involved advertising of money funds' current yields. Shortly after the rule was adopted, the industry became concerned that investors might be confused because different money funds could use different mathematical formulas to compute and advertise their current yields. Therefore the Investment Company Institute developed a uniform seven-day yield formula that was adopted by the SEC as the standard for computing money fund yields in advertisements and prospectuses. Subsequently, the industry suggested that the SEC permit the use of compound yields, just as banks are permitted to advertise compound interest, and the SEC amended its rules to permit this.[10]

Although it was relatively easy to develop advertising standards for money market funds, it proved far more difficult to do so for bond funds. Bond funds were the industry's star attraction in the 1980s—many Americans moved from buying bank certificates of deposit to investing in higher-yielding bond funds. Bond funds posed a number of tricky disclosure and advertising issues. How should they convey to investors that as interest rates rise, the prices of bonds and bond funds tend to fall? How should they alert investors that the prices of funds investing solely in U.S. government obligations are not guaranteed? What period should be used for computing bond fund yields? Seven days, as the case with money market funds? Thirty days? A year? Should advertisements of compound yields be permitted as with money funds? Funds that invested in bonds backed by mortgages posed a series of special problems, because homeowners could and did pay off mortgages well before the stated maturity dates.

Many bond funds employed investment techniques that boosted their current returns at the expense of principal. For example, a fund could sell a call option on a bond in its portfolio.

The amount paid for the option would increase the fund's current income, but if the bond went up in price, it would be called away, depriving the fund of the appreciation. Moreover, accounting rules gave bond funds freedom to select accounting treatments that would raise their current returns. For example, a fund might pay $900 for a bond that was due in five years for $1,000. Under generally accepted accounting principles, the fund could accrue $20 of the discount as income each year, rather than waiting to recognize the entire $100 gain in the fifth year. Conversely, a fund might pay $1,100 for a bond that was to come due in five years for $1,000. Under accounting rules the fund could decide *not* to amortize a portion of the $100 premium each year, but instead wait and recognize the entire loss in the fifth year. These treatments were legal but could convey misleading impressions to investors.

I recall returning to the office after a summer vacation in 1985 and having lunch with the institute's tax attorney, Cathy Heron, who had been meeting with industry accountants about bond fund accounting practices. She related to me example after example of ways some funds were increasing their current returns at the expense of principal. It reminded me of ways to get more miles per gallon from a car while gradually destroying the engine. I was convinced that these abuses had to be addressed. So I asked Cathy to begin cataloging the issues and possible solutions. In September, the Institute's Executive Committee appointed an Ad Hoc Committee on Income Fund Yield Calculations, chaired by Ben Korschot, a former chairman of the institute, to develop a uniform method of computing yield and related disclosures in advertisements and other communications to investors. In October, Kathryn McGrath, director of the SEC's Division of Investment Management, delivered a speech in which she noted formation of the industry committee and warned, "I encourage you to move ahead. If you don't, we will."[11]

The committee faced a daunting task. There were many types of bond funds, including corporate, Ginnie Mae, global, high-yield, national municipal, state municipal, and U.S. government funds, many with their own unique issues. Fund managers employed an array of different investment techniques. Most important, generally accepted accounting principles permitted bond funds to make choices in the ways they accounted for income and expense items. The committee formed a number of subcommittees. Over fifty individuals, including senior executives, attorneys, accountants, portfolio managers, and communications personnel, from approximately thirty-five fund organizations participated. It was the one of the largest and most complicated efforts ever undertaken by the institute.

The committee had three choices in developing a uniform method for calculating bond fund yields:

- First, base the yield calculation on distributions made by the fund out of net investment income. (This would cause funds with similar portfolios, income, and expenses to quote different yields because they used different accounting principles in determining their net investment income.)

- Second, base the yield calculation on distributions made by the fund out of net investment income and change numerous generally accepted accounting principles to mandate one result. (This approach, if at all feasible, would take forever.)

- Third, base the yield calculation on distributions made by the fund out of net investment income and develop a special set of rules for performing the calculation. (This would require the committee to develop numerous rules covering matters such as original issue premiums and discounts, market premiums and discounts, mortgage pay-downs, equalization accounting, option premiums, etc.).

The committee chose the third approach, developing a special formula for calculating bond fund yields, despite the complex work required, so that investors could compare yields of similar funds without awaiting changes in generally accepted accounting principles. On March 11, 1986, the institute submitted the committee's recommendations to the SEC. Under the proposal, yields in bond fund advertisements had to be computed

according to this uniform formula, and an advertisement setting forth the fund's distribution rate had to give equal promi-
nence to the yield number.[12]

In September, the SEC proposed to adopt the institute's yield
formula, prohibit the use of distribution rates, and require yield
advertisements to contain total return numbers for the past five
years. The SEC also proposed to require total return numbers
in performance advertisements for equity funds, even though
they had not been part of the debate. The institute objected to
many of the commission's proposals, particularly the proposal
to include stock funds. In February 1988, the SEC adopted final
advertising rules that used the institute's yield formula, prohibited advertisement of distribution rates, and required performance advertisements for both bond and stock funds to contain
total return numbers for the prior one, five, and ten years.[13]

Although the SEC and the industry disagreed over many
points as the standards governing performance advertising
were being formulated, the debate helped produce a sensible set
of rules. The industry developed yield formulas for money market funds and bond funds, and the SEC developed the overall
regulatory package. The SEC's performance advertising rules are
simple but comprehensive. They have worked. There have been
few abuses or complaints. The advertising rules have helped
no-load funds reach more investors, thus placing pressure on
other funds to reduce costs. Shortly after the SEC adopted the
1988 package, I concluded that the commission was correct
to have included equity funds because some stock funds had
started running advertisements using carefully selected time
periods to tout their performance. I advised the SEC staff of
my change of heart. More generally, I thought that a number of
bond funds had engaged in shady (though legal) practices, and
I was glad that the institute had assisted the SEC in addressing
this matter.

After I retired as president of the institute in 2004, I joined
the board of the Oppenheimer Funds as an independent director. At one of my first meetings, Ron Fielding, head of
Oppenheimer's municipal bond funds and an old friend, made

a presentation about his funds. Ron sat at the head of the conference table, and I was off to the side. We couldn't see one another, and I don't believe that he knew that I was in the room.
After his presentation, Ron took questions from directors. One
asked about an exhibit that Ron had handed out. Ron said, "Oh,
those are SEC yield numbers that Matt Fink and his friends at
the SEC make us publish."

The explosion in media coverage of mutual funds created
the need to create other types of advertising standards. A number of financial publications and services, including *Barron's*,
Kiplinger's, Lipper, Money, and *Morningstar,* began publishing
rankings of mutual funds based on their performance over specified periods compared to similar funds. As might be expected,
many funds that received high rankings ran ads proclaiming
this fact. Just as there had been a need to develop standards for
advertisements presenting performance information, there arose
a need to develop standards for advertising rankings. The need
for standards was highlighted when in 1993 the Pilgrim fund
group ran an ad claiming that five of its income funds were at
the top of *Lipper's* rankings. *Morningstar* published a piece titled
"Lies, Damn Lies, and Fund Advertisements," pointing out how
Pilgrim had manipulated the numbers to produce these results.
Pilgrim sued *Morningstar,* and the court dismissed the suit. The
National Association of Securities Dealers (NASD) fined Pilgrim
for violating its general antifraud rules and suspended its CEO
from the industry for a period of time.[14]

Shortly thereafter, the Investment Company Institute submitted to the NASD proposed guidelines regarding the use of
fund rankings in advertisements and sales literature. The NASD
went on to file proposed guidelines with the SEC, and in July
1994, the SEC approved the ranking guidelines. The guidelines
require that the ranking be produced by an independent "ranking entity" and not be procured by the fund. The advertisement
must disclose the name of the category (e.g., growth funds), the
number of funds in the category, the length of the period and
the ending date, the criteria on which the ranking is based,
and the names of both the ranking entity (e.g., Lipper) and the

publisher (e.g., *ABC Magazine*, June 1993). The headline cannot state or imply that the fund is the best performer in a category unless it is ranked first in that category.[15] The NASD's ranking guidelines appear to be working well; I am not aware of any abuse in this area.

Newsletters

As fund complexes grew in terms of number of funds and services offered, they began publishing regular newsletters for shareholders covering such matters as market developments, personal investing topics, and particular funds offered by the complex. I received a number of newsletters and found them to be a good deal more interesting than prospectuses and shareholder reports. In 1987, I received a letter from Stanley Judd, a senior member of the SEC staff, concerning fund newsletters.[16]

I had trouble fully understanding all of the legal points in Stan's letter, but I gathered that he was raising the possibility that some newsletters might be in violation of the Securities Act of 1933 because some articles could be viewed as offering fund shares without being accompanied or preceded by a prospectus. This struck me as a crazy result but totally in keeping with the way the 1933 act just doesn't fit mutual funds.

I was tempted to write back to Stan to tell him to forget the whole thing or to retain outside counsel to challenge his line of argument. But knowing and respecting Stan, I thought that he probably was correct from a purely legal point of view. I decided that the best course of action would be to engage him in a high level of intellectual discourse, hoping that somehow it might lead to a reasonable solution. I thought of just the debater—Steve West, a partner at Sullivan & Cromwell, longtime counsel to the institute and a guru in federal securities law theology. I called Steve; he immediately understood what I wanted, and the debate began. Learned missives written in a language that I often thought of as "olde SECese" went back and forth between Steve and Stan discussing 1933 act concepts and the way they might impact fund newsletters. Much of the discourse was well over my head, but I did not care as long as a respectful dialogue continued. At one point, Stan's boss, Kathie McGrath, called me to ask, "What the hell is going on?" I told her that all of this was beyond mere mortals like the two of us, and I urged her to allow the debate to go on in the hope that it might produce good results.

Steve and Stan worked out a series of guidelines that permit fund newsletters to contain both material that would constitute fund advertisements and nonoffering material, provided there is proper segregation between the two and the inclusion of appropriate legends.[17] Just as in other situations, common sense and creative lawyering on the part of the SEC staff and industry representatives came up with a workable solution that advanced the interests of investors and met the four corners of the federal securities laws.

Shelf Space

The development of SEC standards governing advertisements and newsletters demonstrates how disclosure requirements can be adjusted to meet new conditions in the interests of investors and the industry. In contrast, the history of disclosure, or rather the history of nondisclosure, of "shelf space" demonstrates how problems can get worse when they go unaddressed.

In 1995, I was approached by a former CEO of a mid-size fund group who expressed great concern about arrangements between mutual funds on one hand and broker-dealers and banks on the other that he thought could threaten the fund industry's legal structure and viability. It took me several days to figure out exactly what he was getting at. I felt as though I was untangling a very snarled fishing line. After several phone calls and much thought, I had it: many broker-dealers and banks were requiring payments in addition to sales loads and 12b-1 fees to sell particular mutual funds. These require-ments came in many shapes and sizes (percentages of sales, percentages of assets, reimbursement of expenses, etc.), had many different names (preferred lists, due diligence, etc.) and were generically referred to as payments for "shelf space" or "revenue sharing." It struck me that these arrangements raised a major disclosure issue. If a broker or bank was recommending a particular fund to a customer, didn't the customer have the right to know that the firm was receiving extra compensation for selling that particular fund?

I decided that the industry had to address this issue as promptly as possible. The institute formed a committee of fund CEOs and representatives of a variety of sales organizations. As a result of the committee's deliberations, on October 19, 1995, the institute wrote to the NASD, proposing that it amend its rules to require fund prospectuses to contain general disclosure about such payments and also require that on request fund under-writers provide a separate "cash compensation disclosure document" with respect to each particular broker-dealer. In October 1997, the institute modified its suggestions and proposed that fund prospectuses be required to set forth general disclosure and that broker-dealers also be required to provide general written disclosure when or before they sell fund shares (e.g., in the account application form). The institute emphasized that as the result of these two general written disclosures, "Investors would be put on notice as to the existence of cash compensation arrangements and thus would be in a position to inquire further, if they so wished, when purchasing shares of a particular fund."[18] The NASD did not act on either our 1995 or 1997 suggestions.

The institute staff, outside counsel, committee members, and, I imagine, the NASD all assumed that issues relating to shelf space fell exclusively within the NASD's purview because they involved sales practices. It never occurred to us that the SEC also might have jurisdiction. But in 2000, the SEC asserted that payments for shelf space are subject to disclosure under the SEC confirmation rule, which requires broker-dealers to send customers written evidence of transactions. Although it struck me as pretty far-fetched to argue that the confirmation rule applied to payments for shelf space, the SEC's assertion of jurisdiction provided the institute with another place to seek regulatory action. Therefore, on May 8, 2000, the institute wrote to the SEC, urging that the commission impose disclosure requirements on both mutual funds and broker-dealers along the lines of our 1997 submission to the NASD. The Securities Industry Association, representing the broker-dealer industry, submitted similar suggestions.[19] But the SEC, like the NASD, took no action. The industries' suggestions were placed in the back of the medicine cabinet and forgotten.

In September 2003, almost eight years after the industry first called for regulatory action, the NASD issued a proposal to require broker-dealers to provide extensive disclosure about shelf space. However, the proposal was pushed offstage by the flood of government actions following revelation of the fund trading scandals. Bills were introduced in Congress with provisions requiring disclosure of shelf-space arrangements. The SEC proposed a rule requiring disclosure. In an Orwellian move, the SEC brought enforcement actions against funds and brokers for failure to provide adequate disclosure about shelf space, despite the fact that the SEC had ignored the industry's pleas to adopt a disclosure rule in this area: "Winston Smith, you are found guilty of violating a law that is not on the books but that you called for". There recently has been positive movement. The SEC's new summary prospectus rule requires funds to provide disclosure regarding shelf space. FINRA (the successor to the NASD) has revived its proposal to require broker-dealers to provide disclosure. But as this edition goes to press, FINRA has not yet adopted a rule.

Since 1995, when the institute first called upon regulators to require revenue sharing disclosure by both mutual funds and brokers, fund assets have more than tripled, fund companies have paid billions of dollars to brokerage firms for shelf space, there have been five SEC chairs and four heads of the NASD-FINRA. But the shelf space issue still is not fully addressed and goes on and on and on. It brings to mind Dickens' famous case:

> Jarndyce and Jarndyce drones on. The scarecrow of a suit
> has, in course of time, become so complicated, that no man

alive knows what it means. The parties to it understand it least; but it has been observed that no two Chancery lawyers can talk about it for five minutes, without coming to a total disagreement as to all the premises. Innumerable children have been born into the cause; innumerable young people have married into it; innumerable old people have died out of it. Scores of persons have deliriously found themselves made parties in Jarndyce and Jarndyce, without knowing how or why; whole families have inherited legendary hatreds with the suit. The little plaintiff or defendant, who was promised a new rocking-horse when Jarndyce and Jarndyce should be settled, has grown up, possessed himself of a real horse, and trotted away into the other world. Fair wards of court have faded into mothers and grandmothers; a long procession of Chancellors has come in and gone out; the legion of bills in the suit have been transformed into mere bills of mortality; there are not three Jarndyces left upon the earth perhaps, since old Tom Jarndyce in despair blew his brains out at a coffee-house in Chancery Lane; but Jarndyce and Jarndyce still drags its dreary length before the Court, perennially hopeless.[20]

Proxy Votes

Another disclosure issue ignited heated debate. In 2002, the American Federation of Labor–Congress of Industrial Organizations (AFL-CIO) filed a petition with the SEC seeking action requiring mutual funds to publicly disclose their proxy votes. The industry, the SEC staff, and reporters noted the filing but assumed that it was frivolous and likely part of the battle then going on between the AFL-CIO and Fidelity.[21] In fall 2002, the Investment Company Institute selected a new chairman, Paul Haaga of Capital Research, and Paul, the institute's general counsel, Craig Tyle, and I paid a courtesy visit to SEC Chairman Harvey Pitt. We had known the chairman for decades and felt a bit awkward because he was under intense criticism and likely was on his way out. After the normal greetings, Pitt dropped a bombshell by telling us that he wanted the SEC to adopt a rule requiring mutual funds to publicly disclose their proxy votes. We were stunned, both because no one (other than a few unions) had ever urged this requirement and because the SEC apparently was going to propose public disclosure of proxy votes only for mutual funds and not for any other types of institutional investors. In September, the SEC proposed to require mutual funds to make available to shareholders the specific proxy votes they cast, either by responding to telephone calls, by postings on the fund's Web site, or by postings on the SEC's Web site. The SEC also proposed to require investment advisers to clients other than investment companies to disclose to clients on a one-on-one basis how they could obtain information as to how the adviser voted their proxies.[22] Thus under these proposals, mutual funds alone would be required to make their proxy votes public.

The SEC's release offered two rationales for singling out mutual funds—using mutual funds to police corporate America on behalf of all investors, and overcoming potential mutual fund conflicts of interest.

First, "Proxy voting decisions by funds may play an important role in maximizing the value of the funds' investments, having an enormous impact on the financial livelihood of millions of Americans. Further, requiring greater transparency of proxy voting by funds may encourage funds to become more engaged in corporate governance of issuers held in their portfolios, which may benefit *all investors* and not just fund shareholders" (emphasis added).

Second:

> Moreover, in some situations the interests of a mutual fund's shareholders may conflict with those of its investment adviser with respect to proxy voting. This may occur, or example, when a fund's adviser also manages or seeks to manage the retirement plan assets of a company whose securities are held by the fund. In these situations, a fund's adviser may have an incentive to support management recommendations to further its business interests.... Shedding

light on mutual fund proxy voting could illuminate potential conflicts of interest and discourage voting that is inconsistent with fund shareholders' best interests.

The SEC's proposal produced a firestorm. The AFL-CIO organized a massive letter-writing campaign in support of it. The
fund industry was dead opposed and was as angry as I could
ever recall due to a combination of the general environment (the
bear market, the controversy over portfolio disclosure, etc.) and
the proxy proposal itself. In its comment letter, the Investment
Company Institute stressed the fact that ironically, the proposal
would cause mutual funds to lose the ability to vote confidentially
(a right that reform groups supported to shield voters from pressure from management), and would politicize the proxy voting
process by making the funds an easy target for special interests.
Fund independent directors were irate that the SEC completely
ignored their role in deciding how proxies should be voted. In
an unprecedented development, the heads of the two largest
fund organizations, Jack Brennan of Vanguard and Ned Johnson
of Fidelity, normally tough rivals, coauthored a piece in the *Wall
Street Journal* criticizing the proposal. The SEC went on to adopt
the proposal.[23]

I hardly thought that this was the most important issue
facing the fund industry, but I found it outrageous that the SEC
had singled out proxy votes cast by mutual funds for public
disclosure, allegedly to benefit all investors. This rationale was
reminiscent of the argument that community reinvestment
requirements should be imposed on mutual funds to benefit
local communities, an argument that the SEC had castigated as
being contrary to the Investment Company Act, which mandates
that funds be managed solely in the interest of fund shareholders.
The SEC's second argument, potential conflicts, was equally
applicable to all money managers, but the commission was only
directing its fire at mutual funds. It was true that mutual funds
owned approximately 19 percent of U.S. equities. But other institutional investors owned over 30 percent. If public disclosure of
institutional proxy votes was such a good idea, why didn't the

SEC require it for *all* institutions within its jurisdiction, such as broker-dealers holding customers' stock, and investment advisers to retirement plans, universities, foundations, hedge funds, and so on? Why didn't the SEC call on other regulators (the Department of Labor, the comptroller of the currency, state insurance regulators) to follow its lead with respect to entities (such as pension funds, bank trust departments, and insurance companies) they regulated?

The proxy vote episode highlighted the very different ways that the mutual fund industry and the media viewed things. The industry thought that its standards were far higher than those of other money managers, and therefore it should not be called on to do more. The media believed that what other money managers did was irrelevant and mutual funds, as the main vehicles for Americans' savings, should be held to the highest possible standards. The industry bristled at this argument and felt that only because it was subject to far greater government control than other investment vehicles (i.e., bank common trust funds, bank collective funds, pension funds, insurance company separate accounts, hedge funds, commodity pools), it was being subjected to more and more regulation. I termed this the "only ape in captivity" phenomenon: because the zookeeper, the SEC, had pervasive jurisdiction only over mutual funds, it kept trying out the latest regulatory remedies on mutual funds, while the other great apes, such as bank funds, hedge funds, and so on, roamed free in the wild. This difference in viewpoints was to play itself out again and again, for example, in connection with personal investing by portfolio managers and application of parts of the Sarbanes-Oxley Act to mutual funds. When I was president of the institute, there were many days when I received angry calls from members complaining that the institute had gone too far in capitulating to regulators or critics, while on my desk there were editorials blasting the industry for not having gone far enough.

My own negative reaction to the proxy vote disclosure issue was not based on some gut antiregulatory bias. In fact, I was quite concerned that the SEC had not acted on a series of suggestions made by the institute to *increase* regulation in a number of areas, including disclosure of shelf space, hedge funds, rating agencies, asset-backed arrangements, and industry compliance systems. Indeed, I was upset precisely because the SEC was ignoring the critical need for regulatory actions in these vital areas while pursuing something as trivial, though headline-grabbing, as proxy vote disclosure.

1940 Act Regulation

In addition to seeking to address new conditions through adjustments in disclosure requirements, the SEC and the mutual fund industry sought changes in regulations governing fund operations in areas such as permissible investments by money market funds, 12b-1 plans, personal investing by fund managers, and the qualifications and duties of fund directors.

Money Market Funds

One reason for money market funds' success was that the SEC had adopted rule 2a-7, which permits the funds to maintain $1 per share net asset values, provided specified conditions relating to matters such as the short duration and high quality of the portfolio are maintained. In 1989, Integrated Resources defaulted on its commercial paper, which was held by a number of money funds. Kathryn McGrath, director of the SEC Division of Investment Management, asked for the industry's views regarding regulatory changes designed to reduce risks to money funds. The institute formed a committee of money market fund CEOs, who concluded that no changes were needed. Then a second company, Mortgage & Realty Trust, defaulted on its commercial paper.[24] The committee reconvened.

At its next meeting, the committee split into two groups. The majority believed that if a single money market fund were to "break a buck" (i.e., its share price were to fall below $1), the entire industry's reputation would be damaged, and therefore the majority favored tightening the standards in rule 2a-7.

The minority felt that a fund group with good portfolio management or the resources to make its funds whole in the event of losses should not be forced to adhere to tougher standards to protect weaker groups. It was an excellent debate. The best presentation was made by Dan Maclean of Dreyfus, who argued passionately in favor of the minority position, speaking eloquently of the benefits of competition and the need to avoid "dumbing down" the entire industry. His presentation almost brought tears to one's eyes. The only thing that surprised me was that Dan was opposing tougher standards, whereas his boss, Howard Stein, was well known for his aversion to risk.

Sure enough, at the committee's next meeting, it was apparent that Dan had received new marching orders. He now argued passionately in favor of tightening the standards, speaking eloquently of the need for each firm to put aside its own interests and of the moral requirement that everyone work together for the common good. Again, he was inspirational and moved his audience to the verge of tears, although he was now arguing the opposite case. In any event, the committee determined that the institute should propose changes to rule 2a-7 designed to reduce risk. For example, the existing rule required that portfolio securities that were rated by a rating agency must receive one of the two highest ratings; the committee decided to require the highest rating. As to duration, the committee concluded that the average dollar-weighted portfolio maturity requirement should be shortened from 120 to 90 days.

The institute forwarded these and other suggestions to the SEC. The SEC also was lobbied by issuers of lower rated commercial paper and the securities firms that underwrote that paper not to amend rule 2a-7 so as to discriminate against lower rated paper. The final changes adopted by the SEC reflected most of the committee's recommendations and adopted a compromise on lower rated commercial paper, permitting a money fund to invest up to 5 percent of its assets in that paper.[25]

The rule as amended has worked well. Until 2008, only one money market fund broke a dollar. Ironically, it was a fund created by several banks for the investment of their own reserves,

Community Bankers U.S. Government Money Market Fund. Just before the fund broke a dollar in 1994, several of the bankers who ran the fund came to see me. They had read reports that the fund industry had a "secret bailout agreement" to rescue money funds that were in trouble, and they asked what the institute was prepared to do in their situation.[26] I was as polite as I could be and told them that there was no secret agreement, and the institute could do nothing to help them. The fund then broke a dollar and fell to ninety-six cents a share, but there was not a ripple. This hardly was a fair test case because the fund was tiny and didn't have retail investors.

There have been numerous instances in which sponsors of money funds have purchased portfolio securities from the funds or taken other measures to maintain the funds' $1 per share net asset values. In November 2007, an executive at Moody's Investors Service reported, "Prior to this year, there were 145 cases where money funds received some type of support from sponsors to prevent or mitigate losses."[27] In the first edition of this book, I stated that "I hope that we never have to learn what would happen should a large well-known money market fund break a dollar." As discussed in chapter 12, in 2008, a large money market fund, Reserve Primary Fund, broke a dollar, resulting in competing calls to regulate money funds as "near banks" or to tighten SEC regulation of money funds under rule 2a-7.

12b-1 Plans

As discussed in chapter 5, in 1980 the SEC adopted rule 12b-1, which permits mutual funds to pay for the distribution of their shares to investors. The first plans adopted under the rule were used to supplement existing marketing activities and front-end sales loads. Then a new type of 12b-1 plan, one that substituted 12b-1 payments for front-end sales loads, came into existence. The development of these spread-load and level-load 12b-1 plans led to concerns regarding investor protection under the federal securities laws, which were enacted when there was a simple front-end load/no-load fund universe. The SEC took two major steps to address these concerns.

First, in 1988, the SEC sought to improve investors' understanding of 12b-1 and other fees by requiring the inclusion of a fee table at the beginning of every fund prospectus. The table shows (1) transactional expenses, including front-end loads and contingent deferred sales loads, paid directly by fund shareholders; (2) the fund's annual operating expenses (including 12b-1 fees); and (3) an example showing the cumulative amount of all of these fees over various periods of time, based on a hypothetical investment in the fund.[28]

Second, in 1992, the SEC approved an NASD proposal to amend its existing front-end sales charge rule to encompass both CDSLs and 12b-1 fees, in recognition of the fact that spread-load and level-load plans are substitutes for front-end sales charges. The rule in effect limits 12b-1 fees to 0.75 percent of a fund's average annual assets. The rule also permits a service fee of 0.25 percent a year. Both the SEC and NASD have stated that it is unlawful for to describe a fund with a CDSL or an "asset-based sales charge" greater than 0.25 percent as "no-load."[29]

Despite these reforms, criticism of rule 12b-1 continues.

Some, concerned that 12b-1 fees are not sufficiently transparent to investors because the fees are borne by the fund rather than by investors, as is the case of sales charges, call for repeal of the rule and the end of all 12b-1 fees.[30] But this would return us to the uncertainty that prevailed before 1980 as to the permissibility of various types of arrangements, such as a fund adviser reallocating part of its fee to dealers, a fund paying dealers directly, or a fund paying recordkeeping fees to brokers, pension fund administrators, or fund supermarkets that also distribute fund shares.

Some would prohibit use of 12b-1 fees for purposes they believe were never intended, "including compensating financial intermediaries who sell the mutual funds."[31] But this ignores the fact that this was precisely one of the situations that led the SEC to adopt the rule, and the rule expressly refers to "compensation of underwriters, dealers, and sales personnel."

Some would prohibit funds that are closed to new investors from charging 12b-1 fees.[32] But this misses the point of spread-load and level-load 12b-1 fees, which are not used to pay for current sales but rather to pay for past sales by reimbursing the fund's underwriter who had advanced up-front payments to dealers.

Some would amend the rule to require that 12b-1 fees be charged against each shareholder's account, rather than against the fund.[33] But this change would raise major operational and tax problems. In 1992 the SEC staff stated, "tax law complications would make the method [charging each shareholder's account] essentially impossible. Unless and until the tax laws change, we think spread loads generally should be permitted."[34]

Some fund directors and their legal counsel express concern that some factors for director consideration in the SEC's 1980 release, which were designed for supplemental 12b-1 plans, are not relevant to 12b-1 arrangements that substitute for front-end loads. But the SEC release makes it clear that directors are not required to consider these factors.

I have attended numerous meetings where just about everyone declares that "something needs to be done about Rule 12b-1." When pressed, each participant points to a different issue and therefore proposes a different solution. In 2004, the SEC invited comments on a wide range of questions concerning rule 12b-1, and as one would expect, many different views were expressed. In 2007, the SEC held a public 12b-1 roundtable, and again, views were all over the lot. In July 2010, the SEC issued a 270 page release proposing changes that would reduce some fees. Commentators were quick to point out that fee reductions in one area are likely to be offset by increases in other areas.[35] I have no doubt that these issues will be with us for years to come.

I believe these issues can be resolved only by ending the fruitless effort to segregate fees paid by mutual funds into neat and unrealistic categories of advisory, distribution, and administrative fees and by moving to a single unitary fee, as recommended by the SEC staff in 1992.

Personal Investing

A third regulatory issue involved personal investing by employees of mutual fund organizations. In the 1960s, members of the SEC staff had been concerned over the possibility of fund insiders engaging in personal trading based on their knowledge of the fund's investment activities (e.g., buying a security that the fund currently is buying or is about to buy). In response to this concern, the 1970 amendments to the Investment Company Act added new section 17(j), which authorized the SEC to adopt rules in this area, most important, rules requiring fund organizations to adopt codes of ethics governing personal investing by fund insiders. One of the first projects I worked on when I joined the legal staff of the Investment Company Institute in 1971 was drafting a proposed rule and a model code of ethics that the institute submitted to the SEC. The lack of urgency in this area was demonstrated by the fact that it was not until 1980, ten years after the authorizing legislation, that the SEC adopted rule 17j-1.[36]

Fund codes of ethics had three key provisions:

1. Fund insiders were prohibited from purchasing or selling any security that the fund was considering for purchase or sale or was currently purchasing or selling.

2. Insiders had to report *all* of their personal securities transactions to the fund organization.

3. The fund organization could impose sanctions for violations of its code, including termination of employment.[37]

The system mandated by section 17(j) was unique to mutual funds. No other types of money management, such as pension funds, endowments, bank common trust funds, insurance company portfolios, separately managed accounts, or hedge funds, were subject to these types of regulatory requirements. The system seemed to work well in deterring abuse, and relatively little attention was paid to this area.

Then, in January 1994, the Invesco fund group fired a well-known portfolio manager, John Kaweske, for failing to report his personal securities transactions as required by its code of ethics. I naively thought the media and policy makers might praise the fund industry for establishing standards governing personal investing and for punishing violators, including superstars. Boy, was I wrong. The press, regulators, and members of Congress ripped into the industry. The *Washington Post* ran the Kaweske story on the front page with the headline "Fund Managers' Own Trades Termed a Potential Conflict." The story in the *Chicago Sun-Times* began, "The mutual fund industry's seemingly perpetual honeymoon with the media is suddenly on hiatus. At issue is whether the press—and more important, the public—can continue to trust the funds to do what's right."[38] Members of Congress wrote to the SEC demanding an explanation. The SEC initiated an investigation of personal investing practices at the thirty largest fund groups. There were calls to prohibit fund insiders from engaging in any personal investing, other than investing in their groups' mutual funds.

Most people in the fund industry were astonished at what they regarded as an overreaction. After all, mutual funds were required by law to have codes of ethics and were enforcing them, as evidenced by Invesco's firing of Kaweske. Meanwhile, similar controls were not imposed on any other money managers, and the mutual fund industry asked, "what about the other guys?"[39]

In retrospect, the difference in reactions between the fund industry, on one hand, and the media and policy makers, on the other hand, was understandable. The fund industry viewed personal investing as a relatively minor problem, and one that was being dealt with. Moreover, the industry was concerned that a total ban on personal investing by fund personnel would result in a brain drain, as fund managers left to manage pension plans, hedge funds, and other investment vehicles that did not have such restrictions. Outsiders had a completely different perspective. One publication observed:

> The extraordinary response to the Invesco incident reveals
> a pent-up demand for scrutiny of an industry with a

wholesome image that, up to now, has not received a
great deal of critical attention from Congress, the SEC or
the news media. Although the remarkable growth of mutual funds is not a new story—the industry boomed in the
1980s—only now has it seemed to dawn on everyone that
a mouse has grown up to be an elephant.[40]

Many in the fund industry advised me that the issue would
blow over. But if anything, the controversy became even more
intense. I began to think of actions the industry could take to
end the matter, short of agreeing to a total ban on personal
investing, which I regarded as a severe mistake. I sought advice
from Dick Phillips, a well-respected fund attorney, and he said,
"Whatever you do, it can't be a half measure but must be so
draconian as to end the debate." Dave Silver, my former boss,
surmised that the core problem was extremely short-term trading by fund insiders. On a Sunday in late January, I was flying
from Washington and almost jumped out of my plane seat when
I read a story in the *New York Times* quoting Stanley Sporkin, a
U.S. District Court judge, formerly a legendary director of the
SEC Division of Enforcement, and an old friend, as saying there
should be a total ban on personal trading. "They should put it
in a blind trust....If a person is getting paid well to manage
money, that should be his job."[41] I called Stanley on Monday,
and found myself yelling at a federal judge, "Stanley, you jerk!
Don't you realize that there is a section of the 1940 act dealing
with this, and that funds are required to have codes of ethics,
etc.?" Stanley said, "Matt, calm down, calm down. Close your
door and do three things. First, calm down. Second, write down
a list of possible reforms. Third, appoint a blue ribbon committee to recommend reforms." The following Friday my wife and I
attended a dinner party at a neighbor's house. Standing behind
me in the buffet line was a fellow who identified himself as a
local investment adviser. When I told him that I was president
of the mutual fund trade association, he said, "The personal
investing issue is killing you guys. You better do something,
and soon."

That Saturday, as I drove around town doing errands, I thought of all this advice (draconian measures, short-term trading, blue ribbon committee, "do something, and soon"), and formulated a plan. I called Harvey Pitt, one of the institute's outside counsel, to retain him to work with a blue ribbon committee of industry CEOs that would, within ninety days, promulgate a series of draconian measures, including a ban on short-term trading. Harvey said, "Matt, you're a genius." First thing Monday morning, I called Ron Lynch, the institute's chairman, and by that afternoon he had appointed a blue ribbon committee of fund CEOs, the Advisory Group on Personal Investing. The advisory group met in person with experts, including former SEC officials, representatives of the accounting and legal community, and noted ethicists and academicians. I recall one professor of ethics telling the group, "You don't have an ethical problem. You have a public relations problem."

On May 9, 1994, well within the ninety-day deadline, the advisory group issued its report. It called for a number of stringent measures to be included in fund codes of ethics.

- *Initial Public Offerings.* A flat prohibition against investment personnel acquiring securities in any initial public offering.

- *Private Placements.*A requirement for express prior approval of the acquisition of securities by investment personnel in a private placement.

- *Blackout Periods.* Fund personnel cannot trade a security any day the fund has a pending buy or sell order. A portfolio manager cannot trade a security seven days before or after the fund he or she manages trades that security. Any profits on trades within the proscribed periods must be disgorged.

- *Ban on Short-Term Trading Profits.* Investment personnel cannot purchase and sell securities within sixty days. Any profits on such short-term trades must be disgorged.

- *Gifts.* Investment personnel cannot receive gifts of more than de minimus value from persons doing business with the fund.

- *Service as a Director.* A requirement for investment personnel to obtain prior authorization to serve on the board of a publicly traded company.

- *Six Specific Compliance Procedures.* Includes preclearance of all personal securities transactions, timely records of all securities transactions and accounts, annual disclosure of personal securities holdings, and annual reports to fund boards.[42]

These recommendations were endorsed unanimously by the institute's Board of Governors and were adopted throughout the industry. Regulators, members of Congress, and industry observers commended the advisory group's work. SEC chairman Levitt stated that the recommendations "constructively address the conflicts of interest that arise when portfolio managers purchase and sell securities for their personal accounts." John Dingell, chairman of the House Energy and Commerce Committee, praised the report as "a series of tough and far-reaching procedural requirements." *Investment Lawyer,* a publication aimed at attorneys representing various types of money management firms, wrote, "The fund industry could easily have argued that the problem of personal trading by fund personnel had been sensationalized. The reported abuses were in fact isolated and modest. Instead, the fund industry accepted responsibility for restoring public confidence and largely achieved this through self-regulation."[43]

The fund industry itself expressed strong support for the advisory group's report. Several years after the report was issued, I hosted a dinner in Los Angeles for institute members. One attendee complained about the stringent nature of the personal investing standards that applied only to his firm's mutual fund business and not to its other money management activities. Before I could respond, another member, Ron Robison, then with Trust Company of the West, said, "These are the rules of the mutual fund business. If you don't like them, you should get out of the fund business." Ron's views were seconded by many other attendees, who represented a broad spectrum of different types of fund organizations.

The report has not put the matter to rest. In his address at the institute's 1996 General Membership Meeting, SEC chairman Levitt stated, "If I were a director, I would have reservations about portfolio managers trading for their own account." Later that year, an editorial in the *Economist* recommended that mutual funds prohibit their portfolio managers from engaging in any personal trading for their own accounts.[44] I confidently predict that a new scandal involving personal investing by a fund portfolio manager will revive the controversy.

The personal investing episode offered a textbook example of my "only ape in captivity" theory. Because mutual funds were subject to pervasive SEC regulation, regulators felt free to impose tough controls on investments made by mutual fund employees, and outside observers felt free to urge a total ban on their investing activities. Meanwhile, investments by employees at other money managers went totally unregulated. More important, the episode demonstrated the precarious situation the fund industry faced. Because mutual funds had become so popular with millions of investors, the media and policy makers expected a great deal from us. An infraction that the industry viewed as minor could ignite calls for extreme government action. In the case of personal investing, the outstanding work of the advisory committee headed by Ron Lynch forestalled government action. I guessed that it would be hard to repeat this exercise every time the industry faced a problem.

Directors

Over the years, perhaps the most divisive issue in mutual fund regulation has been the role of fund directors. In one camp are those who would abolish fund directors. At the other extreme are those who would greatly expand their role, for example, have directors regularly determine which outside firm should serve as the fund's adviser or even have the directors regularly decide whether they should dismiss the adviser and have the fund itself assume management functions. Both positions would surprise the drafters of the 1940 act. On one hand, they viewed independent directors as a device to help prevent management from going too far, and they never considered doing away with this tool. On the other hand, the drafters regarded directors as a "check on," not a replacement for, management. The SEC's original version of the 1940 act would have required that a majority of directors be independent, but the commission abandoned this approach in favor of a 40 percent requirement, testifying:

> the argument was made that it is difficult for a person or firm to undertake the management of an investment company, give advice, when the majority of the board may repudiate that advice. It was urged that if a person is buying management of a particular person and if the majority of the board can repudiate his advice, then in effect, you are depriving the stockholders of that person's advice.
>
> Now, that made sense to us. If the stockholders want A's management, then A should have the right to impose his investment advice on that company. *However, we felt that there should be some check on the management and that is why the provision for 40 percent independents was inserted.*[45]

The Investment Company Act gave fund directors only four specific responsibilities: approval of the advisory agreement, approval of the underwriting agreement, selection of the fund's outside accountant, and valuation of portfolio securities for which market quotations are not readily available. Directors' responsibilities successively increased in the years following passage of the act. Fund groups made director oversight one of the proposed conditions in the exemptive orders they sought. The SEC adopted a series of exemptive rules that required transactions to be approved by directors.[46] This process of "director creep" was greatly accelerated by the 1970 amendments to the Investment Company Act that placed more responsibility on directors regarding approval of management fees. In subsequent years, the SEC adopted many more exemptive rules requiring actions by directors, and in 1980, the SEC adopted rule 12b-1, which permits the use of fund assets for distribution of fund shares conditioned on approval by the independent directors. Moreover, directors' work has increased in areas not addressed by law and regulation, including assigning responsibility for paying for errors and the allocation of expenses between funds and their advisers. Thus, the role of independent directors that had played a limited (albeit important) part in the system of checks and balances devised by the drafters of the 1940 act had mushroomed. Meanwhile, directors almost never fired fund advisers. In fact, when directors sought to change the adviser, they were rebuffed by fund shareholders.[47]

There were very different reactions to these developments. Some, like Warren Buffett, scoffed at fund directors because they almost never changed advisers. In 1993 he wrote, "a monkey [would] type out a Shakespeare play before an 'independent' mutual-fund director [would] suggest that his fund look at other managers, even if the incumbent manager has persistently delivered substandard performance." A year later, after revelation of the fund trading scandals, Buffett wrote, "So what are the directors of these looted funds doing? I have seen none that have terminated the contract of the offending management company (though naturally that entity has often fired some of its employees). Can you imagine directors who have been personally defrauded taking such a boys-will-be-boys attitude?"[48]

Others proposed doing away with directors. In 1980, Stephen K. West, a partner in the law firm of Sullivan & Cromwell and outside counsel to the Investment Company Institute, proposed that the Investment Company Act be amended to permit the creation of a new type of mutual fund, a unitary investment fund (UIF), similar to investment companies in other countries. A UIF would be created by a corporate trustee (the UIF's adviser) with the indenture spelling out fundamental investment policies and the management fee, and investors owning interests in the UIF. There would be a single management fee covering all expenses, and the UIF would not have directors or shareholding voting. More recently, Peter Wallison of the American Enterprise Institute and Bob Litan of the Kauffman Foundation and Brookings Institution have advanced a similar proposal for the creation of managed investment trusts.[49]

At the other extreme are those who urge that the role of directors be expanded tremendously. Some would require that directors regularly decide which outside firm should serve as the fund's adviser, just as directors currently select the fund's accountant, transfer agent, custodian, and other service providers. Others would go further and have directors regularly decide whether the fund should dismiss its adviser and have the fund itself assume management functions.[50]

Between the extremes of "first let's kill all the directors" and "let's have the directors manage the fund" are those who would retain the current system of independent directors as a check on management but seek to have the system work more effectively. In 1999, the SEC held a roundtable on the role of independent investment company directors. At the conclusion of the roundtable, SEC chairman Levitt challenged the industry and the SEC staff to offer recommendations to improve the current system. Both the industry and the SEC staff responded. The Investment Company Institute established a blue ribbon committee that issued a report endorsing a series of best practices, including having at least two-thirds of fund directors be independent, having new independent directors selected by incumbent independent directors, having independent directors represented by their own legal counsel, having audit committees composed entirely of independent directors, and having one or more "lead" independent directors coordinate activities of the independent directors.[51] The SEC amended a number of exemptive rules and rule 12b-1 to require that independent directors constitute a majority of the board, new independent directors be selected by incumbent independent directors, and any legal counsel for independent directors be "independent." Following disclosure of the mutual fund trading scandals in 2003, the SEC adopted additional amendments requiring 75 percent independent boards and independent chairs.

My own view is that, while independent directors were given a secondary role in 1940, they now play a critical function.

Their presence alone forces advisers to think things through and deters questionable actions. Directors' policing of potential conflicts protects shareholders, just as the drafters of the Investment Company Act intended. Directors help allocate expenses between the fund and its adviser, as well as among funds, and help determine responsibility for errors. It would be a serious mistake, from the point of view of both fund shareholders and the fund industry, to eliminate independent directors.

However, the fee-setting function, stapled on in 1970, is unnecessary. The decline in total shareholder costs in recent years appears to have resulted from the replacement of front end sales loads with rule 12b-1 fees and the movement by investors to lower cost funds, rather than from actions taken by directors.[52] Moreover, directors' focus on fees has reduced their time and energy available to identify and police conflicts. Indeed, concentration on fees and performance has caused some to forget that directors' key role is to identify and police conflicts of interest. For example:

> Notorious investor Phillip Goldstein of the Bulldog Investors Hedge fund group says mutual fund directors are nothing more than expensive "hood ornaments" consumed by red tape.
>
> "I have actually long believed that for open-end mutual funds, you don't really need a board of directors," he says. "I question whether the benefits justify the cost because there's an economic incentive to perform well. If you don't perform well, you get hit with redemptions and you lose money. So what do you need a board for?"[53]

The mutual fund industry will be in serious trouble if directors themselves adopt the view that their principal role is setting fees, rather than identifying and policing conflicts of interest.

I believe that the only way to fix this mess is for Congress to enact the reform urged by the SEC staff in 1992. In that year, the SEC staff proposed the creation of a new type of mutual fund, the unified fee investment company (UFIC). The UFIC would have a single fixed fee that could not be "unconscionable or grossly excessive," and that would not require shareholder approval or negotiation by directors. (More recently, Steve West modified his earlier proposal and suggested that fund directors be retained but be removed from approving management contracts and fees.) Implementation of the reform proposed by the SEC staff and Steve West would get directors out of the business of rate regulation, an area for which fund directors (or anyone else for that matter) are not well equipped. It would permit directors to concentrate on conflicts of interest, the very type of check on the management that the drafters of the 1940 act intended.[54]

Hedge Funds, Asset-Backed Arrangements, and Rating Agencies

The mutual fund industry had an interest in improving SEC regulation of entities that impacted fund operations, such as hedge funds, asset-backed arrangements, and rating agencies.

The growth of hedge funds (investment companies that are not regulated under the Investment Company Act because they either have 100 or fewer shareholders or are only offered to wealthy investors) raised a series of issues of concern to the mutual fund industry and, indeed, to all investors. First, the collapse of one hedge fund, Long-Term Capital Management, threatened the entire financial system and necessitated a rescue by a group of banks orchestrated by the New York Fed. Second, I received complaints from a number of mutual funds that hedge funds were using portfolio information in mutual fund regulatory filings to front-run and piggy-back mutual fund trades. Finally, there were reports that some hedge funds and brokers were seeking to sell interests in hedge funds to smaller investors. In December 2000, I spoke on a panel sponsored by the Council of Foreign Relations on market vulnerabilities. I warned that, as illustrated by the Long-Term Capital debacle, hedge funds' total lack of transparency posed a danger to other market participants, and therefore I suggested that hedge funds be required to publicly disclose their positions, leverage, and counterparties on a periodic basis. In 2003, the SEC held a roundtable on hedge funds. In its testimony, the Investment Company Institute urged that the existing limits on permissible hedge fund offerings, such as the prohibition on advertising, should be strictly enforced and that investment advisers to hedge funds should be required to register with the SEC under the Investment Advisers Act of 1940.[55] But neither Congress nor the SEC took any action to regulate hedge funds. Only after the fund trading scandals discussed in chapter 11 did the SEC seek regulation in this area, and its attempt was struck down in court.[56]

I often have said that if President Roosevelt and the first Chairman of the SEC, Joseph P. Kennedy, were to come back today, they would be astonished to find that hedge funds are not regulated by the SEC and would say, "These are the types of risky arrangements that led to the enactment of the federal securities laws and the creation of the SEC seventy-five years ago."

In 1992, the SEC sought to assist the process of securitization (the issuance of debt securities based on pools of assets such as mortgages and credit card receivables) by adopting a rule exempting these arrangements from regulation as investment companies. The Investment Company Institute strongly objected to the proposal, stating that it was "one of the most important rule proposals ever considered by the Commission under the Investment Company Act," and that asset-backed arrangements are "classic investment companies" that "raise the very same policy concerns that exist in the case of traditional investment companies."[57] Despite these warnings, the SEC adopted the proposed exemptive rule. I recall telling Marianne Smythe, director of the Division of Investment Management, that this was one of the greatest mistakes the SEC ever made and, jokingly, "you will hang for it."

This exemptive rule also marked the beginning of a lengthy and heated debate over the role and regulation of credit rating agencies. One of the conditions in the rule was that the securities had to be rated "investment grade" by at least one rating agency. The institute objected, stating that if ratings were to be used as a substitute for regulation, there needed to be "far greater SEC oversight over rating agencies."[58] The institute subsequently objected to the use of risk ratings prepared by rating agencies in bond fund sales literature, and consistently called for improvements in the regulatory oversight of rating agencies.[59] In 2006, Congress enacted the Credit Rating Agency Reform Act of 2006, which required the SEC to establish clear guidelines for determining which agencies qualify. However, the act did not address core conflicts, such as rating agencies being paid by the very issuers whose bonds they are rating.

In sum, in three critical areas—hedge funds, asset-backed arrangements, and rating agencies—the mutual fund industry called for modernization of SEC regulation to meet new conditions. But in all three areas SEC regulation lagged the facts on the ground: it took the SEC years to promulgate a hedge fund rule and that rule was struck down in court; the SEC exempted asset-backed arrangements from regulation; and the 2006 rating agency legislation failed to address key issues. These failures helped produce the 2008 crisis discussed in chapter 12.

Compliance

Modernization of SEC disclosure requirements and substantive rules to meet the dramatic growth of the mutual fund industry were important. Equally important were improvements in systems, both these conducted by industry participants and those carried out by the SEC, that monitor for compliance with law and regulation.

Industry Compliance Systems

As discussed in chapter 8, in 1993, SEC Chairman Levitt delivered a speech in which he renewed the issue of self-regulation of the mutual fund industry. Paul Stevens, then the institute's general counsel, and I considered what position the institute should take. Paul mentioned to me that defense contractors are required to maintain their *own* systems of self regulation by having their own compliance procedures and compliance officers, and he suggested that such a system might fit the fund industry. I thought the idea was excellent, and the institute submitted a comprehensive proposal to Levitt providing that the SEC mandate a system of self-regulation at the individual fund level by requiring each fund to have compliance standards and procedures and a senior compliance officer reporting to the fund's independent directors and board.[60]

Unfortunately, the SEC did not act on our submission during the 1990s. Only after the Enron and WorldCom scandals and the enactment of the Sarbanes-Oxley Act did the SEC issue proposals in this area, and only after revelation of the mutual fund trading scandals in 2003 did the commission adopt specific mutual fund compliance requirements.[61] My sense is that they are working quite well. I have often wondered whether adoption of these requirements in the mid-1990s, as urged by the institute, might have prevented the fund trading abuses.

SEC Inspections

For decades, inspections of mutual funds had been conducted under the supervision of the SEC unit responsible for fund regulation, the Division of Investment Management. Similarly, inspections of broker-dealers were overseen by the unit responsible for regulating them, the Division of Market Regulation. Having inspections overseen by the operating divisions had two benefits. First, the inspectors served as the eyes and ears of the divisions, informing them about areas in need of regulatory attention. As Joel Goldberg, a former director of the SEC Division of Investment Management, stated, "the inspection program was adept at finding problems when they were small and had not burgeoned into enforcement issues."[62] Second, the head of a division could order inspectors to examine specific areas of regulatory concern to that division.

In 1995, the SEC moved inspections out of the operating divisions and into a new unit, the Office of Compliance Inspections and Examinations (OCIE).[63] I was concerned at the time that this reorganization could be harmful to the regulatory process by depriving the operating divisions of their agents on the ground. A number of parties, both inside and outside the SEC, have told me that this is in fact what has occurred. According to Goldberg, "The program lost its way ... as it became more focused on making referrals to the enforcement division."[64] This fragmentation, however well intended, may have contributed to the SEC's failure to detect the mutual fund trading abuses. Not surprisingly, proposals have been made to restore examination responsibility to the operating divisions. The 2007 report of a commission established by the U.S. Chamber of Commerce flagged the problem and the solution:

> The oversight of policy implementation [by OCIE] requires a great deal of judgment and necessarily results in policy formulation. Given the significant separation of Market Regulation and Investment Management from OCIE, this leads to the unfortunate result of OCIE making policy on a case-by-case basis, separate from the policy-making expertise within the SEC Divisions.... The rule-interpretation functions that occur in SEC examinations should be better aligned with the rule-development functions that occur in the SEC Divisions. One way to do this would be to fold OCIE's functions back into the SEC's other operating divisions.[65]

Summing up the SEC Regulatory Scorecard

The transformation of the mutual fund industry during the 1982–2000 bull market from a small cottage industry to the world's largest financial industry necessitated accompanying changes in SEC regulation. In many areas involving disclosure and mutual fund operations, SEC requirements were modernized. Despite the industry's urging, compliance requirements were not upgraded, and the SEC's own ability to check for compliance may have declined due to changes in its internal structure. Perhaps most importantly, despite recommendations made by the mutual fund industry, other parts of the U.S. financial system—hedge funds, asset-backed arrangements, and rating agencies—remained unregulated.

10

Updating Other Regulation

If a thing is bad, the longer it has done harm the worse, and the sooner abolished the better. Establishment by law is no plea. They who make laws can repeal them.

—John Burgh

As earlier chapters have made clear, mutual funds not only are subject to Securities and Exchange Commission (SEC) regulation under the federal securities laws but also must meet requirements imposed by other bodies of law. The vast changes in the mutual fund industry that occurred during the bull market of 1982–2000 led the industry to seek changes in state securities laws, federal tax law, and federal pension law. Against all odds, the industry obtained federal legislation ending state regulation of mutual funds. The industry was also successful in obtaining modernization of provisions of the Internal Revenue Code dealing with mutual funds. However, federal pension law and regulation were not updated to take account of the major shift from defined benefit plans to 401(k) and other types of defined contribution plans.

Changes in State Regulation

The greatest change in mutual fund regulation during the record bull market of 1982–2000 took place with respect to regulation by the states. From the start of the first mutual fund in 1924, each state was free to regulate a fund offering shares in that state. Most of the time, state regulators were not active. They simply received filings to register fund shares for sale in the state and collected registration fees. Periodically, state regulation involved more than filings, fees, and administrative headaches. (The North Carolina secretary of state had a habit of not depositing checks for registration fees, which drove fund accountants crazy.) Once in a while, a particular state would impose a unique requirement. Because almost all mutual funds as a practical matter are obliged to offer their shares in all fifty states, an idiosyncratic requirement imposed by a single state became, in effect, a nationwide requirement. Many of these unique requirements frustrated national policies set forth in the Investment Company Act and SEC rules implementing the act. Every sizable mutual fund firm had several professionals who did nothing but make state filings and deal with state problems. The two major fund groups with their own sales forces, IDS and Waddell & Reed, had experts who spent their time traveling from state to state. Law firms specializing in mutual fund work had "blue sky" (state law) departments. The Investment Company Institute spent a good deal of its time and resources on state matters.

The SEC was well aware of the problem. Less than one year after the Investment Company Act of 1940 became law, the acting director of the SEC division responsible for mutual fund regulation told state securities regulators, "it seems to me that the persons regulated are entitled to the convenience of uniform regulations when, as here [in the case of periodic reports] no local peculiarities of any consequence exists which justify diversity of treatment." However, understandably, the SEC shied away from telling state regulators what to do. Indeed, the acting director assured state regulators, "It is not my business to suggest that any substantive regulation of any state should be modified because the same subject is covered by the Investment Company Act, and I am not making any suggestion to that effect."[1]

In the early 1970s, Henry Hopkins of T. Rowe Price suggested that the institute prepare a loose-leaf reference service of state requirements regarding mutual funds, some of which were written but many of which were based on custom or unpublished understandings. Olivia Adler, an institute attorney, spent years compiling the institute's *Blue Sky Guide*, which summarized each state's requirements and was updated on a regular basis. The guide was of immense help to people responsible for state filings. In addition, by compiling all fifty states' requirements in one place, the guide demonstrated how awful the situation was. For example:

- The Investment Company Act and SEC rules set forth substantive standards regarding what a mutual fund can invest in. These include matters such as illiquid securities, options, and borrowing. At least eight states had express provisions imposing portfolio limitations that were inconsistent with federal law. To make matters worse, different states had different restrictions in the same area, such as fund investment in options and warrants. Moreover, when the SEC sought to modernize its standards in a particular area, a single state's refusal to follow its lead blocked the SEC's reform. For example, in 1992, the SEC issued a policy statement dealing with restricted securities and liquidity. A number of states followed suit, but Ohio refused to budge, in effect vetoing the SEC's reform.

- The SEC requires that fund prospectuses set forth specified information in a particular order. More than a dozen states routinely imposed their own prospectus disclosure requirements. Some required that items be rewritten, the order of presentation be changed from the SEC's order, and additional disclosures be included.

- State requirements on fund portfolio investments and prospectus disclosure not only varied from the SEC's requirements and among the individual states but were

constantly changing on an ad hoc, case-by-case basis.
A modern mutual fund complex with scores of different
funds could never be sure which standards would be
applied to any of its funds by a given state at a particular
point in time.[2]

Moreover, the situation was getting worse. In many cases, when
the SEC simply announced that it was going to look at a particular area or there was a press story on some alleged problem,
one or more states would start imposing its own requirements.
For years, the institute dealt with state problems on a case-by-
case emergency basis. The number of problems accelerated when
the fund industry took off in the early 1980s—funds became
more visible, and the SEC and the media became more active,
thus precipitating more actions by individual states. The institute could barely keep up with state emergencies. We needed a
new approach.

We first tried working with the association of state securities regulators, the North American Securities Administrators
Association (NASAA). In 1984, we succeeded in having NASAA
adopt five resolutions urging state uniformity with respect to
expense limitations, filing of sales literature, uniform registration requirements, sales reports, and oversales.[3] However, these
resolutions barely helped. Individual states would comply with
the recommendations, if at all, only if the institute visited each
state a number of times with respect to each particular issue.
Moreover, the refusal by a single state to follow NASAA's recommendation would leave a nationwide problem in place.

I thought of another approach. Many states based their securities laws on the Uniform State Securities Law, which had been
prepared in 1956 by the Commissioners on Uniform State Laws
under the leadership of Louis Loss of Harvard Law School. The
Uniform Law did not have any special provisions dealing with
mutual funds. The National Conference of Commissioners on
Uniform State Laws was preparing a revised Uniform State
Securities Law. I thought this might provide the opportunity to
obtain a provision dealing with the state mutual fund issue.

We retained Loss to lobby the commissioners for a provision that would exempt qualified mutual funds from state regulation. I asked Loss how he would explain his failure to include such a provision in the 1956 Uniform Law. He replied, "The idea simply did not occur to me." We succeeded in having the revised law contain a "blue chip" exemption from state registration for a mutual fund with an investment adviser that has been registered for three years under the federal Investment Advisers Act of 1940 and has acted as an investment adviser to an SEC-registered mutual fund for three years.

We now had a model blue chip exemption to try to implement in the states. We knew we would only be successful if we provided states with the full authority to prosecute sales fraud and did not reduce the amount of fees states collected. As to fees, I was reminded of what year-round residents of Nantucket allegedly say about the summer people, "We wish they would not come, but still send the money." Similarly, we decided that a fund that qualified for the exemption would not register shares but would still send the money. We planned to approach individual states with legislative proposals containing the blue chip exemption, giving the state the right to collect fees from funds claiming the exemption, and providing the state with full antifraud authority with respect to sales practices.

By coincidence, as the Revised Uniform Securities Law was being finalized, the New Jersey legislature began consideration of a new securities law. The existing law exempted securities registered with the SEC, and the proposed new law had a similar exemption, so mutual funds were and would continue to be exempt. It struck me as an ideal first situation to seek a blue chip exemption because we could not be accused of seeking to change the substance of New Jersey law. We succeeded. New Jersey enacted a new securities law containing the provisions we sought. We now had an actual example of a blue chip exemption to use in other states. Next, the securities commissioner in Oregon called me to complain about the huge amount of paper being filed by mutual funds when they registered shares. I told her, "Boy, do we have a deal for you," and the commissioner helped us obtain legislation with the blue chip exemption. We went on, state by state, as opportunities presented themselves. By 1995, we had obtained blue chip exemptions in twelve states.

We heard complaints from two quarters. First, NASAA adopted a resolution urging states not to adopt blue chip exemptions and encouraging those that had adopted them to reexamine their positions.[4] Second, employees at individual fund organizations complained that the institute was concentrating its efforts on obtaining blue chip exemptions, especially in states like New Jersey that were not problems, rather than fighting battles in problem states. I was convinced our priority had to be to obtain as many blue chip exemptions as possible, on the theory that once funds were statutorily exempt in a particular state, that state was unlikely to become a problem in the future.

I also periodically had the institute's in-house lobbyist, Julie Domenick, check with members of Congress to see if there was any chance of obtaining federal legislation that would address the state problem. Each time, she reported that there was no chance. Democrats tended to favor regulation, state as well as federal, and Republicans were wary of federal regulation and tended to favor states' rights. It appeared that we were stuck with a grinding state-by-state strategy. It would be difficult. We already had picked off the easiest states. NASAA was up in arms. However, it seemed as though we had no choice but to press on at the state level.

In early 1995, the new chairman of the House Subcommittee on Telecommunications and Finance, Jack Fields, introduced HR 2131, the Capital Markets Deregulation and Liberalization Act. The bill represented a major attempt to cut back on both federal and state securities regulation. Among other matters, the bill would have ended state regulation of all new issues of securities including mutual funds, repealed the Trust Indenture Act, repealed key provisions of the Williams Act dealing with takeovers, and reduced the number of SEC commissioners from five to three. The bill was sharply criticized by federal and state regulators, Democratic members of Congress, and the consumer press.

Money ran a story titled "How Washington Could Tip the Scales against Investors."[5]

It was clear that the bill did not stand a chance of enactment. However, it provided the mutual fund industry with our first opportunity to raise in Congress the problems caused by state regulation of mutual funds. Moreover, if the bill could be revised to take more moderate approaches on a variety of issues, maybe it could serve as the vehicle to address the state mutual fund issue. Paul Stevens, the institute's general counsel, urged that the institute make the attempt. I asked Paul what he thought the odds were, and he replied, "One out of a thousand. But normally they are one out of a million. This is the best chance we will ever have." I agreed with his assessment, and the executive committee determined that the institute would use the introduction of HR 2131 as the occasion to seek federal legislation addressing state regulation of mutual funds. At our first internal staff meeting on the matter, we made a number of decisions to guide our efforts in what was certain to be a long and difficult campaign: we would seek a provision prohibiting states

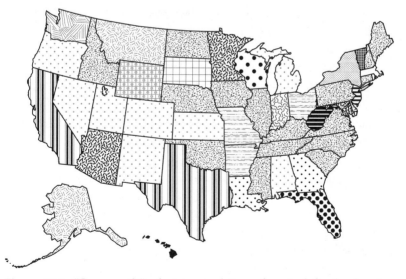

Figure 10.1. "Crazy quilt" of state regulation of mutual funds showing sixteen different systems of state regulation. Courtesy of the Investment Company Institute.

from regulating funds; we would seek a provision providing states with full antifraud authority regarding sales practices; we would seek a provision providing states with the ability to collect fees; and we would concentrate on the state mutual fund issue and avoid involvement with other matters in which we had an interest (such as state regulation of investment advisers). We also decided that our banner would be a map of the fifty states detailing the crazy quilt of state regulation of mutual funds.

We presented our case in testimony on HR 2131. Two critical events occurred. First, SEC chairman Arthur Levitt delivered a major speech on federal and state securities regulation in which he credited Fields for raising basic issues, and noted that the SEC-state regulatory structure "looks more like the product of Rube Goldberg than of Thomas Jefferson." Levitt went on to outline his thoughts regarding a new division of responsibilities between the SEC and the states in a number of areas, including investment advisers, broker-dealers, registration of corporate securities, enforcement authority, and mutual funds. As to mutual funds, the chairman stated:

> Some of the stories told about the current system sound like Kafka: What is a national investment company supposed to do when several states impose investment limitations that conflict with federal law—and conflict with one another? As I see it, investment companies would be exempt from state review, but would continue to file documents with the states and pay the same fees. The Commission would continue to seek input from NASAA in our rulemaking process with respect to investment companies. And of course, the states would still enforce sales practice violations.[6]

Second, Fields abandoned his support for the highly controversial deregulation bill. He and the ranking Democratic member of the subcommittee, Ed Markey, introduced a far more moderate bill, HR 3005, the Securities Amendments of 1996. At the center of the bill were provisions prohibiting state regulation of mutual funds, while leaving the states with antifraud authority and the ability to collect fees from mutual funds. We now had provisions, supported by the SEC, in a bipartisan bill that would end the nightmare of state regulation of mutual funds.

We had reached first base. There was still a long way to go. NASAA continued to oppose enactment of the mutual fund provisions and called for a study. There were sharp differences of opinion in Congress over other provisions, such as the allocation of federal and state regulatory authority over investment advisers and the manner in which the SEC should be funded. Failure by Congress to reach consensus on any issue could doom the entire effort. The Senate always was a problem for securities legislation. *Congressional Quarterly* noted, "In the Senate, bills affecting the financial services industry are never prime candidates for floor time, and mid-level bills affecting securities regulation have a history of dying at the end of a Congress."[7]

We also encountered another problem we had not foreseen. Over the years, when the mutual fund industry wanted legislation, it sought to add provisions to bills that were moving through Congress. Now, for the first time, mutual fund provisions were the steam engine that was driving legislation, and other interest groups sought to add provisions to our bill. The day after HR 3005 was approved by the House subcommittee, I received calls from a variety of groups that wanted to use it as the vehicle to add new exemptions to the Investment Company Act. These included a Presbyterian church organization, Enron Corporation, and representatives of different hedge fund groups. All callers stated that if we allowed them to add provisions to our bill, they would help get it enacted. Several implied that if we did not let them on our bill, they would work to have it defeated. In most cases, such as the church groups and Enron, I suggested that the callers meet with the SEC staff to see if their problems could be worked out administratively.

Hedge funds posed a particular problem. Historically, they had avoided regulation under the Investment Company Act by relying on section 3(c)(1), which excludes from regulation an investment company that has one hundred or fewer shareholders and is not making a public offering of its securities to investors.

The hedge funds wanted a broader exemption that would permit them to offer their securities to an unlimited number of investors. The SEC staff's 1992 report on investment company regulation recommended legislation that would permit hedge funds to offer their securities to an unlimited number of "qualified purchasers," with the SEC given authority to define this term.[8] As discussed in chapter 9, I thought (and I still think) that hedge funds pose serious dangers to mutual funds, other investors, and the securities markets as a whole. I believe we will come to regret not having subjected hedge funds to regulation. The last thing I wanted was the use of HR 3005 to provide an unwise expansion of hedge fund operations. I wanted a strict definition of "qualified purchasers," and I wanted this test set in law and not left to SEC rule making. The institute's executive committee shared my concerns and determined that the institute would not object to a provision being added to the bill that would permit hedge funds to sell their securities to an unlimited number of investors, provided each investor had substantial investments, for example, institutions with $100 million in investments and individuals with $25 million. During the legislative process, the hedge funds kept getting the dollar amounts reduced. The bill passed by the House retained the $100 million test for institutions, but reduced the test for individuals to $10 million. The Senate bill lowered the tests to $25 million and $5 million. If the tests had gotten any lower, I was prepared to recommend to the executive committee that we oppose enactment of legislation, even though this meant that we would be opposing legislation that would address state regulation of mutual funds. Fortunately, the final legislation maintained the $25 million/$5 million tests.

Early in the legislative process, it became clear that the mutual fund provisions were largely settled and the fate of the bill would turn on the resolution of other issues. I assigned the institute's lobbyist, Julie Domenick, to monitor the numerous congressional negotiations taking place. SEC chairman Levitt called me on a periodic basis to compare notes. I recall an instance when he telephoned me to say that negotiations between two key members of Congress had broken down and the legislation was dead. I told the chairman that I thought that this particular problem had been solved but that I would double-check with Julie and get back to him. Julie confirmed that my recollection was correct. I asked her to come to my office so we could call the chairman. Before we could do so, Levitt called me. I turned the speakerphone on so Julie could participate in the conversation, but I forgot to tell the chairman about it. Levitt began, "Matt, I don't know how the institute does it. I spoke with my people and they were wrong. I spoke with two congressional staffs and they were wrong. It was only when I just spoke with the Senator himself that I learned that you were right. The problem has been solved. How does the institute do it? Your lobbyist, Julie Domenick, is phenomenal. How does she do it?" I replied, "Mr. Chairman, there are three factors. First, Julie is very bright. Second, she works extremely hard. Finally, and most important, I provide great leadership." All three of us burst out laughing, and Levitt thereby learned that Julie was on the call.

Members of the House and Senate committees worked out their differences with respect to the regulation of investment advisers, funding for the SEC, and other matters. On October 11, 1996, President Clinton signed into law the National Securities Markets Improvement Act of 1996 that ended state regulation of mutual funds while retaining state antifraud authority and the payment of fees. Our one-in-a-thousand bet had come through. The SEC was now the exclusive regulator of the mutual fund industry. Future generations of fund executives and attorneys will not have to contend with fifty-one different mutual fund regulators.

Changes in Tax Law

As discussed in chapter 1, the first federal law governing the activities of mutual funds was a tax law, the Revenue Act of 1936. The act provided that a mutual fund would be exempt from federal income tax if it met a number of conditions. Three of the conditions were that the fund had to derive at least 95 percent of its income from dividends, interest, and gains on the sale of securities; the fund had to diversify by not having more than 5 percent of its assets invested in any one issuer; and the fund could not receive more than 30 percent of its gross income from sales of securities held for less than three months. Few changes were made over the years. Most notably, in 1942 the 95 percent "good income" test was changed to 90 percent, the diversification test was made less stringent, and mutual funds were permitted to pass through long-term capital gains to shareholders as capital gain dividends.

On the whole, the mutual fund tax system worked extremely well. It was simple to administer, there were few problems, and it generally placed shareholders in the same tax position as direct owners of securities. Although there were occasional problems, the industry determined that it was preferable to live with them rather than run the risks inherent in the legislative process. We knew that mutual funds had an extremely good deal since they were generally ignored for tax purposes. Dave Silver and I once attended an event honoring the retirement of Eddie Cohen, the institute's long-time tax attorney, from the faculty of the University of Virginia Law School. Dave and I were sitting at the bar in our hotel when I fellow came up to us, introduced himself as a tax attorney in New York, and said "You guys are getting away with murder. Mutual funds are the only corporations in the world that don't pay any tax." When younger lawyers in the industry urged the institute to seek Congressional action in tax and other areas, Arthur Haussermann, an experienced attorney at Vance Sanders, would tell of the times in his youth that he went duck hunting with his Uncle Oscar. Uncle Oscar had many rules of shooting—"Stay low in the blind," "Lead the duck," and "Squeeze, don't pull the trigger." But Arthur would always remind us that "Uncle Oscar's first rule of shooting" was "Don't shoot yourself." However, as markets changed and the fund industry grew in size and complexity, problems increasingly arose under both the 90 and 30 percent tests. The Investment Company institute determined that, despite the risks involved, legislation was essential.

The 90 Percent Test

The 90 (originally 95) percent test was put in place at a time when investors in securities sought to earn only dividends, interest, and capital gains, and the test encompassed all of these types of "good income." By the early 1980s, mutual funds were earning other types of income in connection with their securities activities, such as gains from currency transactions, options, futures, and forward contracts. A number of parties, including the Committee on Financial Institutions and Insurance Companies of the New York State Bar Association, the Tax Section of the American Bar Association, and the Investment Company Institute, concluded that there was a need to expand the 90 percent test to include these types of securities-related income. The institute met with the many governmental bodies involved with tax legislation, including the Department of the Treasury, the Congressional Joint Committee on Taxation, the Senate Finance Committee, and the House Ways and Means Committee. The joint committee staff did not raise any objection to a limited expansion of the 90 percent test, and the Treasury Department testified in support of expansion. The Tax Reform Act of 1986 amended the 90 percent test to include gains from the sale of foreign currencies and from options, futures, and forward contracts derived from the fund's business of investing in stock, securities and currencies. Thus in a relatively short period of time, the industry obtained needed expansion of the 90 percent test.[9]

The 30 Percent Test

Elimination of the 30 percent or "short-short" test proved to be far more difficult. Although there was no legislative history explaining the rationale for the test, it had been put in place in the midst of the Great Depression and presumably reflected the predominant "buy and hold" investment philosophy of that time. The test constantly caused problems for mutual fund portfolio managers. There were situations in which a fund would purchase a security, the security would shoot up in price, and the manager would want to realize the gain but was precluded from doing so for fear of generating short-short income. In other cases, funds had to decline tender offers for securities they held for less than three months. If a fund did receive a large short-short gain, it had to realize enough long-term gains and other income to bring the ratio below 30 percent, thus raising the possibility that some portfolio decisions were being driven by tax requirements rather than investment considerations. These problems were particularly acute for new funds that started with short fiscal years (e.g., a fund that began operations on October 1 with a December 31 end of the fiscal year). In these cases, if there was a major short-short gain at the beginning of the short year, there was little time in which to generate sufficient good income.

There was a wonderful apocryphal story told by fund accountants about the 30 percent test. The star portfolio manager of a fund in a major complex realized a huge short-short gain at the start of the fund's fiscal year. The top executives of the group realized that it would be very difficult for the fund to avoid flunking the 30 percent test, so they transferred management of the fund from the star manager to the accounting department, which was told to realize as much good income as possible during the remainder of the year so as to prevent the fund from failing the test. The accountants did a great job, the fund earned a huge amount of good income, and passed the 30 percent test. Moreover, the story goes, it was the best-performing fund in the complex that year.

The industry lived with these types of problems for decades. The development of new types of investments, such as index futures, index options, exchange-traded stock options, debt options, and financial futures, greatly exacerbated the problem by giving rise to short-term gains. The New York State Bar Association, the Tax Section of the American Bar Association, and the Investment Company Institute all concluded that the 30 percent test made no sense, was inhibiting prudent investment strategies, and should be repealed. As was the case with the 90 percent test, the institute made the rounds of the various governmental bodies that dealt with tax legislation. The Department of the Treasury supported repeal, and members and staffs of the Senate Finance and House Ways and Means Committees were sympathetic, but the staff of the Joint Committee on Taxation was another story.

The staff argued that Congress wanted mutual funds to be passive investors and asserted that the 30 percent test furthered this goal by deterring trading. The Investment Company Institute countered that passivity meant that a fund had to be an investor in corporations and not seek to manage or control them and had nothing to do with the length of time a fund held securities. At a meeting between industry representatives and the joint committee staff, a portfolio manager of a bond fund unfortunately argued that application of the 30 percent test was reducing returns to investors. The committee staff used this argument as the basis for the theory that repeal of the test would reduce tax revenues: as yields on bond funds increased due to repeal, investors would move from investing in bank deposits to investing in bond funds, which did not pay tax, thus decreasing bank earnings and the corporate taxes they paid. Based on this argument, the joint committee assigned a small tax revenue loss to the proposal to repeal the test. Although an estimate of revenue loss was not an absolute killer, it did raise another roadblock to the enactment of legislation.

The industry plowed ahead. On two occasions, provisions repealing the 30 percent test were included in major tax reform legislation passed by Congress, but both times the legislation was vetoed for unrelated reasons. Meanwhile, the problem got worse. One well-known mutual fund portfolio manager correctly predicted the steep 1987 market decline and took action in advance to reduce the fund's exposure. Unfortunately, the manager's astute behavior produced such large short-short gains that the fund flunked the 30 percent test. In 1989, a very successful money manager cited the 30 percent test as the reason for abandoning his plans to manage a closed-end fund, stating that the test "makes it impossible for the public to get the best management for its money."[10]

Finally, after a twelve-year effort, the Taxpayer Relief Act of 1997 repealed the 30 percent test. Repeal permitted fund managers to use modern investment techniques and led to the creation of new types of mutual funds that generate large amounts of short-short income. To my knowledge, repeal has not led to any abuse.

In the early 1990s, a friend in the industry chided me about how long it was taking to achieve repeal of the 30 percent test. Given all the effort we had expended and the disappointments we had endured, I felt like punching him. This incident led me to make the following observations in my keynote address at the next annual Mutual Funds and Investment Management Conference:

> First, to initiate a U.S. tax law change, one must secure approval from four technical staffs—the tax staffs of the Treasury Department, the Joint Committee on Taxation, the House Ways and Means Committee and the Senate Finance Committee. If successful at garnering OKs from these four staffs, you then need to find a member of the House Ways and Means Committee and a member of the Senate Finance Committee to sponsor the proposed change. Most likely, each sponsor in turn will ask you to obtain a number of co-sponsors on each committee. The U.S. Budget Act adds another wrinkle....you have to demonstrate that enactment of your provision would not result in any significant loss of tax revenue. This introduces you to the mysterious world of revenue estimating, where 2 plus 2 often equals minus 7. Finally, you need to make sure that your provision gets attached to a suitable vehicle—that is, to a tax bill which is likely to be passed by Congress and signed by the president.
>
> This system seems intentionally designed to produce failure. The saddest moments in Washington occur when your tax counsel closes the door, and advises you in hushed tones that your tax problem cannot be solved administratively, but requires legislation.[11]

Changes in Pension Regulation

The nation's pension law, the Employee Retirement Income Security Act of 1974, was largely intended to address issues involving defined benefit (DB) plans, by far the predominant type of plan at the time the law was enacted. As might be expected, the federal agency responsible for the administration of the law, the Department of Labor, focused on DB plans. Due to the shift from DB plans to 401(k) and other defined contribution (DC) plans, the mutual fund industry repeatedly urged the department to become more active with respect to DC plans, but to little avail.

Disclosure

Perhaps the most important issue involves decision making by employees. Typically, a DC plan provides that an employee may select investments from a menu of options provided by the employer. Section 404(c) of ERISA provides that if, pursuant to Department of Labor regulations, employees can select their own investments from a broad range of alternatives, the employer will not be responsible for employees' investment decisions.

In 1976, the Investment Company Institute submitted extensive suggestions for regulations to the department. In its submission, the Institute wrote: "*most importantly*, in order to really exercise full investment control over his individual account, a participant or beneficiary must *receive* adequate information on which to base his investment decisions."[12]

However, the regulations that were adopted by the Department of Labor do not require employers to provide full information to employees. Instead, (1) only some information, such as a general description of each investment option, must be provided to employees; (2) in the case of a mutual fund, the fund's prospectus must be provided to employees; (3) in the case of investment vehicles without prospectuses (such as bank collective funds and insurance company separate accounts), however, certain key information, such as the vehicles' annual operating expenses and historical investment performance, need only be provided on the employee's request.[13]

The institute repeatedly criticized the regulation's failure to require that employees receive all critical information concerning all investment options. In a 1992 letter to the secretary of Labor, I wrote:

> We fail to see how a participant or beneficiary can be considered to be "informed" if he is not furnished adequate information, but simply is told that "information is available in room 1096" or that "information can be obtained by writing to our Personnel Department." This very type of pseudo-disclosure was criticized by Louis Brandeis [who wrote] "But the disclosure must be real. And it must be disclosure to the investor. It will not suffice to require merely the filing of a statement of facts.... To be effective, knowledge of the facts must be actually brought home to the investor."[14]

The institute also advised the department that the regulations fail to require disclosure of plan administration fees borne by employees, and stated, "the Department should require plan fiduciaries to affirmatively disclose to all participants the nature of any plan-level fees that affect participant accounts." Finally, the institute pointed out that the regulations affect only plans that qualify under section 404(c) and has urged the department to adopt regulations requiring disclosure to employees in all participant-directed plans, whether or not they seek to qualify under section 404(c).[15]

Although the institute and other parties repeatedly urged the Department of Labor to require disclosure to employees in all participant-directed plans of all material information concerning their investment options and any fees they pay, the department did not act in any of these areas. Nor, assuming the department lacked authority to impose these requirements, did it call for legislation that would provide it with the necessary authority.

A newspaper column by financial writer Humberto Cruz highlighted the problem by relating the writer's personal experience:

> I had invested in Wellington [Fund] on my own years earlier. Before accepting my money then, Vanguard had sent me a prospectus explaining Wellington's investment strategy, potential risks and fees. I received detailed reports every six months discussing the fund's performance and listing every security it owned.
>
> I got all this information even though I made only an itsy-bitsy investment. The Securities and Exchange Commission requires funds to make this disclosure to all investors, big and small.
>
> But years later, when I had a much larger amount in Wellington through my employer's 401(k) plan, precious little was disclosed. I was never given a prospectus or shareholder report, or anything beyond a cursory explanation of the fund's strategy or possible risks.
>
> I wasn't told how many shares my 401(k) contributions were buying and at what price. My account statements showed the total value of my investment but not how many shares I owned.[16]

A similar problem exists with respect to information that employers receive, or rather do not receive, about the costs of products and services offered by competing plan service providers. In 2004, the Investment Company Institute urged the Department of Labor to require that employers receive complete information about fees and expenses at the time they are considering service providers and investment options. The institute also urged the department to require that employers receive information about any "revenue sharing" arrangements, arrangements under which a plan service provider receives compensation from another party (e.g., a plan record-keeper is compensated by a fund adviser or the fund itself). In 2005, the institute provided the department with a model disclosure schedule designed to provide employers with information about revenue-sharing arrangements.[17] (In 2010, thirty-six years after the enactment of ERISA, due to congressional pressure, the Department of Labor finally required disclosure of fees to employers and appeared ready to do so for employees.)

Complexity

There are other issues regarding DC plans. Over the years, Congress authorized the creation of different types of DC plans—401(k) plans for businesses, 403(b) plans for school systems and charities, and 457 plans for state and local governments. Each plan's purpose is identical—to encourage working Americans to save for retirement. Largely due to historical accidents, the statutory rules governing the various types of plans are a kaleidoscope of different, complex, and sometimes conflicting requirements. About twenty-five years ago, the Concord Coalition, the nonprofit organization where my wife worked, decided to install a 403(b) plan. I went to hear the sales presentations made by two firms, one an insurance company and the other a mutual fund group. The parts of both presentations regarding investment options were outstanding. But the parts summarizing rules as to the permissible level of contributions were incredibly dense and almost unintelligible. It became clear to me that the 403(b) contribution rules are designed for actuaries and pension consultants, not the rest of us. In 2003, the Bush administration proposed to consolidate 401(k), 403(b), 457, and other DC plans into a single employer-sponsored defined contribution plan, an employer retirement savings account, with a set of simple universal rules. This reform, like requiring full and fair disclosure to workers and employers, is long overdue.

Summing up the Regulatory Scorecard

The transformation of the mutual fund industry during the bull market of 1982–2000 not only necessitated updating of SEC mutual fund regulation but also required modernization of other systems of regulation that impacted mutual funds. This occurred with respect to state securities regulation and federal tax law. In contrast, in the case of federal pension law, there was a failure to update regulation in recognition the fact that the world had moved from DB plans to DC plans.

Snapshot of the Industry in 2000

The mutual fund industry looked very different in 2000 than it had in 1980. The number of households owning mutual funds had grown more than elevenfold, from 4.6 million in 1980 to over 52 million in 2000. In 1980, money market funds dominated the industry, with 57 percent of total industry assets. The boom in equity and bond funds during the record bull market of 1982–2000 changed everything. At year end 2000, stock funds accounted for 57 percent of industry assets, money market funds for 26 percent, bond funds for 12 percent, and hybrid stock and bond funds for 5 percent.[18] The five largest funds were Vanguard 500 Index Fund, Fidelity Magellan Fund, Investment Company of America, Smith Barney Money Fund: Cash, and Vanguard Prime Money Market Fund. The five largest fund complexes were Fidelity, Vanguard, Capital Research & Management, Putnam, and Janus.[19]

By 2000, no-load funds and no-load share classes accounted for a majority of sales of both equity funds and bond funds, reflecting the growth of 401(k) plans, the increased use of financial planners, and funds' ability to advertise their past performance.[20]

By 2000, the percentages of fund complexes by category of fund sponsor were approximately:

Independent investment advisers	58%
Insurance companies	16%
Banks	15%
Broker-dealer wirehouses	11%[21]

By 2000, retirement plans played a major role in the mutual fund business. Mutual funds had become the largest funding vehicle for individual retirement accounts (IRAs), with fund IRA assets amounting to $1.2 trillion. Similarly, funds constituted the largest funding vehicle for 401(k) plans, with over $800 billion in 401(k) assets invested in fund shares. In 2000, 36 percent of mutual fund assets consisted of IRAs and DC plans.[22] U.S. mutual funds had become the largest financial industry in the world.

11

The Trading Scandals

Complacency is the Seven Deadly Sins heaped into one.
—Louis D. Brandeis

The record 1982–2000 bull market ended with a bubble in high-technology and telecom stocks, followed by a severe bear market and revelations of a number of major corporate and accounting scandals, resulting in enactment of the Sarbanes-Oxley Act. In 2003–2004, there were revelations of illegal market timing and late trading in mutual fund shares at some twenty fund groups, the worst scandal ever in the fund industry. The scandal resulted in over a hundred proposals for legislative and regulatory reform, and led the Securities and Exchange Commission (SEC) to adopt a record number of new regulations. Fortunately for fund shareholders and the fund industry, Congress did not enact punitive legislation in response to the scandals.

The Tech Bubble

The last years of the bull market bore an uncanny resemblance to the end of the bull market of the 1960s. In the late 1960s, the public was enamored with growth stocks and go-go funds investing in those stocks. In the late 1990s, the public was in love with high-technology and telecom stocks and funds investing in them. The difference was that in the 1990s high-tech and telecom stocks constituted a far larger share of the stock market. One writer observed, "By early 2000, technology and telecom stocks would account for nearly 45 percent of the overall market value of the S&P 500." Portfolio managers of mutual funds, pension funds, endowments, and other investment vehicles often were judged by how well their records stacked up against Standard & Poor's 500 index. Because the S&P was being propelled upward by high-tech and telecom stocks, these professional money managers "gritted their teeth and shelled out 50 times earnings, 100 times earnings—whatever the rest of the herd was willing to pay." Meanwhile, individual investors continued to pour money into these stocks and funds owning them: "Of the $259 billion invested [in stocks funds] in 2000, $130 billion, or roughly half, went into what the Investment Company Institute characterized as 'Aggressive Growth' equity funds. This was three times more than they had invested in 1999."[1]

When the record bull market inevitably ended and was succeeded by a sharp bear market, investors suffered huge losses.

By February of 2002, 100 million investors had lost $5 trillion, or 30 percent of the wealth they had accumulated in the stock market—just since the spring of 2000. There was nowhere to hide. At year-end, $10,000 invested in an S&P 500 index fund three years earlier was worth less than $6,300. $10,000 stashed in a large-cap growth fund had shriveled to $4,900. Just 43 of 5,500 diversified U.S. stock funds wound up in the black.

The bear had taken no prisoners. After three consecutive years of losses, the Dow now stood at just over 8341—down from a bull market peak of 11,722. Meanwhile, the Nasdaq had plunged from roughly 5048 to 1335.[2]

The bear market demonstrated the wisdom of investing through mutual funds because of their diversification. *Morningstar* calculated that in the first quarter of 2001, 14.6 percent of individual stocks lost 50 percent or more in value. In contrast, less than 1 percent of equity mutual funds experienced a loss that large.[3] In other words, at the start of 2001, an investor's chances of choosing a stock that would lose at least 50 percent of its value was one out of seven. An investor's chance of choosing an equity mutual fund that would lose that much was less than one out of one hundred. However, the fact that investors in equity funds may have lost less money than many direct investors in stocks was small consolation. Both groups of investors had been hit hard and were not happy.

The Corporate and Accounting Scandals

As is often the case following a major stock market break, there were revelations of financial misdeeds by corporations that had been among the hottest investments during the boom and talk about legislation. First came Enron. "The unraveling of Enron Corp., a direct product of the era's financial fantasia, began in late 2001 and escalated in early 2002, heightening already high marketplace anxiety. Even then, however, investors held on, markets held sideways, and politicians began hearings but kept them on the sidelines."[4] Revelations about Enron were followed by news about Global Crossing, Adelphia Communications, and Tyco International. Then came revelations about WorldCom, that shifted the odds in favor of legislation. "The ultimate tipping point arrived in June 2002 with a true and pure accounting deception of such a large scale that there was no turning back from an Act of Congress, even for President Bush and his fellow free-market Republicans. That month WorldCom Inc.'s internal auditors revealed that top dogs had cooked its books to the tune of several billion dollars."[5]

The result was enactment of the Sarbanes-Oxley Act, which has been described by President George Bush as "the most far-reaching reforms of American business practices since the time of Franklin Delano Roosevelt" and by SEC commissioner Harvey Goldschmid as "the most sweeping reform since the Depression-era securities laws."[6] The act covered a host of areas, including auditing standards and processes, governance and disclosure requirements for public companies, required certifications by CEOs and chief financial officers (CFOs), and enforcement.

Though the scandals that led to passage of Sarbanes-Oxley involved operating companies, many provisions applied to mutual funds because they technically are organized as companies. (Investment vehicles that are not organized as companies, such as bank common trust funds, insurance company separate accounts, and hedge funds, are not subject to Sarbanes-Oxley.) Some in the mutual fund industry were irate that they were burdened with requirements, such as CEO and CFO certifications, even though mutual funds had not been involved in the scandals. Others in the industry noted with pride that mutual funds had avoided scandal and that many requirements of Sarbanes-Oxley mirrored those that had long been followed by mutual funds. Meanwhile, mutual funds faced their own problems in Congress.

Mutual Fund Legislation

For a number of years, the chairman of the House Financial Services Committee, Michael Oxley, and the chairman of its Subcommittee on Capital Markets, Insurance and Government-Sponsored Enterprises, Richard Baker, indicated their intention to have the subcommittee hold oversight hearings on mutual funds. In February 2003, there were reports that members of Oxley's staff had suggested that "the congressional probe might ease up" if the Investment Company Institute replaced its top lobbyist, Julie Domenick, a Democrat, with a Republican.[7] The institute did not replace Domenick (but did hire a Republican lobbyist who reported to both me as president and Domenick). Hearings ensued before the subcommittee.

One of the major issues was the reporting of fund expenses to shareholders. In 2000, the General Accounting Office (GAO) had suggested that funds be required to provide each shareholder in the quarterly account statement with the dollar amount of fund expenses borne by the shareholder during the past quarter. The institute retained PricewaterhouseCoopers (PWC) to study this proposal. PWC's report stated that implementation would be costly. To determine the dollar amount of expenses borne by a shareholder during a quarter, the fund would have to multiply its expense ratio on each day times the value of the shareholder's account on that day and then add up the daily results. Moreover, the report pointed out that in many cases mutual funds do not know the name and account information of the shareholder because broker-dealers and other third parties maintain omnibus accounts with the fund that combine the accounts of numerous individual shareholders. Therefore, to provide each shareholder with individualized expense information, funds would be required to communicate the fund's daily expense ratio to numerous third parties on a daily basis, and those third parties would have to make the calculations for each shareholder. Partly as a result of these complications, the SEC testified in favor of another approach to fee disclosure— requiring fund annual and semi-annual shareholder reports to set forth the dollar amount of fund expenses per $10,000 invested. Unlike the GAO's idea, this reform would require only one calculation and would provide easy comparability among different funds. Another issue involved fund governance. Some suggested that the law require the chairs of fund boards to be independent directors. The SEC testified that this was unnecessary: under legislation being considered by the subcommittee, independent directors would constitute a majority of the board and therefore could choose any chairperson they wanted.[8]

At the March hearing, critics of the fund industry advanced a number of proposals. Jack Bogle urged that funds be required to provide each shareholder with an estimate of expenses the shareholder would bear the coming year and that the chair of fund boards be required to be independent. Gary Gensler, former undersecretary of the Treasury and coauthor of *The Great Mutual*

Fund Trap, testified that it might be appropriate to consider a "requirement that fund directors seek competitive proposals on a periodic basis," and "having all 401(k) and 403(b) plans include as investment alternatives a low cost broad market U.S. equity index fund and a bond index fund." In June, Chairman Baker introduced legislation, HR 2420, the Mutual Funds Integrity and Fee Transparency Act of 2003. The bill included many provisions urged by industry critics, including requiring funds to provide each shareholder with the estimated amount of expenses borne by the shareholder and requiring funds to have independent chairs. Hearings were held on the bill in June.[9]

In sum, Republican leaders of the House committee and industry critics did all they could to find alleged weak spots in the mutual fund industry and its system of regulation. None of them even mentioned the issues of illegal market timing and late trading that soon dominated the financial pages.

It was expected that the subcommittee would take up the bill on July 10. But there was a revolt by the Democratic members and a number of Republicans who opposed efforts at political retaliation for the institute's refusal to fire Domenick, and the subcommittee meeting was canceled. The bill was then considered by the full committee, and the Democrats and the group of Republicans succeeded in deleting most of the controversial provisions, including both the proposed individualized expense disclosure and independent chair provisions.[10]

The mutual fund industry had weathered a very difficult period that included a deep bear market, application of parts of the Sarbanes-Oxley Act to mutual funds, a battle over disclosure of fund portfolio holdings, a far more contentious battle over disclosure of fund proxy votes, a beleaguered SEC chairman and therefore a weakened SEC, attacks on its trade association's chief lobbyist, and proposed legislation that incorporated much of the critics' wish list.

I had planned to announce my retirement earlier in that year but put it off due to these adverse circumstances. By May, it appeared that we were coming out of the woods: we could envision the likely compromise on portfolio holdings disclosure;

the battle over proxy vote disclosure was over (we'd lost); SEC chairman Pitt had been succeeded by William H. Donaldson; and Julie Domenick was still in place as the institute's chief lobbyist. The institute's compensation committee decided that if things continued to improve, the institute would announce my forthcoming retirement and the start of the search for my successor on Friday, September 5, 2003, the day of the next meeting of the executive committee. In July, the most objectionable features were deleted from the House bill. I was particularly pleased that we had defeated proposals that were at least in part a form of political retaliation for the institute's refusal to fire Domenick. By late August, things were looking so good that the institute's chairman, Paul Haaga, suggested that I inform the members of the executive committee and the institute senior staff of the coming announcement. Unknown to us was the fact that a seemingly technical issue relating to the pricing of mutual fund shares was about to produce the greatest scandal ever in the fund industry.

The Anomaly in Fund Pricing

During the bull market of 1982–2000, there had been a tremendous increase in mutual fund investment in foreign securities. Questions arose regarding the pricing of foreign securities for purposes of computing a fund's daily net asset value.

Section 2(a)(41) of the Investment Company Act provides a simple dichotomy for the pricing of portfolio securities. First, "securities for which market quotations are readily available" are to be valued at "market value," and second, all other securities are to be valued at "fair value as determined in good faith by the board of directors."

Funds investing in U.S. securities typically compute their net asset values (NAVs) when the New York Stock Exchange (NYSE) closes, 4 P.M. Eastern Time, using closing prices in U.S. markets to price their portfolio securities and calculate their NAVs as of 4 P.M. When funds began investing in foreign securities, they similarly computed their NAVs at the close of the NYSE but used the closing prices of the foreign securities on the foreign markets on which they traded. In many cases (e.g., Asian markets) the foreign markets closed well before the close of the NYSE, so funds used old prices for their foreign securities. This could be a problem if new information came to light after the close of the foreign market but before the close of the NYSE that might have an effect on the prices of foreign securities had foreign markets been open. Such events might involve a specific foreign issuer (e.g., an earthquake damages the company's plant) or an entire foreign market (the government resigns), or a major move in U.S. markets (because foreign markets tend to follow U.S. markets).

The problem was more than theoretical. Professional arbitrageurs and hedge funds used such new information and the anticipated price discrepancies to profit at the expense of fund shareholders. Many brokers assisted clients to market time funds by creating multiple accounts through omnibus accounts to minimize detection by fund organizations. Similarly, pension administrators permitted plan participants to market time without detection through the use of omnibus accounts. Mutual fund firms fought back, establishing policies set forth in their prospectuses to deter timers, creating "timing police" to detect trades that violated fund policies, imposing redemption fees, and fair valuing foreign securities. A number of academics, including Eric Zitzewitz of the Stanford Graduate School of Business, published papers discussing market timing.[11] The institute held a seminar with academic experts to explore the problem and possible solutions.

The SEC was aware of the problem, but its position went back and forth. Initially, it took the position that if an event occurs after the close of the foreign exchange that is likely to have changed the value of the securities, a fund must use fair valuation. In 1981, the SEC staff stated that it would not recommend that the commission take enforcement action if two Putnam funds used old closing prices for foreign securities, except when an event has occurred since the close of a foreign market that is likely to have resulted in a change in the securities' value (a "significant event"), in which case fair valuation would be used. A footnote in a 1984 SEC release interpreted the 1981 staff letter as requiring the use of fair valuation in these circumstances.[12]

However, in 1997, the director of the SEC Division of Investment Management, Barry Barbash, delivered a speech in which he interpreted the 1981 position as permissive, not mandatory: "Under the staff's 1981 position, a fund may (but is not required to) price portfolio securities traded on a foreign exchange using fair value." A 1998 SEC release also interpreted the 1981 position as permissive: "Funds appear to have relied on a long-standing position of the SEC staff's that a fund may (but is not required to) value portfolio securities traded on a foreign exchange using fair value."[13] In 1997, there was a crash in the Hong Kong stock market. Fidelity decided not to use the stale Hong Kong closing prices but rather to fair value Hong Kong securities using outside pricing services, futures prices, and other factors. For taking the trouble to attempt to use current prices, Fidelity was lambasted by *Business Week*.[14] Later that year, in his speech Barbash reported that the staff's investigation of the Asian crash indicated that some fund groups used fair value for Asian securities held by all of their funds, some used it only for certain funds, whereas a third group used market quotations. He emphasized, "All of these procedures can be undertaken in accordance with the Commission's fund pricing rules and the staff's interpretations of the rules." He spelled out the reasons that some groups gave for not using fair value or for using it only in limited circumstances: "Some noted that fair value pricing can involve complicated judgment calls that are susceptible to second-guessing. Others pointed out that fair value pricing takes more time and is more costly to implement than pricing by reference to market quotations. Moreover, these funds asserted, the possibility of significant dilution in the value of their shares was not high enough to warrant the additional costs of fair value pricing." Finally, he stated that the SEC would undertake a comprehensive analysis of fund pricing issues and consider updating fund pricing requirements.[15]

Then, in 2001, without such a comprehensive SEC analysis or change in pricing rules, the SEC staff simply issued a letter that discussed a fund's obligation to fair value securities when market quotations are not available because of significant events, including market volatility, that occur after closing market prices are established but before the time set for calculation of the fund's NAV.[16] The 2001 letter marked a return to the SEC's 1984 position that fair valuation was mandatory in certain circumstances and, for the first time, articulated the staff's view that market volatility could constitute a significant event.

There were very different reactions to the 2001 letter. On one hand, funds that had been fair valuing foreign securities in cases of market volatility felt vindicated. The Investment Company Institute sought to assist funds in complying with the staff's position by publishing a supplement to its earlier paper on valuation and liquidity issues.[17] On the other hand, many fund groups resisted the use of fair value, citing the same reasons that Barbash had mentioned in 1997—fair valuing necessitated complicated judgment calls, the fear of second-guessing, costs, and the objectivity of market quotations. These groups felt that they would be damned either way. If they used fair value, they could be accused of making up prices. If they used market quotations, they would be out of whack with the 2001 letter. Fund directors were concerned over the number of securities they might be required to fair value, and the SEC official who had authored the 2001 letter expressed sympathy with them: "I'm sure that Congress didn't have in mind the possibility that so many securities might be subject to fair valuation by boards of directors," and "it's a legitimate point to question whether the act should be amended, or perhaps exemptive rules could be adopted, to reassess the fair value standard."[18]

Funds took other steps to deter arbitrageurs. Some complexes imposed redemption fees on short-term trades in their international funds. Redemption fees offered only limited relief: the SEC staff historically took the position that redemption fees could not exceed 2 percent of the amount redeemed, and many intermediaries, such as broker-dealers with omnibus accounts, 401(k) plan administrators, and insurance company variable annuities, could not or would not apply redemption fees. The Investment Company Institute sought the SEC staff's concurrence that delayed exchanges between funds aimed at market timers were permissible under the Investment Company Act. The SEC staff interpreted the act to allow funds to delay exchanges between two funds for a day or more after the order was received. However, the staff declined to interpret the act to permit an arrangement under which shares would be redeemed from the first fund on the day the order was received but the proceeds would not be used to purchase shares of the second fund until the next day.[19]

More generally, the SEC was of two minds about measures to deter market timers:

> According to the SEC, the Investment Company Act of 1940 required all open-end funds to provide investors easy and regular access to their funds....The Commission believed that placing onerous restrictions or penalties on investors seeking to redeem shares was a violation of the rules under the 1940 Act. On the other hand, the SEC agreed that mutual fund companies ought to protect the majority of shareholders, who were long-term investors, from the risks posed by market timers.[20]

With the advantage of hindsight, it is clear that the SEC, with the assistance of the fund industry, should have undertaken a comprehensive analysis of all issues relating to market timing, including both the proper valuation of fund shares and various measures aimed at combating abusive market timing, and devised a comprehensive regulatory package. But the SEC and the industry were knee deep in a host of other matters, including the drafting and implementation of the Sarbanes-Oxley Act, the House hearings on proposed mutual fund legislation, and SEC proposals regarding disclosure of fund portfolio holdings and proxy votes. To my knowledge, no one at the SEC, at the National Association of Securities Dealers (NASD), in the fund industry, in Congress, or in the media ever suggested such a comprehensive approach to the market timing problem.

The Crisis Hits

On the morning of Saturday, August 23, 2003, I played tennis with a friend on a court near my home in Maryland. As we finished our game, Eliot Spitzer, the New York State attorney general, and his playing partner walked onto the adjacent court. I had met Spitzer briefly at an SEC get together, so I reintroduced myself and asked what brought him to Washington. He explained that his sister lived nearby and introduced me to his niece, who was his tennis partner. We chatted for a minute, and my partner and I headed toward the exit. Spitzer asked, "Matt, how are mutual funds doing?" I turned to him and replied, "Just fine. We've been undergoing some tough scrutiny, but at least you aren't giving us a hard time." He said, "Just you wait. Have a good weekend." When I got home, I told my wife about the exchange. She said, "Matt, you always worry, you always catastrophize. Calm down. Take a shower. Eat breakfast. Relax." The incident stayed in my mind. On Monday, I sent an e-mail recounting the episode to members of the institute's compensation committee. Jack Brennan, CEO of Vanguard, said, "You should take up golf."[21]

The summer days went on. I recall driving to the office on Monday, September 1, and thinking that on Friday, the institute would announce my forthcoming retirement. I was tired from a rather rough period but was proud that the industry and the institute had come through it in good shape. On Wednesday morning, my assistant, Carole Hall, knocked on my door and said that we had just received a phone call recommending that we turn on CNN or Fox News. We did. We watched Spitzer announce a case against a hedge fund, Canary Capital Partners, beginning revelations of the worst scandal ever in the mutual fund industry.[22]

The complaint alleged that Canary was involved in two types of illegal activities. First was illegal market timing through funds advised by Bank of America, Bank One, Janus, and Strong. Although these funds' prospectuses stated that their advisers sought to prevent market timing of fund shares, it was alleged that the advisers permitted Canary to do so in exchange for other business, such as Canary investing in other mutual funds or hedge funds managed by the adviser. Second was late trading. SEC regulations require purchase and redemption orders for fund shares to be submitted to the fund, broker, or other intermediary by 4 P.M., the time funds are required to price their shares. Bank of America allegedly permitted Canary to submit orders for its funds after 4 P.M. but to receive 4 P.M. prices, clearly an illegal practice under the 1940 act. Three academics also observed, "Perhaps most scandalous is how Bank of America leveraged its broad platform of financial services to advance market timing of its funds. The bank provided a $300 million credit line and derivative facilities that were used to time the firm's own funds. Bank of America also provided Canary its own trading terminal that it could use to trade fund shares as late as 6:30 P.M.—two and a half hours after he close of the market."[23] Similarly, Bank One allegedly lent money to facilitate Canary's market timing activities. Canary's profits from illegal market timing and late trading came out of the pockets of long-term fund shareholders.

The facts alleged in the complaint were shocking. They reminded me of the most horrendous case studies in the SEC's *Investment Trust Study* that led to the Investment Company Act and of the abuses that resulted in the Glass-Steagall Act. Moreover, Attorney General Spitzer did a brilliant job in presenting a complicated case, for example, stating that "Allowing timing is like a casino saying that it prohibits loaded dice, but then allowing favored gamblers to use loaded dice," and "Allowing late trading is like allowing betting on a horse race after the horses have crossed the finish line."[24]

As I watched the press conference and read the complaint, I felt physically ill. Four major fund groups apparently had violated not only the law but also the most basic principles of fiduciary fair dealing. Decades of hard work by hundreds of people in the mutual fund industry and the SEC to create the industry's reputation for integrity had been obliterated. How could these firms and individuals, some of whom I knew personally, have engaged in such flagrant misconduct? What were they thinking? I felt personally betrayed. At the same time that the institute was imploring the SEC to provide funds with more tools to combat market timers, these four fund groups were cutting deals with timers.

I also wondered how could we (and by "we" I meant the SEC, the NASD, the institute, industry leaders, fund attorneys, compliance officers, the media, and industry critics) all have totally missed the existence of these illegal and immoral trading activities. We knew of the widespread existence of market timing. We had read studies by Zitzewitz and others. We had noted high turnover rates in international funds. The SEC had issued a staff letter on fair value. The institute had published a white paper to assist funds in fair valuing. The institute's research department had sponsored an academic seminar on market timing. Many funds were vigorously combating market timing by creating timing police, imposing redemption fees, and fair valuing. The institute was seeking SEC permission for funds to adopt additional tools to deter timers. No one had dreamed that individuals at some fund organizations were making arrangements to facilitate market timing. Late trading, if anything, was even worse. The 4 P.M. cutoff for the receipt of sale and redemption orders was one of the most basic tenets of the mutual fund industry. In all my time at the institute, I had never once heard of a violation, even an inadvertent one, of the 4 P.M. rule.

Navigating the Crisis

On the afternoon of September 3, my immediate concern was the likely political fallout from the Canary complaint and Spitzer's press conference. The SEC and the NASD, like the institute, were caught flat-footed. I received a barrage of phone calls from institute members, regulators, legislators, and the media.

Some urged me to issue a statement damning the behavior of a few rotten apples. However, I was concerned that there might be more bad news to come. Tim Forde, the institute's vice president for strategic analysis, and I agreed that the only thing that could possibly make the situation worse would be the revelation that fund officials had profited personally from illegal trading in fund shares. I issued a statement declaring, "The legal standards and duties regarding trading and valuation of mutual fund shares are clear and long standing," and supporting "strict compliance with and vigorous enforcement of the law."[25] The next day, SEC chairman Donaldson wrote to me asking that I urge institute members to seek assurances from broker-dealers and other intermediaries that they were following all relevant rules and policies regarding timely handling of fund orders and to review the sufficiency of their own policies and procedures. I immediately complied with this request. The SEC also undertook a full-scale sweep of the mutual fund and brokerage industries.[26]

As I had feared, the next months witnessed a series of revelations implicating over a dozen additional fund firms. Most involved arrangements permitting hedge funds and other outsiders to market-time fund shares in contravention of policies set forth in the funds' prospectuses. As Forde and I had feared, there also were situations where fund officials personally market-timed their own funds: at Putnam, two portfolio managers and four other employees timed their funds; at Strong, the founder and chairman timed his firm's funds; and at Pilgrim Baxter, one of the principals was a major investor in a hedge fund that the firm permitted to engage in market timing.[27]

The political reaction was swift. Congressman Baker, chairman of the House Financial Services Subcommittee, stated that he planned to seek floor amendments to the bill previously passed by the full committee. Senator Richard Shelby, chairman of the Senate Banking Committee, called hearings and told reporters that he would not rule out any legislative reform proposals. Senator Peter Fitzgerald, chairman of the Senate Subcommittee on Consumer Affairs and Public Safety, called hearings, although it did not appear that the subcommittee had legislative jurisdiction over mutual funds.

The fund industry faced as dire situation a situation as I had ever seen. There was a clear danger that Congress would overreact and pass punitive legislation that would harm the industry and millions of fund shareholders. Many investors had lost substantial sums in the 2000–2003 bear market, and there was a search for scapegoats. Congress and the media were still smarting from the corporate and accounting abuses. Many saw mutual funds as the next area in need of a major overhaul. The SEC had been weakened by Spitzer's earlier upstaging of the agency in connection with Wall Street research analysts. Now the SEC was blindsided by his discovery of fund trading abuses and suffered a further loss of credibility. Spitzer was quick to blame the SEC for the fund scandals, stating, "This has been an outrageous betrayal of the public trust by that agency. The regulators who were supposed to have been watching this industry were asleep at the switch." Spitzer was likely to continue upstaging the SEC by bringing additional cases. Experience indicated that officials in other states would seek to emulate Spitzer, thus producing a race among regulators to bring enforcement actions. Some GOP members of the House committee seemed intent on political retaliation against the mutual fund industry because the institute had refused to fire Domenick. Although Fitzgerald's subcommittee lacked legislative jurisdiction, he appeared to be a loose cannon, accusing the mutual fund industry of being "the world's largest skimming operation." Congressional hearings would provide critics with opportunities to blast the industry on all sorts of issues and promote their pet ideas for legislative change. Meanwhile, each month brought a drumbeat of revelations regarding other fund groups—Alliance, Alger, Federated, Putnam, and Strong in October; Pilgrim Baxter in November; Invesco and MFS in December; Fremont in January; Franklin, Columbia, PIMCO, and State Street Research in February. Four members of the institute's fifteen-person executive committee resigned from their organizations and the committee. (Jim Riepe of T. Rowe Price sent me an e-mail stating, tongue-in-cheek, that the "band of brothers" soon would be a "band of brother.") The media predicted that Congress would enact tough legislation. I dreaded picking up the newspapers each morning in my driveway for fear of seeing more bad news.[28]

The fund industry did hold a few cards. The vast majority of fund groups, over 500 in number, were not accused of trading improprieties. SEC chairman Donaldson was well respected in both Wall Street and Washington. Senators Shelby and Sarbanes, the chairman and ranking member of the Senate Banking Committee, were highly regarded as thoughtful and deliberate legislators. Industry critics were likely to lose credibility by overstating their cases and advocating extreme legislation. The institute's chairman, Paul Haaga, was experienced, well respected, and tough. Institute members rallied around the flag. I was contacted by numerous fund executives and independent directors expressing their support and offering to do whatever they could. During the entire period of controversy over the scandals, only one firm threatened to resign from membership in the institute (because it believed that the institute was not sufficiently aggressive in opposing regulation, a course of action I was convinced would be both wrong on the merits and politically suicidal).

Although the scandals had greatly damaged the industry's credibility, it was essential that we do all we could to help produce a sensible outcome. The institute immediately advocated a program centered on strict enforcement, including criminal penalties, the payment of full restitution to injured fund shareholders, and the adoption of rigorous new SEC rules to combat illegal trading and other abuses. We never once minimized the scandals, and as to reform, we testified that "everything is on the table." The institute backed up its program with specific suggestions for reform—advocating a "hard" close under which orders would have to reach the fund (rather than the broker or other intermediary) by 4 P.M., urging adoption of a rule requiring the imposition of redemption fees on short-term trades in all funds, and requiring inclusion in fund codes of ethics of provisions governing trading in fund shares by fund personnel.

Industry officials, including executives from some of the largest groups, small fund representatives, and independent directors, called for strict enforcement of existing rules and the adoption of tough new SEC standards. As had been the case in 1940, all segments of the industry joined in.

Three congressional committees—the Senate Banking Committee, chaired by Senator Shelby; the Senate Subcommittee on Consumer Affairs and Public Safety, chaired by Senator Fitzgerald; and the House Subcommittee on Financial Markets, chaired by Congressman Baker—held hearings on the fund scandals. As I had hoped, industry critics went overboard in search of headlines and testified in favor of extreme measures. Among other matters, they advocated requiring mutual fund boards to regularly put the fund's advisory contract "out to bid" (i.e., to request contract offers from a number of advisers); requiring fund advisory fees to meet a "most favored nation standard" (i.e., the fee could be no greater than the lowest fee the fund's adviser charged any other client); requiring mutual fund advisory contracts to be "cost plus"; requiring mutual funds, when they reach a certain size, to "internalize" (i.e., fire their advisers and assume management responsibilities); prohibiting a fund organization from imposing a new fee (and hence introducing a new service) without prior approval from the SEC; requiring fund boards to employ their own staffs; banning mutual funds, but not other money managers, from using "soft dollars" (i.e., using fund brokerage commissions to acquire investment research); requiring disclosure of compensation received by fund executives and portfolio managers, but not requiring such disclosure by any other money managers; creating a mutual fund oversight board to examine and regulate fund directors; and prohibiting funds from advertising their past performance.[29]

Many of these measures were rolled into a bill, the Mutual Fund Reform Act of 2004, authored by Senator Fitzgerald. Most frightening was the fact that the bill was cosponsored by a number of well-respected Senators from both parties, including Senators Susan Collins, Richard Durbin, Fritz Hollings, John Kerry, Frank Lautenberg, Carl Levin, Richard Lugar, and

George Voinovich. Julie Domenick, Craig Tyle, the institute's general counsel, and I met with a cosponsor and members of his staff about the bill. After the Senator left the meeting, a staff member asked what I believed would happen if the bill were enacted into law. I replied that over time, the bill would commoditize, homogenize, and dumb down the fund industry. The best investment advisory firms would exit the mutual fund business, where fees would be set on a cost-plus basis, to manage hedge funds, pension plans, and endowments, where fees would be set by the market. Fund sponsors would be hesitant to introduce new shareholder services because the associated fees would require preapproval by the SEC. Good portfolio managers and executives would leave the mutual fund business, where their compensation would be disclosed, to manage other types of money, where their compensation would remain private. Competing products would outperform mutual funds because they would have better managers and could use their commissions to obtain research, whereas mutual funds would be barred from the use of soft dollars. As a result of all this, wealthy investors would exit mutual funds in favor of more creative, better-performing forms of investment. This would drive up expenses for the remaining, smaller shareholders. I thought that I was eloquent. The staff member replied to the effect that "That's exactly what we want to do. If the price of making mutual funds safe for middle-class investors would be to commoditize and dumb down mutual funds, so be it." I thanked her for her candor. I left the meeting with the awful realization that my worst fears were well founded: proponents of these measures *intended* to dramatically change the mutual fund industry, to the great detriment of mutual fund shareholders.

Senator Fitzgerald did not seek approval of his bill by his subcommittee, presumably because it lacked legislative jurisdiction. However, in November, the House of Representatives passed by a vote of 418 to 2 the bill that had been reported by the Financial Services Committee, with several floor amendments aimed at fund trading practices. The decision as to whether there would be legislation now lay with the Senate Banking

Committee, which held a series of hearings from September 2003 through April 2004. During this period, the SEC, under Donaldson's leadership, took decisive action. The SEC brought a series of cases against mutual fund firms, broker-dealers, and individuals for trading abuses. The commission also proposed and adopted a record number of new mutual fund rules, including a hard 4 P.M. close, mandatory redemption fees on short-term trading, requiring fund boards to have 75 percent independent directors and independent chairs, requiring funds to have comprehensive compliance systems and chief compliance officers reporting to fund boards, requiring fund codes of ethics to include reporting of employees' personal transactions in fund shares, prohibiting arrangements whereby fund advisers take into account the sale of fund shares in selecting brokers to execute portfolio transactions, and a series of new disclosure requirements. The SEC was no longer asleep at the switch but was moving aggressively on a number of fronts. The institute endorsed all of the SEC actions, except its proposal to require independent chairs, a matter that we believed was best left to each board.

I remembered Bob Augenblick's warnings back in 1971 about the problems created by Congressional reconsideration of the Investment Company Act. My hope was that the SEC's comprehensive regulatory and disclosure program, with the affected industry in support, would render moot the need for legislation. My main concern was that out of the blue there would come a completely new fund scandal that would overshadow all of the SEC's good work and trigger punitive legislation. I recalled that the legislation introduced in the wake of Enron had lain dormant until the WorldCom scandal hit. I kept my fingers crossed.

In January, Senator Shelby said that he was not sure whether the issues should be dealt with by legislation or regulation. By March, he was leaning toward legislation. But in April, following the series of SEC actions, he said that he was "leaning straight up" because the SEC was "showing a lot of leadership and resolve.... We don't want to do anything that would be construed in any way as undermining what the SEC is doing."[30] The legislative battle was over. The fund industry and its shareholders had avoided the enactment of punitive legislation. As the duke of Wellington said of the Battle of Waterloo, "It has been a damned serious business...the nearest run thing you ever saw in your life."

There were a number of heroes. Attorney General Spitzer had uncovered the fund trading abuses (although he subsequently tarnished his reputation by seeking to use settlements in trading cases to lower fund fees). SEC chairman Donaldson reenergized the agency and produced major reforms. Several Republican members of the House committee refused to engage in political retaliation regarding Domenick. Senator Shelby's deliberate approach of seeking results rather than headlines paid off. Paul Haaga kept the fund industry united in favor of regulatory reform. There also were those who sought to identify villains, for example, blaming the scandals on the SEC, the NASD, and the institute.[31] No doubt all of us—the SEC, the NASD, the institute, fund executives, mutual fund attorneys, compliance officers, the media, and industry critics—could have been more alert in detecting abuse. But the real villains were those firms and individuals who breached basic fiduciary obligations they owed to fund shareholders.

In June, with the legislative debate over, I retired as president of the institute and was succeeded by Paul Stevens, who had served as general counsel in the 1990s. I looked forward to spending more time with my wife, writing and lecturing on mutual fund history, sailing, and playing tennis on the courts where I had chatted with Spitzer.

Assessing the Scandals

Many explanations have been offered to explain how the trading abuses occurred in an industry that had long prided itself on a reputation for integrity. Some of these explanations are as follows. The 2000–2003 bear market sharply reduced equity fund assets, and thus reduced the fees earned by advisers, putting pressure on fund executives to acquire assets. Whereas fund complexes once had been run by money managers, marketers had taken over. The industry's explosive growth in the 1990s led to hiring executives and employees with no background in operating a fiduciary business. A number of U.S. and foreign financial institutions without experience in the U.S. fund business had acquired American fund companies at or near the top of the market and were determined to recoup their investments. Financial conglomerates wanted to achieve synergies among their various units, and arrangements with timers provided opportunities for this. Several fund advisers had gone public, and there was pressure from public shareholders to grow earnings. The SEC had gone back and forth regarding the need to fair value. It had not, as it had announced, undertaken a comprehensive analysis of fund pricing issues. It had not been willing to interpret the law to arm fund groups with additional tools to combat timers. Moreover, the SEC's ability to monitor for compliance had been weakened by the transfer of inspections from the Division of Investment Management to a separate unit.

Some of these explanations do not hold up very well. The entire mutual fund industry was hit by the bear market, and presumably most firms had hired a large number of new employees. However, according to my best count, only 19 out of more than 500 fund complexes were parties to SEC, NASD, and state actions. Marketers (beginning with Edward Leffler in 1924) always have played a major role in the industry, which is hardly surprising because a company that offers redeemable securities requires constant sales just to stay even. Conversely, many groups that were involved in the scandals were headed by individuals who had grown up on the money management side of the business. Although the SEC could have been clearer and more consistent, after news of the scandals broke, I learned that Canary and others had approached a large number of other fund groups seeking permission to engage in trading that contravened stated policies. Despite the SEC's lack of clarity, all of these fund groups easily knew enough to turn Canary and its ilk down flat. The conglomerate theory offers more promise. Approximately 40 percent of fund advisers (about 200 groups) are owned by other companies (banks, brokerage firms, insurance companies, foreign firms, and others). But these advisers accounted for over 70 percent (fourteen out of nineteen) of the illegal trading cases. The public adviser theory also may have some merit. Though very few fund advisers, probably fewer than ten, are public companies, three were charged with trading improprieties. In contrast, of the 300 or so private advisers, only 2 were charged with misconduct. There are major exceptions to every explanation, of course. For example, over 90 percent of the complexes owned by conglomerates were not involved in the scandals. None of the theories explains why some fund executives and portfolio managers personally engaged in illegal market timing of their own funds. My conclusion is that good (and bad) behavior is more the result of culture than of economic circumstances or corporate structure.

Overall, how bad were the trading scandals? Relatively few mutual fund companies were involved. (There were far more enforcement cases brought against intermediaries, particularly brokers, than against fund companies.) Although there is a tendency to lump all of the fund cases together, they ran the gamut from gross abuses, such as the Bank of America case, to borderline situations. (For example, NASD fined State Street for not being aggressive enough in blocking timers, rather than for cutting deals with timers.) The monetary harm to individual shareholders was slight. This was in sharp contrast to the Enron and WorldCom situations, in which many employees lost their life savings. Fund shareholders barely reacted to the scandals and continued to put new money into mutual funds. From the height of the scandal at year end 2003 to 2007, industry assets increased 60 percent, growing from $7.4 trillion to over $11 trillion. Based on these facts, it could be argued that the scandals were purely an "inside the Beltway phenomenon," stirred up by politicians and journalists. But this misses the point. Mutual fund advisers, their executives, and employees are fiduciaries whose overriding obligation is always to put the interests of investors first. Illegal market timing and late trading arrangements violate the most basic standards of fiduciary behavior. When I testified before Congress on the scandals, I stated that I was "outraged by the shocking betrayal of trust exhibited by some in the mutual fund industry." I feel the same way today.

The fund industry paid a heavy price. Billions of dollars were levied in fines and payments to injured shareholders. Individuals were barred from the business. Careers were ruined. Many firms that were involved in the scandals were punished by investors and lost significant market share. The innocent suffered along with the guilty. The entire industry was saddled with increased regulatory burdens and costs. The chances of eliminating or reforming misguided or outdated rules have been greatly diminished. It will take decades for the industry to recover the high reputation and credibility it long enjoyed with regulators, Congress, consumer groups, and the media.

I and many individuals I have spoken with in the fund industry, government, academia, and the media are still amazed that none of us spotted the trading problems before they blew up. Larry Greene, an attorney who started working at the SEC in 1938, participated in the drafting of the Investment Company Act, and later served as general counsel of Dreyfus, expressed it well: "I was absolutely aghast that could happen; how could the SEC in their examination of mutual funds have missed the fraud? They go over everything very carefully. The mutual funds have their independent accountants reviewing what goes on in the way of sales; how could that have happened that they would let some firms make special deals and be able to choose their own price? That doesn't make sense."[32]

As a result of the corporate accounting and mutual fund scandals, mutual funds have been provided with new tools to detect abuse, including mandated compliance systems and chief compliance officers, "reporting up" requirements, and whistleblower provisions. These new tools are on top of inspection programs conducted by the SEC and the Financial Industry Regulatory Authority (FINRA; formerly the NASD). These provisions have been in place for several years. It is time for a study, perhaps conducted by a congressional committee or the Governmental Accountability Office, as to the efficacy of these private and governmental detection systems and ways they can be improved. The purpose of such a study would be to ensure that the best possible early detection systems are in place. No one—neither the mutual fund industry, nor regulators, nor the public—can afford a repetition of the fund trading scandals.

Snapshot of the Industry in 2007

The scandals remind us of how abuse can undo decades of success. Fortunately, aggressive enforcement and a series of SEC regulatory initiatives limited the damage. By 2007, the industry had regained its balance and showed every sign of a healthy recovery. The number of individual funds shareholders stood at a record 88 million. The industry enjoyed positive cash flows, with a record inflow of $883 billion in 2007. Assets increased from $7.4 trillion in 2003, to $8.9 trillion in 2005, to over $12 trillion in 2007. Mutual funds' share of household financial assets grew to 23 percent. Mutual funds continued to gain share in key retirement markets, amounting to 55 percent of the 401(k) market and 47 percent of the IRA market. In the 403(b) market, once the *exclusive* preserve of the insurance industry, mutual funds held a 53 percent market share. Fund groups contuinued to introduce new products and services, such as lifestyle and life cycle funds. The mutual fund industry was well diversified, with 54 percent of assets in stock funds, 6 percent in hybrid funds, 14 percent in bond funds, and 26 percent in money market funds. The five largest funds were three Capital Research & Management funds—Growth Fund of America, EuroPacific Growth Fund, and Capital World Growth & Income Fund; Vanguard 500 Index Fund; and CREF Stock Account. The five largest fund complexes were Fidelity, Capital Research & Management, Vanguard, Franklin, and PNC Financial Services.[33]

12

The 2008 Meltdown

All crises have involved debt that, in one fashion or another, has become dangerously out of scale in relation to the underlying means of payment.

— John Kenneth Galbraith

The turn of the twenty-first century witnessed a huge run up in home prices. Despite warnings, the Federal Reserve Board and other regulators did not act to curb speculation. When the bubble burst, there was a severe decline in home prices, failures of major financial institutions, and the worst economic downturn since the 1930s. Mutual funds were hit hard but fared considerably better than institutions that employed leverage far in excess of that permitted for mutual funds. The meltdown resulted in numerous calls for changes in financial regulation, including proposals that would impact mutual funds.

The Housing Bubble and Crash

In the late 1990s and early years of this century, there was a sustained rise in U.S. home prices, accompanied by a general perception that they would continue to go up and up. "Rates of price increase moved above 6 percent in 1999, accelerating to 8 and then 9 percent .... Respondents [to a 2003 survey] expected prices to increase in the future at 6 to 15 percent a year, depending on location."[1] Many factors fueled the housing bubble. Most importantly, the Federal Reserve, fearing that the economy would be in difficulty due to the collapse of the tech bubble and the terrorist attacks of September 11, 2001, kept interest rates low, making cheap real estate financing widely available. Traditional mortgage lenders, who once concentrated on low-risk buyers, increased their loans to the high-risk "subprime" market. New lenders came into being who concentrated on the subprime market. Prime mortgages fell from 85 percent of total mortgage lending in 2003, to 64 percent in 2004, to 52 percent in 2006.[2] Whereas lenders traditionally retained mortgages they originated, there was a massive movement to "securitization," whereby many lenders sold their mortgages, in the form of various types of mortgage-backed securities, to other institutions. These lenders paid less attention to the credit-worthiness of borrowers since they knew that they would not continue to hold the mortgages. Conversely, purchasers of mortgage-backed securities had no first-hand knowledge about borrowers. Because of this fact and the complexity of mortgage-backed securities, buyers became increasingly dependent on the opinions of rating agencies as to the credit-worthiness of the mortgage-backed securities they purchased. Many of these buyers, including banks, broker-dealers, and hedge funds, borrowed short-term to finance their purchases of long-term mortgage-backed securities, a classic use of leverage. As home prices kept rising, consumers increased their own leverage by utilizing no-down-payment mortgages, refinancing existing mortgages, taking out home equity loans, and increasing credit card debt.

There were warnings that the housing bubble, built on ever-increasing leverage by both financial institutions and consumers, was likely to burst. In 2003, Glenn Hubbard, Chairman of the White House Council of Economic Advisers, pushed the Fed to raise interest rates.[3] Federal Reserve Board Governor

Edward M. Gramlich urged Fed examiners to investigate sub-prime mortgage lenders affiliated with national banks.[4] As previously discussed, the Investment Company Institute recommended that the SEC regulate asset-backed securities arrangements as investment companies, and the institute and others advocated SEC regulation of hedge funds and rating agencies. But these warnings fell on deaf ears. Congress and regulators were caught up in the boom and in the prevailing anti-regulatory mood. The last thing policymakers wanted to do was to apply the brakes.

When home prices began to decline in 2006 all the dominos were positioned to fall. In early 2007, several major subprime lenders filed for bankruptcy. The crisis spread to highly leveraged owners of mortgage-backed securities, including hedge funds, commercial banks, broker-dealers, and insurance companies. A number of hedge funds collapsed. The Federal Reserve Board and the Department of the Treasury were forced to provide assistance to major banks. They also arranged for the rescue of a large broker-dealer, Bear Stearns, by a bank, J.P. Morgan Chase, the first time that the federal government had provided support to an investment bank. There was another first when the government shored-up a major insurance company, AIG. But a leading broker-dealer, Lehman Brothers, failed. A major money market fund, Primary Fund, broke a dollar a share, due to its holding of Lehman paper. The resulting panic forced the Treasury Department to offer insurance to all money funds. The stock market tumbled, with the S&P Index falling 37 percent in 2008, and an additional 25 percent in early 2009. Unemployment increased month after month. The country entered its worst economic downturn since the Great Depression.

Impact on Mutual Funds

The severe downturn in the economy and the securities markets took a heavy toll on mutual funds, due to a combination of falling portfolio values and net redemptions. Total fund assets fell from a record $12.2 trillion in May 2008 to just over $9 trillion in February 2009. Equity funds were hurt the most, with assets dropping over 50 percent, from $6.3 trillion to $3.1 trillion. Bond fund assets declined from $1.7 to $1.6 trillion. On the other hand, the flight to safety produced an increase in money market fund assets, which grew from $3.6 to almost $3.9 trillion.

The 50 percent decline in equity fund assets was greater than the 40 percent decrease in the early 1970s. The damage to investors was far worse than in the earlier period, since in the intervening years mutual funds had grown from a tiny "cottage" industry to the principal way Americans invest. The fund industry as a whole did better than in the 1970s due to increased diversification from new products such as money market funds and tax-exempt funds. Thus, total industry assets declined only 26 percent, versus 40 percent in the 1970s. Groups that concentrated on equity funds got hit hard, whereas those that focused on bond funds or money funds held steady or even advanced. For the first time since 1984, money market fund assets surpassed those of equity funds. Most notably, the damage suffered by mutual funds, whose borrowing is strictly limited by the Investment Company Act, was far less than that sustained by other financial institutions, who either have no limits on leverage (hedge funds), or very loose limits (banks and broker-dealers). A 2008 study concluded that, on average, commercial banks were leveraged 9.8 to 1, and broker-dealers and hedge funds nearly 32 to 1, all far in excess of 1940 Act limits.[5]

The 2008 meltdown did underscore one problem in current mutual fund regulation—the creation of leverage not through borrowing, but through investment in derivatives. Buddy Donohue, the Director of the SEC Division of Investment Management, has noted that a number of fixed-income funds suffered one-year losses in excess of 30 percent, and that some of the explanation "likely may rest with the use of derivatives to magnify the economic exposure of the portfolio." He called upon the American Bar Association (ABA) to develop recommendations.[6]

How the ABA, the SEC, the Investment Company Institute, and the fund industry as a whole respond will be critical to the industry's future. As I have repeatedly emphasized, the fund industry's success rests upon regulatory controls that were imposed in the 1930s and 1940, most notably strict limits on borrowing, the only type of leverage that was known in 1940. It is imperative that tough regulatory controls be imposed, as soon as possible, on new types of leverage that may be employed by mutual funds.

As could have been predicted, there were those who announced that the 2008 meltdown meant the end or near-end of mutual funds.[7] On the other hand, many observers, even long-time critics of mutual funds, now proclaimed their virtues. Louis Lowenstein, author of *The Investor's Dilemma: How Mutual Funds are Betraying You and What to Do About It*, declared, "You do not see mutual funds imploding like hedge funds or like private equity funds, and there are several very good reasons for that based on government oversight and regulation." Financial columnist Scott Burns went so far as to call upon Congress to create an entirely new regulatory system for banks under which banks would be subject to the types of controls that are imposed on mutual funds.[8]

Calls for Legislation

Looking back, it is clear that the basic problem was the failure of regulators to act as the bubble grew and grew. The Federal Reserve Board declined to crack-down on unscrupulous sub-prime lending practices. The SEC exempted asset-backed arrangements from regulation as investment companies, repealed its "uptick" rule designed to impede short-selling, and lowered, rather than raised, capital requirements for broker-dealers. Most importantly, the Fed, first headed by Chairman Greenspan and then Chairman Bernanke, refused to raise interest rates in order to curb excessive speculation. *The story of the 2008 meltdown was not the failure of financial laws, but rather the failure of regulators to properly apply those laws.*

No doubt there are serious gaps and inefficiencies in our financial laws and regulations. The meltdown caused administration officials, members of Congress, regulators, academics, think tanks, columnists, and others to offer hundreds of suggestions for reform. Few proposals were new. For the most part, would-be reformers reached into the national medicine cabinet and brought out prescriptions that had been offered, and largely ignored, well before the bubble and meltdown. Some proposals would fill gaps in regulation, for example, at long last providing for regulation of credit rating agencies, derivatives, and hedge funds. Others would seek to reduce inefficiencies, for example, requiring the combination of various federal agencies that regulate banks. The final Dodd–Frank Act reflected many of these proposals.

Policymakers also struggled over what to do about giant financial institutions whose problems can threaten the entire financial system.

Some recalled Justice Brandeis' call for legislation that would limit the size and activities of financial institutions, so that none are "too big to fail." (Several New Deal laws incorporated Brandeis' approach: the Glass–Steagall Act separated commercial and investment banking; the Public Utility Holding Company Act imposed a death sentence on giant utility holding companies; and the Revenue Act of 1936 limited mutual fund control of portfolio companies). Many in the academy (Simon Johnson), in the Administration (Paul Volcker), overseas (Bank of England Governor Mervyn King), in Congress (Senator Kaufman), and even in giant financial conglomerates (former Citicorp CEO John Reed) urged legislation incorporating Brandeis' approach. But the key players had reasons to reject this advice. It is easier for members of Congress to buck responsibility to regulators rather than make difficult decisions. Agency officials are not inclined to admit fallibility and give up turf. Financial firms would prefer to deal with regulators possessing broad discretion rather than abide by strict statutory limits.

So the Obama Administration and Congress rejected the Brandeis approach. Instead they opted for giving regulators, who helped produce the 2008 financial crisis, even more authority.

Thus the Dodd–Frank Act provides the SEC and the Fed with greatly expanded powers and creates entirely new regulatory bodies such as the Consumer Financial Protection Bureau and the Financial Stability Oversight Council.

I hope that this reliance on regulation works. Experience indicates that it won't.

There were also proposals that were of particular importance to the mutual fund industry. Here I will discuss three areas—money market funds, the fate of the SEC, and 401(k) plans.

Money Market Funds

The early 1970s witnessed the introduction of money market funds, funds that invest in short-term debt instruments and seek to maintain a one dollar per share net asset value (nav) pursuant to Investment Company Act rule 2a-7. There have been hundreds of instances in which events (e.g., a sharp rise in short-term interest rates, a default by an issuer of commercial paper) threatened to cause a money fund to "break the buck." Each time, the fund's adviser purchased paper from the fund or took other steps to maintain the fund's one dollar nav. Until 2008, only one money fund, a tiny fund for investment of the reserves of a group of small community banks, broke the buck.

Over the years there have been a number of debates regarding money funds. First, some banks and bank regulators have favored the imposition of bank regulation on the funds. Thus, when he was Chairman of the Federal Reserve Board, Paul Volcker wanted Congress to give the Fed stand-by authority to impose reserve requirements on money funds. The fund industry successfully opposed this proposal. Second, industry participants differed as to how stringent rule 2a-7 should be. Some favored tightening the rule's standards to reduce the risk that any fund would break the buck; others wanted more liberal controls, leaving each fund greater latitude to make its own investment decisions. Finally, individual players in the industry differed as to types of investments money funds should make within the confines of the rule. For years, Bruce Bent, co-founder of Reserve Fund, the first money fund, criticized other money funds for allegedly investing in order to reach for yield.[9]

The 2008 financial crisis resulted in the first major money market fund breaking the buck and the threat of a run on money funds generally, bringing into play all of these old debates and even some of the individual debaters, including Bruce Bent and Paul Volcker.

On September 15, 2008, the financial crisis reached a critical point when a major broker-dealer, Lehman Brothers, failed. Primary Fund, the successor to Reserve Fund, had 1.2 percent of its assets invested in Lehman commercial paper and notes. The fund's adviser, headed by Bruce Bent, was unable to provide assistance to the fund, and its share price fell to $0.97, the first time in history that a major money market fund had broken the buck. There ensued a massive flight to quality. Institutional investors moved from money funds owning commercial paper to "government only" funds; many money funds were hit with massive redemptions; and the commercial paper market, already under severe pressure, tightened further. The federal government stepped in on a massive scale; notably the Treasury Department offered to temporarily guarantee the one dollar per share of participating money funds. This and other government actions calmed the situation.

There ensued a heated debate over the future regulation of money funds. Three alternatives were put forth: first, continue to regulate money funds as mutual funds under the federal securities laws but tighten the standards in rule 2a-7; second, follow that approach and also require money funds to have fluctuating net asset values; and third, subject money funds to regulation as banks.

The first volley was fired by Paul Volcker, who headed a steering committee on financial reform of the Group of Thirty, a private international body of financial experts. The committee's report recommended that money market funds be regulated as banks:

> Money market mutual funds wishing to offer bank-like services, such as transaction account services, withdrawals

on demand at par, and assurances of maintaining a stable net asset value (NAV) at par should be required to reorganize as special-purpose banks, with appropriate prudential regulation and supervision, government insurance, and access to central bank lender-of-last-resort facilities.[10]

The Investment Company Institute countered with a white paper calling for changes in existing SEC regulatory requirements under rule 2a-7 and maintenance of the fixed one dollar nav regime.

Next, the Obama Administration proposed a two-pronged approach—tighten SEC regulation under rule 2a-7 and study requiring the use of fluctuating navs or access to private sources of liquidity:

> The SEC should move forward with its plans to strengthen the regulatory framework around MMFs to reduce the credit and liquidity profile of individual MMFs and to make the MMF industry as a whole less susceptible to runs. The President's Working Group on Financial Markets should prepare a report assessing whether more fundamental changes are necessary to further the MMF industry's susceptibility to runs, such as eliminating the ability of a MMF to use a stable net asset value or requiring MMFs to obtain access to reliable emergency liquidity facilities from private sources.[11]

It is noteworthy that the Administration did *not* put on the table the Group of Thirty option—regulating money market funds as banks.

Then the SEC proposed and adopted amendments to rule 2a-7, generally along the lines suggested by the institute, and also invited comments relating to requiring the use of fluctuating navs.[12]

At this point, the odds favor continued SEC regulation of money funds under a strengthened Rule 2a-7, retention of the stable nav system, and possibly the creation of emergency liquidity facilities. However, a new crisis involving just a single money market fund is likely to reignite calls to regulate money funds as banks.

There are sound policy arguments for moving money funds to fluctuating navs. There are better arguments for maintaining the system of fixed navs under a strengthened Rule 2a-7. However, it would be perverse to adopt the third approach—subjecting money funds to bank regulation. Bank regulators were the main culprits behind the 2008 economic crisis. Taxpayers have paid billions of dollars to bail out troubled banks, whereas money funds, regulated by the SEC, have not cost taxpayers one cent.

The SEC

Mutual funds' success has been based on strict requirements set forth in the federal securities laws *and* firm administration of those laws by the SEC. Fortunately for fund shareholders and the fund industry, for most of its life the SEC has been one of the most effective agencies in the entire federal government. In 1977, the Senate Governmental Affairs Committee released a study that ranked the SEC as the top agency for "technical knowledge, impartiality, legal ability, and hard work."[13]

Criticism of the SEC usually has come from conservatives, who believe that the agency has been too zealous in seeking to protect investors. In 1940, the Washington correspondent for the daily banking newspaper, the *American Banker*, wrote:

> For bankers generally, the Securities and Exchange Commission is the enfant terrible of the Franklin D. Roosevelt era …. While other Roosevelt Administration agencies of the Government have mellowed over the years, the Securities and Exchange Commission has continued on its stormy way, determined to rule.[14]

It is not surprising that in periods when conservatives controlled the White House and Congress there were efforts to reduce the SEC's authority through legislation, budget cuts, and the appointment of pro-business SEC chairmen and commissioners.

What is new is that in recent years the SEC has come under heavy criticism from liberals, who believe that the agency has lost its focus and effectiveness. Gary Weiss, an investigative journalist, has written, "Something happened to the SEC over the years, just as something happens to a lot of us as we get older. All too often we abandon the principles we had when we were young."[15] In 2003, Marty Jezer argued that the SEC no longer is "the kind of government [agency] that Franklin D. Roosevelt introduced in the 1930s," and that what is needed is a "new old deal" to revitalize the agency.[16]

Not unexpectedly, much of the liberal criticism has been aimed at Republican SEC officials, but it also has encompassed Democrats. For example, according to Weiss:

> investors ... didn't have a friend in Arthur J. Levitt, Jr., the SEC chairman during the Clinton administration. Levitt presided over the worst abuses to descend upon Wall Street since the 1920s ... he did a couple of things better than just about any recent SEC chairman in history—give speeches, and court the press ... when in fact thievery was running rampant ....[17]

Liberal criticism of the SEC intensified in 2008 when, despite detailed tips from outsiders, the agency missed the massive Ponzi scheme conducted by Bernard Madoff. A *single* press story contained the following:

> Former SEC Chairman Levitt: "You need new leadership there, and you need new leadership at every level."
>
> Joel Seligman, the leading historian of the SEC: "Although SEC division chiefs normally don't depart with an outgoing chairman, Seligman said the new chief should replace them."
>
> Representative Brad Sherman (Democrat, California): "called for all five SEC commissioners to resign."

Barbara Roper, Director of Investor Protection for the Consumer Federation of America: "This is what government looks like when it's entrusted to people who don't believe in government."[18]

No doubt the SEC has made its share of mistakes. I previously recounted the SEC's decision to exempt asset-backed arrangements from regulation as investment companies and its inaction regarding shelf space, despite the fact that in both instances the mutual fund industry pushed hard for SEC action. In more recent years, the SEC repealed its long-standing "uptick rule" designed to hamper short-selling, and lowered capital standards for broker-dealers, thus permitting them to greatly increase their leverage just as the bubble in asset-backed securities grew. The SEC has lost a series of cases in court in situations where it was seeking to expand its jurisdiction through rule-making. The SEC continues to function under an antiquated organizational structure, with divisions based on the original securities laws, inspections conducted apart from the operating divisions, and no chief operating officer to oversee daily activities. Most famously, the SEC failed to detect Bernard Madoff's massive fraud.

Some of the SEC's wounds may be self-inflicted. But many stem from external forces. Over the last 30 years, Washington has been enamored with deregulation. Legislation has denied the SEC jurisdiction in specific areas, such as over-the-counter derivatives. Leading members of Congress have sought to prevent the SEC from regulating hedge funds, rating agencies, bank holding companies, and other vehicles. The SEC's budget has not kept up with demands. The courts, led by conservative jurists, have handed down a series of cases striking down the SEC's attempts to expand its jurisdiction through rule-making. The SEC has had difficulty in attracting and retaining high-quality employees, whereas in its early years at the height of the Great Depression the SEC attracted outstanding professionals who spent their careers at the agency.

Whatever the source of the SEC's problems—its own errors, external factors, or the simple effects of aging—the agency's lose of effectiveness and declining reputation pose serious problems for mutual funds, whose success has been built on the SEC serving as a tough cop on the beat and the public's confidence in that cop. The fate of the fund industry is tied to the fate of the SEC.

In the closing days of the George W. Bush Administration the Treasury Department issued a blueprint for financial reform that essentially would have wiped out the SEC. After the election, a similar plan was proposed by the Committee on Capital Markets Regulation, a private group of business, legal, and academic leaders.[19] It is not surprising that such proposals emanated from conservative quarters. What is more surprising is that next there were reports that the Obama Administration might move in the same direction. On May 20, 2009, Bloomberg ran a story that began "The Obama administration may call for stripping the Securities and Exchange Commission of some of its powers," and continued "The Fed may inherit some SEC functions, with others going to other agencies …. On the table: giving oversight of mutual funds to a bank regulator or a new agency to police consumer-finance products …."[20]

However, the blueprint for financial services reform released by the Obama Administration in June 2009 would keep the SEC largely intact. In fact, the agency would gain jurisdiction in areas such as hedge funds, securities-related over-the-counter-derivatives, and executive compensation.[21] Part of the credit for the proposed preservation and strengthening of the SEC goes to the continued support of the agency by liberal and moderate policymakers. Credit also must go to the work of the SEC's new chair, Mary Schapiro, in assuring administration and congressional officials that the agency is getting back on track. This is very good news for mutual fund shareholders and the fund industry.

401(k) Plans

It often has been said that "the British Empire was created in a fit of absent mindedness."

The same may be said of 401(k) retirement plans. In 1978, Congress added section 401(k) to the Internal Revenue Code to address a technical tax issue, and had no idea that that it was launching a sea change in the U.S. retirement system. Despite this accidental beginning, 401(k) plans have revolutionized the retirement system and are now the largest component of that system. Mutual funds are the leading funding medium for 401(k) plans. Therefore changes in 401(k) laws and regulations are of utmost importance to the mutual fund industry.

When 401(k) plans first started to gain popularity, advocates of defined benefit (DB) plans criticized 401(k) plans and sought ways to encourage formation of DB plans. But as the movement from DB to 401(k) plans appeared all but inevitable, critics shifted their focus to urging the imposition of limitations and requirements on 401(k) plans. Some of these proposals were drawn from the DB world. For example, the law requires that distributions from a DB plan take the form of a joint and survivor annuity, unless both spouses choose another option. DB supporters urged the imposition of a similar distribution requirement on 401(k) plans. Other proposals sought to affect 401(k) participants' investments, such as imposing a limitation on ownership of employer stock and requiring 401(k) plans to offer low-cost index funds. These and other proposals to impose limitations and requirements on 401(k) plans did not gain traction. Indeed, the Pension Protection Act of 2006 moved in the opposite direction and promoted 401(k) plans by allowing automatic enrollment of participants. Meanwhile DB advocates, the mutual fund industry, and others urged the Department of Labor to require that participants in 401(k) plans be provided with full disclosure regarding their investment options. As previously discussed, the George W. Bush Administration ended without the adoption of disclosure regulations.

The 2008 stock market meltdown changed everything. "As the market was beginning its decline in 2007, 1 in 4 Americans ages 55 to 65 had 90 percent or more of their 401(k) money invested in stock mutual funds."[22] These 401(k) participants, like all investors who over-concentrated in equities, suffered huge losses. Policymakers responded by reaching into the national medicine cabinet and bringing out old prescriptions for 401(k) plans.

The most extreme proposal was reminiscent of the original approach taken by opponents of 401(k) plans—totally abolish 401(k) plans and replace them with a government run guaranteed retirement system. Teresa Ghilarducci, a professor at the New School for Social Research, earned a good deal of notoriety by advocating this approach.[23] Another broad proposal would retain the 401(k) system but would "limit investment options to pre-allocated portfolios consisting solely of low cost index funds, passively managed funds, Exchange Traded Funds and Target Retirement Funds (where the underlying funds are index funds)."[24] There were less sweeping, more rifle-shot approaches. For example, the Brookings Institution published a paper proposing that when retirees take distributions, a substantial portion of 401(k) assets be automatically directed into a two-year annuity-type product, with participants allowed to continue the program after the two year trial period.[25]

In June of 2009, the House Education and Labor Committee approved the 401(k) Fee Disclosure and Pension Security Act of 2009. The bill in essence would require 401(k) plans to offer index funds, and would require that extensive disclosure regarding fees be provided to plan participants and plan sponsors. It appears that fees would include both fees paid directly by the participant and the participant's share of fees paid by vehicles in which the participant invests, a system which, as discussed in chapter 11, would be extremely costly and difficult to administer. In addition, fees would have to be broken out into neat categories such as administration and record-keeping and investment management, whereas mutual funds and other financial firms do not function in this manner. These onerous and likely unworkable disclosure provisions illustrate the price being paid for the failure of the Department of Labor to require sensible fee disclosure years ago. As discussed in Chapter 10, it was not until 2010, 36 years after the enactment of ERISA, that the Department began to act in this area.

At this point it is difficult to predict whether Congress will enact sweeping 401(k) legislation. There are many reasons to bet against Congressional action. The Obama Administration has its hands full with other priorities. Major pension legislation requires the concurrence of the Senate and House tax-writing committees as well as the two labor committees. The bill approved by the House Education and Labor Committee caused sharp partisan divisions. On the other hand, defined contribution (DC) plans are huge, with assets of over $3.5 trillion; the rules for 401(k) and other DC plans have developed on a disjointed and ad hoc basis; and the Department of Labor has not shown leadership in the DC area. All in all, the area cries out for cohesive legislative treatment. Given these conflicting forces, it is likely that the fate of 401(k) legislation will be determined by future events.

I hope that future debate over 401(k) plans is based on facts, not myths. Here are a few key facts. The decline in DB plans largely is the result of the burdens that ERISA placed on DB plans. Many employers who ended their DB plans installed 401(k) plans. Thus, 401(k) plans increased due to the decline in DB plans; but 401(k) plans did not cause that decline. All investors, including 401(k) participants, who over-concentrate in equities will get hammered when the stock market crashes, as it always does from time to time. Long-term investors who make regular contributions to their 401(k) accounts and prudently allocate their investments among stocks, bonds, and cash are likely to fare well. A recent study by the Employee Benefit Research Institute found that balances of 401(k) participants who contributed consistently from 2003 to 2008 dropped 24.3 percent on average in 2008. However, because of employee and employer contributions and investment gains before 2008, during the five-year period participant balances increased at an annual rate of 7.2 percent.[26]

Fee Litigation

Judicial decisions involving fees are likely to prove as important to mutual funds as changes in legislation and regulation resulting from the 2008 economic crisis.

In 1970, Congress added section 36(b) to the Investment Company Act, which provides that a fund adviser has a "fiduciary duty" with respect to compensation received from the fund, and that the SEC or a fund shareholder on behalf of the fund can sue for breach of this duty. Although section 36(b) has been on the books for 40 years and there have been numerous lawsuits, the courts could not agree on what the section means. A recent Supreme Court case sets forth the official interpretation, but most likely the 1970 attempt at rate-making will continue to be a source of problems.

For many years, the leading case interpreting the section had been *Gartenberg v Merrill Lynch Asset Management*, involving a money market fund and decided by the Court of Appeals for the Second Circuit in 1982.[27] *Gartenberg* held that the "fiduciary duty" test means "whether the fee schedule represents a charge within the range of what would have been negotiated at arm's-length in the light of all surrounding circumstances," and that to be guilty of a violation the adviser "must charge a fee that is so disproportionately large that it bears no reasonable

Figure 12.1. Copyright 2009 investment news. Reprinted with permission.

relationship to the services rendered and could not have been the product of arm's-length bargaining." The opinion identified a number of factors that courts should consider in applying this test, including, among others, the nature and quality of the service, the cost to the adviser of providing the service, whether the adviser realizes economies of scale as the fund grows in size, and the independence and conscientiousness of the fund directors. The opinion rejected the argument that fees charged by the adviser to large pension plans should be taken into account since "the nature and extent of the services required by each type of fund differ sharply ... the pension fund does not face the myriad of daily purchases and redemptions throughout the nation which must be handled by the [Merrill Lynch money market] Fund, in which a purchaser may invest for only a few days."

Until recently, the *Gartenberg* case generally has been followed by other circuits. Moreover, courts have been unwilling to find breaches of fiduciary duty provided that a review of the factors enunciated in *Gartenberg* indicates that the fee was in the range of what could have been negotiated at arm's length. The plaintiffs bar was particularly upset that some courts interpreted *Gartenberg* to mean that courts should *never* compare fund fees to fees charged other investors.

Out of the blue, in May of 2008 the Court of Appeals for the Seventh Circuit in the *Jones* case flatly rejected the *Gartenberg* standard and enunciated a completely new test. Instead of focusing on the reasonableness of the advisory fee, the court looked at the investment adviser's behavior during the fee negotiation process:

> We now disapprove the Gartenberg approach. A fiduciary duty differs from rate regulation. A fiduciary must make full disclosure and play no tricks, but it is not subject to a cap on compensation. The trustees (and in the end, investors, who vote with their feet and dollars), rather than a judge or jury, determine how much advisory services are worth.[28]

The Supreme Court heard an appeal in the *Jones* case, and on March 30, 2010 delivered a unanimous opinion overturning the decision by the Seventh Circuit, expressly affirming the *Gartenberg* standard:

> we conclude that Gartenberg was essentially correct in its basic formulation of what §36 (b) requires: to face liability under §36(b), an investment adviser must charge a fee that is so disproportionately large that it bears no reasonable relationship to the services rendered and could not have been the product of arm's length bargaining.[29]

The Court gave great weight to the role played by the fund board:

> Where a board's process for negotiating and reviewing investment-adviser compensation is robust, a reviewing court should afford commensurate deference to the outcome of the bargaining process …. Thus if the disinterested directors considered the relevant factors, their decision to approve a particular fee agreement is entitled to considerable weight, even if a court might weigh the factors differently.

But when "the board's process was deficient or the adviser withheld important information, the court must take a more rigorous look at the outcome."

The Court noted that the parties differed as to the appropriateness of comparing fees the adviser charged the fund with fees it charged other clients. The Court stated that courts may give "comparisons the weight that they merit in light of the similarities and differences between the services" but must be "wary of inapt comparisons." The Court went on to say that Section 36(b) "does not necessarily ensure fee parity between mutual funds and institutional clients." Even if the services are similar, plaintiff must prove that the fund's fees are "outside the arm's-length range."

The Court also cautioned courts "not to rely too heavily on comparisons with fees charged to mutual funds by other advisers." The Court said that these comparisons "are problematic because these fees, like those challenged, may not be the product of negotiations conducted at arm's length."

Both the plaintiffs bar and the mutual fund industry immediately announced that the Supreme Court's decision was a major victory for their side. Plaintiff attorneys were pleased that the Court had rejected Judge Easterbrook's interpretation, and that the Court's opinion permits comparison of mutual fund fees to fees charged other clients. The fund industry was pleased that the Supreme Court had expressly endorsed the *Gartenberg* standard and had warned of the danger of inapt comparisons.[30]

The two sides in the *Jones* case have filed motions with the Court of Appeals for the Seventh Circuit. Plaintiffs argue that the case should be remanded to the district court for a new trial since they allege that the Supreme Court has adopted a new standard. Defendants argue that the Seventh Circuit should reaffirm the district court's summary judgment since they allege that the Supreme Court and the district court adopted the same standard. Meanwhile, new fee suits have been filed in other courts.[31]

In short, there is no indication that the Supreme Court's decision will lessen constant strike-suit litigation over mutual fund fees. This strengthens my conviction that the only real cure is legislation, along the lines recommended by the SEC staff in 1992, that would permit a fund adviser to set a single all-in fee, without the need for approval by shareholders, directors, or the courts. While this simple free-market approach would end the problems that are inherent in attempts at rate regulation, I would not bet on its adoption any time soon.

13

Work of a Trade Association

We must indeed all hang together, or, most assuredly, we shall all hang separately.

—Benjamin Franklin

The trade association for the mutual fund industry, the Investment Company Institute, is unique in several respects. First, membership in the association is almost universal: just about every sponsor of mutual funds, closed-end funds, unit investment trusts, and exchange-traded funds, as well as the funds themselves, are members of the association. Second, the institute has a long history of supporting government regulation of the investment company industry and of opposing unwise deregulation. Third, the institute has adopted a series of best practices that go well beyond law and regulation. Robert Glauber, former president of the National Association of Securities Dealers (NASD), often said to me that "the institute acts more like a self-regulatory organization than a trade association."

As discussed in chapter 2, following enactment of the Investment Company Act of 1940, closed-end funds and mutual funds formed a temporary trade association, the National Committee of Investment Companies, whose primary mission was to assist the Securities and Exchange Commission (SEC) in the administration of the act. It became a permanent association, the National Association of Investment Companies in 1941. In 1961, membership was expanded to include the funds' advisers and underwriters, and the association's name was changed to the Investment Company Institute. Subsequently, sponsors of fixed-unit investment trusts and exchange-traded funds have become members.

Over the years, the association broadened its work to include areas in addition to SEC regulation. Early in the 1940s, it began collecting industry statistics and representing the industry on federal tax issues and state regulatory matters. In the late 1960s, when securities firms that distributed fund shares were experiencing back office problems, the association formed an operations department. In more recent years, the institute created pension and international units and established a captive industry insurance company, ICI Mutual Insurance Company, that provides fidelity bond, directors and officers, and errors and omissions insurance to mutual fund firms. The latest expansion was the establishment of a director services committee, which has become the Independent Directors Council, representing the interests of independent fund directors.

Speaking with One Voice

From the very start, the goal of industry leaders has been to have all industry participants join the association so that the industry can speak with one voice. The industry has been quite successful in meeting this goal. Today, institute members manage 98 percent of total mutual fund assets. Whereas many industries have multiple trade associations that typically spend a good deal of time and effort fighting each other, the mutual fund industry is blessed by having a single association. Certainly there are sharp differences of opinion among members, and fighting goes on, but controversy takes place inside the tent, making it far easier to achieve consensus than would be the case if there were separate, warring associations. There always has been potential for schisms and civil wars. It has taken hard work, good will, and a spirit of compromise to keep the industry together.

The association's original members were closed-end funds and mutual funds. These groups were long-standing rivals. Therefore, for many years the association's executive committee rotated its meetings between the ancestral homes of the two groups, New York and Boston. When I joined the institute in 1971, load and no-load groups viewed each other with a good deal of suspicion. Problems eased as the line between the two types of funds became increasingly blurred.

In the late 1960s, insurance companies became the first "outsiders" to enter the mutual fund business. There had been a long and acrimonious battle between the SEC and the fund industry, on one hand, and the insurance industry, on the other, as to whether the insurance industry's new product, variable annuities, should be required to register with the SEC. The SEC and the fund industry prevailed, and feelings remained frayed. To keep things calm, insurance companies brought their retail mutual funds into membership in the institute, but for many years, the institute's by-laws did not require variable annuity funds to be members. That exception has been removed, so that today almost all insurance company funds of all types are members of the association.

Securities firms entered the mutual fund business in the late 1970s, and banks entered in the 1980s. Securities firms and their funds joined the institute without much fuss. Indeed, many firms hired executives from the mutual fund industry to head their fund units, such as Arthur Zeikel at Merrill Lynch and Charles Fiumefreddo at Dean Witter. However, banks were a different story. When I became president of the institute in 1991, banks, over the institute's strenuous objections, had gained entry into the mutual fund industry through a series of judicial decisions.

Banks managed something on the order of 10 percent of total mutual fund assets, but because of the long and bitter battle over their entry, few banks and bank-managed funds were members of the association. I made it one of my priorities as the new president to have banks and their funds join the institute so that the entire fund industry could speak with one voice. I personally visited numerous banks around the country and told my assistant to accept every invitation for me to speak at banking conferences. On March 25, 1993, I spoke at a conference in New York run by the Bank and Financial Analysts Association. After my talk, I went to the speakers' lounge, took off my name badge, and poured myself a cup of coffee. An older gentleman approached me and said how much he had enjoyed my talk. I thanked him, and he said, "I am so God-damned sick and tired of those people at the Investment Company Institute constantly maligning banks and bankers." I replied, "Oh, you must be referring to my predecessor, David Silver." He said, "No, I mean that son of a bitch Matt Fink." It was clear he had no idea who I was. I muttered something like "Oh, that guy," and snuck off.

These recruiting efforts paid off. During the 1990s, just about every bank that managed mutual funds joined the institute. This near-universal membership proved to be of immense help when Congress considered legislation to formally grant banks full mutual fund powers. An institute task force representing both bank and nonbank members developed a number of provisions that were incorporated in the final legislation.

I am often asked whether the change from an industry consisting almost entirely of mutual fund–only firms to one in which insurance companies, securities firms, banks, industrial companies, and foreign firms play major roles has made it more difficult for the institute to achieve consensus. On the whole, this diversity has not been a problem. The vast majority of legislative and regulatory issues impact funds the same way, regardless of the type of sponsor. In most cases, differences of opinion reflect individual firm positions. Indeed, often the sharpest splits have occur between firms that have very similar business models and markets. (During the height of the money market fund boom, it felt as though Dreyfus and Fidelity disagreed on every issue.)

On rare occasions, issues have raised the potential for schisms between the industry generally and particular types of sponsors. But splits have been avoided because both sides have viewed the issue from the mutual fund perspective. For example, the institute consistently has urged legislation to require bank collective funds and insurance company separate accounts sold to 401(k) plan participants to register with the SEC. In the early 1980s, one of the insurance industry trade associations urged its members who were also members of the institute to "call Dave Silver and Matt Fink and tell them to cut it out." We received calls from three insurance company executives who headed their firms' mutual fund units. All three urged us to *continue* the effort.

Another example involved securities firms. In April 1999, I attended a luncheon meeting of the Exchequer Club, an organization of lobbyists and attorneys who work in the financial services area. At the luncheon, a lobbyist for the trade association of securities broker-dealers, the Securities Industry Association (SIA), mentioned to me in passing that the SIA recently had sent a letter to the Senate Banking Committee that might be of possible interest to investment advisers. I asked him to messenger a copy to me, which he did that afternoon. I was standing as I casually flipped through the letter and almost fell down when I saw that it called for legislation to effectively repeal section 17(a) of the Investment Company Act, a key provision that prohibits dumping (i.e., an adviser selling securities to its fund). The letter had been sent a number of days earlier. We were unable to learn that day if the SIA had already launched a major drive to have such a provision included in the securities bill then being drafted. I concluded that the institute had to act forcefully and quickly to prevent this from occurring. That same afternoon I contacted the institute's executive committee to recommend that we take immediate action. I warned that if the SIA's letter represented the views of securities firms generally, aggressive action by the institute could cause a number of members to resign from the association. The unanimous view of the executive committee, including several members from leading securities firms, was to proceed regardless. I sent a tough letter to the SIA calling for withdrawal of the proposal and provided copies to the SEC and the media. The SEC and the press blasted the proposal, and it was withdrawn.[1] We subsequently learned that a major securities firm, frustrated with the slow pace of the SEC's exemptive process on a technical section 17(a) issue, had persuaded the SIA to call for repeal of the section.

The key to reaching consensus at the institute remains the willingness of participants to hear one another's views and compromise for the common good. The central decision maker is the executive committee of the institute's board of governors. Benjamin Korschot, a former chairman of the institute's board, has written: "Since there are thousands of mutual fund management companies, one of the great achievements of the ICI has been the ability to work, in an unbelievably effective manner, in leading the industry to decisions, where the ICI could speak as one voice for the industry. Much of the credit for this goes to the power that the board of governors has delegated to the executive committee."[2]

The executive committee is charged with representing the long-term best interests of fund shareholders and the industry as a whole, and putting aside the short-term business interests of individual institute members. During my time at the institute there were numerous occasions when the committee supported measures (for example, the code of ethics on personal investing, requiring funds to have chief compliance officers, tightening money market fund rule 2a-7, the yield formula for bond funds) that likely were opposed by many, if not most, members. Dave Silver remarked that executive committee members often must have left meetings wondering how they would justify decisions to their colleagues when they got back to their offices. On several occasions following decisions by the executive committee, I received angry calls and e-mails from members complaining that decisions were harmful to their firms. I delighted in telling them that their bosses were members of the executive committee and had supported the decisions in the interest of the industry as a whole.

The one action by an institute member that is certain to produce unanimity by other members is the threat to quit the institute if the member doesn't get its way. I recall a debate at an institute board meeting as to whether the institute should oppose the SEC's proposal to exempt a new insurance product, variable life insurance, from regulation. One governor indicated that his firm, which was owned by an insurance company, would resign from membership if the institute opposed the SEC's position. Another governor, Justin Dunn of Axe-Houghton, usually said very little at board meetings. This time he spoke up and said something like, "I knew Franklin Roosevelt. I hated Franklin Roosevelt. I hate the entire New Deal. I wouldn't wish the imposition of the Investment Company Act on my worst enemy. But when someone holds a gun to my head, I have only one response. Go ahead. Quit." The board voted to have the institute oppose the SEC's position. The institute entered the proceeding, the SEC reversed itself, and variable life insurance had to register with the SEC. The insurance company did not resign from membership.

Support for Regulation

Although the scope of its activities and the types of members have expanded over time, the institute has continued to follow the course outlined by its first executive director, Paul Bartholet, and has supported pro-investor regulation. David Silver, the institute's president from 1977 to 1991, noted in an interview:

> The success of the Institute is very, very closely correlated with its ability to engage in the continuing dialogue with the SEC and other regulators…[a]s necessary and not starting from the proposition that the government is evil and therefore must be combated at every foxhole—"fight them in the streets and fight them in the hills" kind of thing. But with

the recognition that while government agencies may not be right, there is, most of the time, some reason they're acting the way that they're acting and therefore it is not only expedient but prudent to look at what the agency is saying while trying to satisfy a public need. And we've had our arguments and fights with the SEC over the years—sometimes public and sometimes not, but the Institute I think today has been fundamentally trusted by the SEC. When we say something there's a foundation underneath it.[3]

The institute also opposed unwise efforts at deregulation, even when deregulation was all the rage in Washington. As previously discussed, in 1992, the association successfully opposed efforts to repeal the anti-dumping provisions of the Investment Company Act, despite the fact that this could have alienated some large members. In 2003, the institute opposed proposals by a securities law professor and two SEC commissioners to change the securities laws to permit mutual funds to engage in hedge fund activities, such as the use of leverage, short selling, and asymmetrical performance-based advisory fees.[4]

The institute's unique attitude toward regulation has been noted by industry observers, consumer advocates, and regulators. In 1993, as commercial banks were entering the mutual fund business and becoming members of the institute, the *American Banker* warned, "Banks that join the Institute may be in for a bit of culture shock" due to the association's support for strict regulation. In 1995, a *New York Times* article on the institute quoted Barbara Roper, director of investor protection at the Consumer Federation of America, as saying, "Anything the I.C.I. says is treated like word from on high on Capitol Hill.... They are treated with a degree of respect that other groups don't necessarily have." In 1999, the *Financial Times* reported, "Widely respected for its behind-the-scenes, non-confrontational approach to its opponents, the industry has won support in Washington the quiet way. Even consumer groups— the traditional thorn in the side of the largest players in financial services—are unnervingly nice about mutual funds."[5]

In 2000, at the sixtieth anniversaries of the Investment Company Act and the institute, then SEC chairman Arthur Levitt stated:

> Tonight is also a celebration of cooperation—of a truly remarkable and longstanding partnership between the SEC and the ICI. Over the years, investors have reaped the benefits of this special alliance as it has worked to promote the investor interest and preserve the public trust....
>
> The partnership forged 60 years ago is alive and well today. The ICI and the Commission continue to work together towards making the mutual fund industry the most trusted, transparent, and respected in the world. Time and again, the ICI has supported laws and regulations designed to protect fund investors. It has established tough voluntary standards that go well beyond requirements of the law, creating best practices for personal investing and providing additional guidance for mutual fund directors.[6]

Criticisms

On the other hand, the institute has come in for its share of criticism. Though the association has often been praised for its close working relationship with the SEC, critics alleged that that relationship helped produce the 2003 late trading and market timing scandals. Thus the *New York Times* reported, "Critics and former [SEC] officials also say that the industry's trade organization, the Investment Company Institute, exerted enormous influence—both at the Commission and in Congress—in shaping what critics believe has been a lax set of policies that have further hampered enforcement efforts." Similarly, *Business Week* claimed that "a highly persuasive and aggressive trade association—of 400 fund complexes that make up the Investment Company Institute—for years overpowered or co-opted most attempts to tighten fund regulation."[7]

The institute certainly has made its share of mistakes, many under my leadership. But I find it Orwellian to see the institute criticized for allegedly "shaping...a lax set of policies" and co-opting "most attempts to tighten fund regulation." In fact, in the years leading up to the scandals, the institute repeatedly called for *increased* SEC regulation, in areas such as disclosure of shelf space, requiring mutual funds to have formal compliance systems, regulation of hedge funds and rating agencies, and providing mutual funds with additional tools to combat market timers. Moreover, when I read that some of the criticism comes from former officials at the SEC, an agency that the institute has supported through thick and thin, I am reminded of Harry Truman's advice: "You want a friend in Washington? Get a dog."

14

Looking Back and Ahead

There is no inevitability in history except as men make it.
—Felix Frankfurter

Looking Back

Congressman Ed Markey was correct when he called mutual funds "a genuine American success story." Mutual funds began as an unnoticed investment vehicle in the 1920s, weathered the Depression, and took off after World War II, only to be threatened with near extinction by the bear market of the 1970s. The industry rebounded by creating money market funds, and then myriad new types of funds and new ways to distribute shares to investors. Today, mutual funds are the principal means by which Americans save and invest for their futures.

Some of this success is attributable to external factors. Since 1940, financial markets generally have been positive: large company stocks have produced an average annual return of 10.9 percent, small company stocks 14.6 percent, and long-term corporate bonds 5.8 percent.[1] Investors who have been willing to take the long-term view and ride out the ups and downs of the financial markets have been amply rewarded for their patience. During this period, there also was a steady increase in the size of the American middle class, tens of millions of individuals and families with the need and the wherewithal to save for their first homes, their children's education, and their retirement years. Beginning in 1962, Congress enacted a series of laws that encouraged Americans to save and invest for their retirement. In addition, one of those laws, the Employee Retirement Income Security Act of 1974, was an unintended factor in the shift from defined benefit pension plans to defined contribution plans, plans where individuals make their own investment decisions.

These and other external factors benefited all types of investment vehicles and services, including mutual funds, brokerage accounts, individual investment advisory arrangements, bank trust departments, hedge funds, closed-end funds, and fixed-unit investment trusts. Yet mutual funds have been uniquely successful for several related reasons.

First, mutual funds have benefited from three of their most basic characteristics, characteristics that are so embedded in their DNA that we take them for granted.

1. Mutual funds' defining characteristic, daily redemptions and sales of new shares at current net asset value (NAV), prevents the development of premiums and discounts from actual portfolio values.

2. Federal tax law requires mutual funds to diversify their portfolios, thus imposing by statute the number one rule of prudent investing, "don't put all of your eggs in one basket."

3. The Investment Company Act severely limits mutual funds' use of leverage through borrowing. As John Kenneth Galbraith observed, all financial debacles can be traced to leverage.[2]

These very basic concepts—daily redemptions and sales at current NAV, diversification, and tight limits on borrowing—have kept mutual funds out of a good deal of trouble. The experiences of go-go funds in the late 1960s, high-tech and telecommunication funds in the late 1990s, and stock funds generally in 2008 were bad enough. They would have been far worse had the funds traded at premiums-discounts, concentrated in a handful of stocks, and borrowed heavily. Just compare mutual funds' record in difficult times with that of employees of Enron and WorldCom, who loaded up their 401(k) plans with company stock, and with the recent problems encountered by highly leveraged hedge funds.

These unique attributes of mutual funds did not descend from the heavens. Each was due to the actions of specific individuals. In 1924, Edward G. Leffler came up with the concept of daily redemptions and sales at current NAV. In 1935, President Franklin Roosevelt declared that mutual funds must be diversified to receive favorable tax treatment. In 1940, the Securities and Exchange Commission (SEC) and industry representatives drafted the Investment Company Act to severely restrict borrowing.

Second, on top of these core principles are the numerous strictures of the Investment Company Act of 1940 that spell out standards of fiduciary behavior. At the same time, the 1940 act provides flexibility for change and innovation.

However, standing by itself, the act is just a collection of words. For the law to work, it must be administered in a wise but firm manner. I probably have written more words than anyone criticizing specific SEC actions and inactions in the mutual fund area. However, I also have repeatedly stated that on the whole, the SEC has done an excellent job in breathing life into the 1940 act, to the great benefit of mutual funds and their shareholders. My four decades in Washington convince me that a regulated industry suffers when its governing statutes, regulations, and regulators seek to protect the industry rather its customers. The decline of the banking industry and the demise of the savings and loan industry offer graphic examples. The mutual fund industry needs an SEC that is focused aggressively on investor protection and is not bent on seeking to help the mutual fund industry. The fund industry pays the price when, in New York State Attorney General Eliot Spitzer's words, the SEC is "asleep at the switch." For this reason, the mutual fund industry consistently has supported a well-funded, well-staffed SEC and repeatedly has opposed efforts to fragment regulatory authority among the commission and other regulators, to move from the SEC regime of investor protection regulation to bank-type safety and soundness regulation, and to replace direct SEC oversight of mutual funds with industry self-regulation.

The mutual fund laws and regulations administered by the SEC are extensive, but they cannot possibly address every situation. By its very nature, law always plays catch-up. Most issues that fund officials face have no clear answer in law. In fact, overconcentration on law and regulation can impair decision making. Kathryn McGrath, former director of the SEC Division of Investment Management, put it well: "More rules don't necessarily make for better results. Each new proposal, each legislative proposal standing alone, seems to have a good idea behind it. But I worry that the cumulative effect...is going to impair the ability of people in the business to sit back and think about whether what they're doing is right."[3] A fiduciary's primary obligation is not to become expert in law, but rather is *always* to do what is right for beneficiaries. As Supreme Court Justice William O. Douglas stated: "Service to stockholders cannot be a passive thing. It is not something to be rendered with the lips. It calls for constant diligence and tireless devotion to the standards of fiduciary responsibility."[4]

I am clearly a biased observer, but looking back over the past seventy years, I believe that on the whole, mutual fund managers have acquitted themselves well in serving their beneficiaries, mutual fund shareholders. There have been lapses and mistakes, and the 2003 trading scandals gave the industry a terrible and deserved black eye. All in all, the fund industry has had quite a good record, certainly when compared with most other industries. This record, along with the unique attributes of mutual funds and the requirements of the Investment Company Act, has formed the underpinning of the industry's remarkable success since 1940.

Frequently Asked Questions

Since publication of the first edition, I have lectured on mutual fund history at over twenty venues, including think tanks, historical societies, universities, industry conferences, law firms, and mutual fund boards. Some of the most frequently asked questions about mutual fund history and my responses are as follows.

What was the most important event in mutual fund history? The Revenue Act of 1936, which provided favorable tax treatment for mutual funds, was the first time the federal government regulated funds, and was the critical factor that led Congress to enact the Investment Company Act of 1940.

What is the most important regulation governing mutual funds? Section 18 of the Investment Company, which severely limits mutual funds' use of leverage through borrowing. As John Kenneth Galbraith has observed, all financial debacles can be traced to excessive borrowing.

What was the most important innovation in fund history? The development of money market funds, which gave Americans market rates of return on their savings, provided the industry with millions of new shareholders, and led to the removal of interest rate ceilings on bank deposits.

Who was the most important figure in mutual fund history? I'd like to say Matt Fink, but beginning in 1924 there have been a series of key individuals, including Edward Leffler, Paul Cabot, Merrill Griswold, Jon Lovelace, Howard Stein, and Jack Bogle. If I had to name one individual in recent years, it would be Ned Johnson. Under his leadership Fidelity has introduced a long series of innovations, including check-writing on money market funds, tax-exempt money funds, and no-load tax-exempt funds. The industry is populated executives who got their start, and their training, at Fidelity under Ned Johnson.

What was the worst event in fund history? First prize must go to the deals fund executives cut with market timers, leading to the 2003 trading scandals, The runner-up is the 1970 Amendments to the Investment Company Act that sought to impose a form of rate regulation on the fund industry. We are still living with the consequences.

What event are you personally most proud of? It actually was a non-event—helping see to it that Congress did *not* enact punitive legislation in response to the 2003 trading scandals. At a time when the scandals had severely weakened the industry's credibility, I used all of the knowledge and experience I had gained over the past thirty-three years to help prevent enactment of legislation that would have commoditized, homogenized, and dumbed down the industry, to the great detriment of investors.

In the course of your research, what surprised you the most? Discovery of a 1937 internal SEC staff memorandum that confirmed my hypothesis that the Revenue Act of 1936 was the critical factor that led to the enactment of the Investment Company Act of 1940. The 1936 Act gave tax relief only to mutual funds, and not to closed-end funds. The memorandum made it clear that the SEC would block legislation extending tax relief to closed-end funds unless they agreed to the Investment Company Act.

Looking Ahead

Prophecy is a risky business, as evidenced by the numerous incorrect predictions (set forth in the introduction) that have been made about mutual funds over the years.

Obviously, much of mutual funds' future will depend on external factors, including the markets, government policies, and competing products.

As previous chapters have indicated, bull and bear periods in the securities markets, and in the fund industry, tend to run for long stretches of time, usually well over a decade. The period 1940–68 was positive, the years 1968–82 negative, and the period 1982–2000 spectacular. History indicates that the bear market that began in 2000 still has a way to run.

Prophecy is particularly dicey when it comes to government policies. In 1940, everyone predicted that the Investment Company Act would *not* be enacted. In 1974, no one guessed that ERISA would prove to be so detrimental to defined benefit plans. In 1978, no one forecast the phenomenal growth of 401(k) plans. Following the 2003 trading scandals, many predicted that Congress would enact punitive legislation.

Therefore it is with some hesitation that I offer predictions in three areas. First, my belief, and certainly my hope, is that at long last the United States will address the run away federal deficit. This will require curtailment of government entitlement programs, making private saving even more important than today, thus spurring investment in mutual funds. Second, the industry's future success will depend on the SEC's ability to act as the investor's advocate. The SEC's once stellar reputation has diminished a good deal. No one is better equipped by both experience and temperment to lead the SEC's renaissance than its new chair, Mary Schapiro. I believe that she will succeed. Finally, the greatest threat to mutual funds, and to economy as a whole, will come from the misguided attempt to institutionalize a too-big-to-fail regulatory regime. As discussed in chapter 12, a financial system based on the principle of "all power to regulators" is likely to fail just when needed—in a financial crisis. A far better approach would be to limit the size and activities of financial firms so that none is too big to fail. But that approach appears to be off the table. As a result of the increased size and complexity of financial conglomerates and a commitment to a super-regulatory approach, I fear that the next financial crisis is likely to be even worse than the 2008 meltdown.

I believe that mutual funds remain by far the best way for the vast majority of Americans to achieve their financial goals. (For what it's worth, I have literally put my money where my mouth is. Aside from fixed annuities that were part of my retirement package, all of my own financial assets consist of mutual funds.) There are a number of financial products that compete with mutual funds. Someone is always claiming that one of them is superior to mutual funds and soon will be eating funds' lunch.

It is beyond the scope of this book to fully contrast and compare these products (including separately managed accounts, bank collective funds, hedge funds, and exchange-traded funds) with mutual funds. I simply note that none of them possesses all of the core attributes of mutual funds (e.g., daily redemptions and sales at current NAV, required diversification, strict limits on borrowing, SEC-mandated disclosure). For this reason, my guess is that none of them will overtake mutual funds.

For example, the recent unhappy experiences of numerous hedge funds vividly demonstrate the dangers of unlimited leverage. Proponents of exchange-traded funds initially maintained that ETFs, like mutual funds, would trade at (or at least near) their current net asset values. But a series of articles indicate that many ETFs, like closed-end funds, trade at substantial discounts.[5] Someday someone may invent a better personal financial mousetrap. But I've yet to see it.

In recent years, the mutual fund industry has become somewhat more concentrated, but it remains a highly competitive, fragmented business with low barriers to entry.[6] The regulatory regime is not designed to protect industry participants. Over the years, different mutual fund firms have been the biggest players. For years, the giant was the nation's first mutual fund, Massachusetts Investors Trust. Then came the rise of the direct marketers, IDS and Waddell & Reed. Next was the turn of the large money market fund groups—Dreyfus, Federated, Fidelity, and Merrill Lynch. Today, the big three are American Funds, Fidelity, and Vanguard. The top ten, twenty, and fifty firms are in constant flux. Some of the once largest and best-known groups, such as Calvin Bullock, Citigroup, Hugh W. Long, J. and W. Seligman, Merrill Lynch, Scudder, Stevens & Clark, and State Street Research are no longer in the mutual fund business or in business at all.

Competition has produced constant innovation. The fund industry is so young that we can still meet the individuals who came up with specific innovations. Bruce Bent, Jim Benham, and the late Harry Brown invented the money market fund. Ned Johnson added check writing. Stan Judd thought of a way funds could legally advertise. Dave Silver conceived of the universal IRA. Jack Bogle introduced index funds. Given the openness of the fund industry and the flexible nature of its regulatory regime, I see no reason why such innovation should not continue.

One important contributor to the industry s success has been the unusual role played by its trade association, the Investment Company Institute. The institute is unique among trade groups in that it was created, at the suggestion of regulators, to assist them in supervising the industry. Despite ups and downs over the decades, the association generally has continued to play a constructive role. It is easy for a trade association to advocate positions that provide short-term benefits to its members. I've done that. It's easy for an association to complain about government policies. I've done that too, on countless occasions. But it is extremely unusual for an association to support government actions that are painful to its dues-paying members. It is even more unusual for an association to *initiate* laws, regulations, and private actions that constrain its members. The institute has done so numerous times in order to advance the long-term best interests of fund shareholders. There is no reason that the institute cannot continue to do so. A telltale will be how often members of the executive committee leave committee meetings wondering how they will explain the committee's decisions, which will be painful to fund sponsors in the short-term, to their colleagues back home.

But the institute, like the SEC and other regulators, is not omnipresent. My bet is that the industry's future, like its past, largely will turn on the internal workings of the industry, specifically on the willingness of individual fund officers, employees, and directors to act as fiduciaries, with an eye single on the best interests of fund shareholders. Since retiring as president of the Investment Company Institute in 2004, I have kept up with the industry. I lecture on fund history at industry conferences and fund board meetings. I am a member of FINRA's Investment Companies Committee. I serve as an independent director of a family of mutual funds. I regularly see officials and directors at many other fund groups. I am impressed by their commitment to not just following law and regulation, but to doing the right thing for fund shareholders, particularly by their determination never to allow a situation like the fund trading abuses to occur again.

One incident has given me pause. In December 2005, I participated on a roundtable of mutual fund directors on the issue of whether mutual fund governance is different from corporate board governance. I was asked to kick off the discussion. I did so by expressing my opinion that mutual fund governance is very distinct in that the primary role of fund directors is overseeing compliance with law and fiduciary standards. Thomas A. Theobold, a trustee of the Columbia Group of mutual funds, disagreed with my position, stating: "There's nothing unique about a mutual fund board versus a window company board. It's understanding the business and doing your very best and acting in the right way....I'd say 95 percent of the job either is having some influence on investment management results or on costs. That's where we as trustees can be most effective. Hopefully, with all of the compliance mechanisms now in place, we need not spend more time than is necessary on compliance."[7] I replied at length:

> This is where I disagree with Tom. We are not like his hypothetical window company. Mutual funds are not like other businesses. This is a fiduciary business. Our shareholders are not people on the other side of transactions. We and the management company are trustees to those people. They're like widows and orphans. Therefore, the independent directors' role is to make sure that the fund management company acts as a fiduciary. The key to being a fiduciary is that the beneficiary's interests must come ahead of your own. That's the only test. In most other businesses, if somebody said "if you let me do a little trading or market timing in fund A, I will put a ton of assets in fund B," that would be considered a great business deal, right? The trouble is, in the course of that you're injuring...[the beneficiaries] in fund A. If anything, that's where the troubles happened! Directors of a mutual fund have a unique role in a unique governance context.[8]

I left the roundtable quite concerned about the future of the mutual fund industry. If many fund directors and management company officials believe that ensuring compliance with fiduciary standards is not their number one priority, the industry is in for some very rough times. There will be numerous ethical if not legal violations, resulting in draconian legislation that will make Senator Peter Fitzgerald's 2003 bill look mild by comparison. The industry will be homogenized, commoditized, and dumbed down, all to the detriment of fund shareholders. On the other hand, if industry participants strive to act as fiduciaries, the industry and fund shareholders will do well. The industry's future is in its own hands.

I have a well-deserved reputation as a worrier; nonetheless, I am optimistic. As I hope this book has demonstrated, the

"Faith, hope, spiritual peace of mind ...
That's what mutual funds are all about."

Figure 14.1. Copyright 1993 Tribune Media Services, Inc. All rights reserved. Reprinted with permission.

extraordinary success of mutual funds has been due to many factors. The key has been the understanding of industry participants that they are engaged in an endeavor where success depends on adherence to high standards of fiduciary behavior. I am further comforted by the fact that experts continue to declare that the mutual fund industry is fully mature and is about to be overtaken by competitors. I wouldn't count on it.

In sum, as an expert worrier, my concern is far less about the mutual fund industry than about the overall financial system.

Notes

Introduction

1. Over the years, different numbers have been offered as to the size of the mutual fund industry in 1940. See Natalie R. Grow, "The 'Boston-Type Open-End Fund'—Development of a National Financial Institution: 1924–1940," doctoral thesis, Harvard University, 1977, 410, 602, and 630. For many years, the Investment Company Institute has reported that at year end 1940 mutual fund assets amounted to $450 million, which is the generally accepted number.

2. The various predictions are from William D. Carter, "Mutual Investment Funds," *Harvard Business Review*, 27, no. 6 (November 1949): 716; "What Ails the Mutual Fund Industry," *Business Week* (March 3, 1973): 47; speeches of Marshall and Porter in the files of the Investment Company Institute; Jaime Punishell, Ron Shevlin, and Tom Watson, "The End of Mutual Fund Dominance," Forrester Research, December 8, 2000; *Red Herring*, "The Death of Mutual Funds," August 31, 2000, from http://www.redherring.com/Home/268; and *Financial News Online*, "Mutual funds in peril, study says," December 24, 2008, from http://www.medvedhost.info/2008/12/24.

3. Hugh Bullock, *The Story of Investment Companies* (New York: Columbia University Press, 1959).

4. The history and misuse of the term *investment trust* are discussed in William Howard Steiner, *Investment Trusts: American Experience* (New York: Adelphi, 1929), 4–5; Theodore J. Grayson, *Investment Trusts: Their Origin, Development, and Operation* (New York: John Wiley, 1928), 1–2; and John Francis Fowler Jr., *American Investment Trusts* (New York: Harper & Brothers, 1928), 1–2.

Chapter 1

1. Brussels is cited by Grow, "'Boston-Type Open-End Fund,'" 16; Bullock, *Story of Investment Companies*, 1; Steiner, *Investment Trusts*, 17; and Grayson, *Investment Trusts*, 11. The claim for Amsterdam is made in K. Geert Rouwenhorst, "The Origins of Mutual Funds," Yale International Center for Finance Working Paper no. 04–48 (December 12, 2004). John T. Flynn, *Investment Trusts Gone Wrong!* (New York: New Republic, 1930), 14, defines an investment trust as "an association—incorporated or voluntary—in which a number of persons pool their funds primarily for investment in securities."

2. Marshall H. Williams, *Investment Trusts in America* (New York: Macmillan, 1928), 22–23.

3. H. Burton and D. C. Corner, *Investment and Unit Trusts in Britain and America* (London: Elek Books, 1968), 28–44.

4. John Kenneth Galbraith, *The Great Crash: 1929* (1954; rpt., Boston: Houghton Mifflin, 1997), 54.

5. Max Rottersman and Jason Zweig, "An Early History of Mutual Funds," *Friends of Financial History*, 51 (Spring 1994): 14.

6. Galbraith, *The Great Crash*, 57.

7. Robert Sobel, *The Great Bull Market: Wall Street in the 1920s* (New York: Norton, 1968), 92.

8. U.S. Securities and Exchange Commission, *Investment Trusts and Investment Companies, 1939–1942* (Washington, DC: SEC), part III, chap. 1, 4.

9. Twentieth Century Fund, *The Security Markets: Findings and Recommendations of a Special Staff of the Twentieth Century Fund* (New York: Twentieth Century Fund, 1935), 196; Luther Harr and W. Carlton Harris, *Banking Theory and Practice* (New York: McGraw-Hill, 1930), 487; Steiner, *Investment Trusts*, 122–23; Grayson, *Investment Trusts*, 190–91; Fowler, *American Investment Trusts*, 154–56: and Leland Rex Robinson, *Investment Trust Organization and Management* (New York: Ronald Press, 1926), 345.

10. Leffler is discussed in H. Lee Silberman, *50 Years of Trust: Massachusetts Investors Trust 1924–1974* (Boston: Massachusetts Financial Services, 1974), 9. The history of the first three mutual funds is set forth in Grow, "'Boston-Type Open-End Fund,'" 46–178.

11. Michael R. Yogg, *Passion for Reality: Paul Cabot and the Boston Mutual Fund* (Xlibris, 2006), 45.

12. Ibid., 56.

13. Paul C. Cabot, "The Investment Trust," *Atlantic Monthly* (March 1929): 401–408.

14. Griswold and the Boston press are discussed in Silberman, *50 Years of Trust*: 18. Cabot is quoted in Yogg, *Passion for Reality*, 52.

15. Grow, "'Boston-Type Open-End Fund,'" 116–20.

16. Burton and Corner, *Investment and Unit Trusts*, 205.

17. Bullock, *Story of Investment Companies*, 29

18. Cabot, "The Investment Trust," 402.

19. Fowler, *American Investment Trusts*, 231.

20. George V. McLaughlin, *Proceedings of the Twenty-Seventh Annual Convention of the National Association of Supervisors of State Banks* (July, 25, 1928), 46. The discussion of constitutionality and the unlikelihood of federal action are discussed in Fowler, *American Investment Trusts*, 236.

21. Bullock, *Story of Investment Companies*, 43–44.

22. Grow, "'Boston-Type Open-End Fund,'" 245.

23. Edward Angly, *Oh Yeah?* (1931; rpt., Burlington, VT: Fraser, 1988), 37.

24. SEC, *Investment Trusts*, part II, chap. 4, 276.

25. Ibid., part III, chap. 4, 1021.

26. Bullock, *Story of Investment Companies*, 62–65.

27. Burton and Corner, *Investment and Unit Trusts*, 207–208.

28. The figures are from Grow, "'Boston-Type Open-End Fund,'" 410, with the mutual fund asset number in 1940 reduced from $532 million to the now accepted $450 million number. See note 1 in the introduction.

29. Flynn's initial suggestions are set forth in Flynn, *Investment Trusts Gone Wrong!* 65–66 and 189–93. His subsequent proposals are contained in John T. Flynn, *Graft in Business* (New York: Vanguard Press, 1931), 303–304.

30. Felix I. Shaffner, *The Problem of Investment* (New York: John Wiley, 1936), 75. Frank A. Vanderlip, *Tomorrow's Money* (New York: Reynal & Hitchcock, 1934), 191. Barnie F. Winkelman, *Ten Years of Wall Street* (1932; rpt., Burlington, VT: Fraser Publishing, 1987), 192–93.

31. William O. Douglas, *Go East Young Man: The Early Years; The Autobiography of William O. Douglas* (New York: Random House, 1974), 297 and 269.

32. James M. Landis, *The Administrative Process* (New Haven, CT: Yale University Press, 1938), 27.

33. U.S. House, *Report of the Committee Appointed Pursuant to House Resolutions 429 and 504 to Investigate the Concentration of Control of Money and Credit*, 1913, 62d Cong., 3d sess., 119–27 and 162–63.

34. Vincent P. Carosso, *Investment Banking in America: A History* (Cambridge, MA: Harvard University Press, 1970), 176.

35. A. Newton Plummer, *The Great American Swindle Incorporated* (New York: A. Newton Plummer, 1932), 313. Raymond Moley, *The First New Deal* (New York: Harcourt, Brace & World, 1966), 307.

36. Moley, *The First New Deal*, 310. The development and enactment of the 1933 act are discussed in Moley, *The First New Deal*, 310–15; Joel Seligman, *The Transformation of Wall Street: A History of the Securities and Exchange Commission and Modern Corporate Finance*, 3rd ed. (New York: Aspen, 2003), 39–72; Michael E. Parrish, *Securities Regulation and the New Deal* (New Haven, CT: Yale University Press, 1970), 42–72; and Ralph F. de Bedts, *The New*

Deal's SEC: The Formative Years (New York: Columbia University Press, 1964), 30–55.

37. Parrish, *Securities Regulation*, 114. The development and enactment of the 1934 act are discussed in Seligman, *Transformation of Wall Street*, 73–100; Parrish, *Securities Regulation*, 108–44; and de Bedts, *The New Deal's SEC*, 56–85.

38. Seligman, *Transformation of Wall Street*, 98–99.

39. Parrish *Securities Regulation*, 129.

40. Matthew P. Fink, "The Strange Birth of the SEC," *Financial History*, 86 (Summer 2006): 16–19.

41. Grow, "'Boston-Type Open-End Fund,'" 446 and 450.

42. Ibid., 452.

43. Merrill Griswold, "Taxation of Investment Companies and Their Shareholders," typed paper labeled "11th Draft, January 6, 1958," 13, in files of Massachusetts Financial Services.

44. Grow, "'Boston-Type Open-End Fund,'" 454–58.

45. The White House meeting is described in a number of works, including Griswold, "Taxation of Investment Companies," 16; Edwin S. Cohen, *A Lawyer's Life: Deep in the Heart of Taxes* (Arlington, VA: Tax Analysts, 1994), 136–37; and Yogg, *Passion for Reality*, 91–93.

46. "Tax Law Means Change for Many Investing Trusts," *Wall Street Journal*, June 30, 1936. For a discussion of New Deal policy goals and their impact on the Revenue Act of 1936 and the Investment Company Act of 1940, see Mark J. Roe, "Political Elements in the Creation of a Mutual Fund Industry," *University of Pennsylvania Law Review*, 139, no. 6 (June 1991): 1469–511.

47. Griswold, *Taxation of Investment Companies*, 3.

48. Ibid.

49. The issue of whether mutual funds intentionally froze out closed-end funds in their discussions with administration and congressional officials leading to the Revenue Act of 1936 has been debated over the past seventy years. See Griswold, *Taxation of Investment Companies*, 17–18; Grow, "'Boston-Type Open-End Fund,'" 458–69; Diana B. Henriques, *Fidelity's World: The Secret Life and Public Power of the Mutual Fund Giant* (New York: Scribner's, 1995), 90–91; and Yogg, *Passion for Reality*, 91. It appears that mutual funds did work to prevent closed-end funds from becoming involved. However, it also appears likely that had closed-end funds become involved, they would not have been included in the legislation. Closed-end funds had been the predominant investment companies and the source of greatest abuse in the 1920s, and it is doubtful whether Congress would have granted them special tax treatment. Moreover, it is likely that had closed-end funds become involved, there would not have been any legislation, even legislation confined solely to mutual funds.

Chapter 2

1. "Investment Trust Law Unlikely This Year," *Barron's*, March 18, 1940, 9. John W. Crider, "SEC Reaches Out for Wider Power," *New York Times*, March 24, 1940.

2. "Chances of Regulatory Legislation This Session Fade Still Further," *Wall Street Journal*, April 27, 1940.

3. A *New York Times* editorial stated that "investment trusts seriously need regulation" but criticized the SEC's bill. Editorial, "Investment Trust Control," *New York Times*, April 27, 1940.

4. Groh, " 'Boston-Type Open-End Fund,' " 516.

5. Dwight P. Robinson Jr., *Massachusetts Investors Trust: Pioneer in Open-End Investment Trusts* (New York: Newcomen Society in North America, 1954), 17. "The Prudent Man," *Time*, June 1, 1959, 75.

6. Fred Schwed Jr., *Where Are the Customers' Yachts? Or, a Good Hard Look at Wall Street* (New York: Simon and Schuster, 1940), 98. Percentages are based on the closed-end and mutual fund asset numbers in Groh, " 'Boston-Type Open-End' Fund,' " 410, with the mutual fund asset number in 1940 reduced from $532 million to the now accepted $450 million number.

7. Statement of Raymond D. McGrath, Executive Vice President, General American Investors Co., *Investment Trusts and Investment Companies,* Hearings, Senate Banking Subcommittee, 76th Cong., 3d sess., 1940 (hereafter, *Senate Hearings*), 440.

8. Statement of Raymond D. McGrath, Executive Vice President, General American Investors Co., *Senate Hearings,* 440. Statement of Alfred Jaretzki Jr., Partner, Sullivan & Cromwell. *Investment Trusts and Investment Companies*, Hearings, House Commerce Subcommittee, 76th Cong., 3d sess., 1940 (hereafter, *House Hearings*), 117.

9. R. W. Goldschmidt, "Taxation of Investment Companies," typed memorandum, October 26, 1937, to Paul B. Gourrich, in files of the SEC.

10. Framework of Proposed Investment Company Bill (Title I) Embodying Suggestions Resulting from Conferences Between Securities and Exchange Commission and Representatives of Investment Companies, *House Hearings*, 98.

11. Senate Report no. 1775 to Accompany S. 4108, 76th Cong., 3d sess., 1940, 12. The report of the House Committee on Interstate and Foreign Commerce contained similar language. House Report no. 2639 to Accompany H.R. 10065, 76th Cong., 3d sess.,1940, 10.

12. *Senate Hearings*, 1130. Leslie Gould, "Schenker Dinner Harmony Example for Wall St.," *New York Journal American*, July 3, 1941.

13. Louis D. Brandeis, *Other People's Money and How the Bankers Use It* (New York: Frederick A. Stokes, 1913), 162–88. Irving Fisher, *The Stock Market Crash—And After* (New York: Macmillan, 1930), xii.

14. Statement of David Schenker, *Senate Hearings*, 247.

15. Statement of Merrill Griswold, Chairman, Massachusetts Investors Trust, *Senate Hearings*, 496.

16. *Time*, "The Prudent Man," 75. L. Douglas Meredith, *Life Insurance versus the Ups and Downs of Mutual Funds* (Montpelier, VT: National Life Insurance, 1960), 15. Henry Kaufman, "Structural Changes in the Financial Markets: Economic and Policy Significance," *Economic Review*, Federal Reserve Bank of Kansas City (Second Quarter 1994): 5–15.

17. Statement of David Schenker, *Senate Hearings*, 227.

18. Statement of Robert S. Adler, President and Director, Selected American Shares, *Senate Hearings*, 539.

19. Timothy Peter Ansberry, "Investment Company Act of 1940," *Georgetown Law Journal*, 29, no. 5 (February 1941): 626.

20. *Senate Hearings*, 477.

21. Ibid., 1113.

22. Roe, *Political Elements*, 1489; emphasis added.

23. Murray L. Simpson and Scott Hodes, "The Continuing Controversy Surrounding the Uniform Price Maintenance Provisions of the Investment Company Act of 1940," *Notre Dame Lawyer*, 44, no. 5 (June 1969): 719.

24. Division of Investment Management, U.S. Securities and Exchange Commission, *Protecting Investors: A Half Century of Investment Company Regulation* (Washington, DC: Government Printing Office, May 1992), 298–315.

25. William A. Campbell, "The Investment Act of 1940: 'Reasonable and Intelligent,'" *Friends of Financial History* 52 (Fall 1954): 14.

26. Statement of Cyril J. C. Quinn, Vice President, Tri-Continental Corporation and Partner of J. & W. Seligman & Co., *Senate Hearings*, 441–50.

27. U.S. General Accounting Office, *Long-Term Capital Management: Regulators Need to Focus Greater Attention on Systemic Risk* (Washington, DC: Government Printing Office, October 1999), 7.

28. Alfred Jaretzki Jr., "The Investment Company Act of 1940," *Washington University Law Quarterly*, 26, no. 3 (April 1941): 346.

29. Ibid., 344.

30. Ibid., 345.

31. The New York meetings are discussed in Fowler, *American Investment Trusts*, 238–39. The writer urging formation of an association was Steiner, *Investment Trusts*, 304–305.

32. "Rounding Out the SEC," Editorial, *Wall Street Journal*, September 23, 1938. "Trusts Outline Own Regulation Bill," *Business Week* (May 4, 1940): 15.

33. "From Our Washington Correspondent," *FundScope*, 13, no. 3 (March 1970): 27. Schenker is quoted in Grow, "'Boston-Type Open-End Fund,'" 545.

34. Letter dated September 9, 1941, from Paul Bartholet, Executive Director, National Committee of Investment Companies, to Walter L. Morgan, in files of the Investment Company Institute.

35. Paul Bartholet, "Investment Companies and Their Regulation," *Blue Sky News* (December 1942): 5 and 7.

36. Ibid., 7.

37. Letter dated November 27, 1942, from James H. Orr to Harry S. Middendorf, in files of the Investment Company Institute.

38. The origins and nature of the various funds in existence in 1940, in addition to the three original funds, are discussed in Grow, "'Boston-Type Open-End Fund,'" 125–29, 302–18, and 409–22.

39. *The History of Scudder, Stevens & Clark* (Boston: Scudder, Stevens & Clark, 1994), 39 and 61.

40. Arthur Wiesenberger, *Investment Companies and Their Securities: 1942 Edition* (New York: Arthur Wiesenberger, 1942), 1.

Chapter 3

1. *House Hearings*, 144.

2. Industry assets are from Investment Company Institute, *2007 Investment Company Fact Book* (Washington, DC: Investment Company Institute, 2007), 93. Other statistics were provided by the Research Department of the Investment Company Institute.

3. Harry A. McDonald, "The S.E.C. Looks at Mutual Funds," speech, First Annual Mutual Fund Conference, New York, August 18, 1949. Bullock, *Story of Investment Companies*, 97. *Time,* "The Prudent Man," 74.

4. Morningstar, *Stocks, Bonds, Bills, and Inflation: 2007 Yearbook* (Chicago: Morningstar, 2007), 286 and 292. Paul Bartholet, "Investment Funds' Second Decade Lays Foundation for Sound Growth," *Investment Dealers' Digest*, May 28, 1945, 75. Hugh Bullock, "The Investment Company in 1945," speech, Twenty-Eighth Annual Convention of the National Association of Securities Commissioners, Chicago, November 17, 1945.

5. Figures for 1940 are from a list of funds presented by Mahlon A. Traylor, President, Massachusetts Distributors, *Senate Hearings*, 459–61. 1958 figures are from Bullock, *Story of Investment Companies*, 156–59.

6. Bullock, *Story of Investment Companies*, 156–59.

7. IDS Financial Services, *Investing in the Future: A Century of IDS* (Minneapolis: Investors Diversified Services, 1994), 63.

8. Sales information was provided by the Research Department of the Investment Company Institute.

9. Bullock, *Story of Investment Companies*, 156–59.

10. *Time,* "The Prudent Man," 74–75.

11. McDonald, "The SEC Looks at Mutual Funds."

12. Ibid., 80.

13. *Forbes,* "The Odd Couple," October 15, 1971, 83.

14. *Time,* "The Prudent Man," 80.

15. Meredith, *Life Insurance*, 7 and 16.

16. William C. Greenough, *It's My Retirement Money: Take Good Care of It; The TIAA-CREF Story* (Homewood, IL: Irwin, 1990), 79–128.

17. Ibid., 129–30.

18. Paul J. Mason and Stephen E. Roth, "SEC Regulation of Life Insurance Products—On the Brink of the Universal," *Connecticut Law Review*, 15, no. 3 (Spring 1983): 515–21.

19. *Business Week*, "Insurance Men Stick to Their Funds," November 21, 1970, 75. John C. Bogle, "Marketing Mutual Funds in the 1970's," in *How to Start, Operate & Manage Mutual Funds*, ed. Lucile Tomlinson (New York: President's Publishing House, 1971), 13.

20. The 3 percent approximation for funds started by insurance companies is based on the report in *Business Week*, "Insurance Men," 75, that *all* mutual funds managed by insurance companies accounted for 15 percent of fund industry assets, and the estimate in Bogle, "Marketing Mutual Funds," that funds *acquired by* insurance companies amounted to 12 percent of industry assets.

21. "Are They Compatible?" *Forbes*, August 15, 1969, 86.

22. Ibid., 91.

23. *Business Week*, "Insurance Men," 75.

24. Alan A. Thaler, "Life Insurance Sales of Investment Company Shares: A Survey," *Mutual Funds Forum*, April 1973, 6. *Forbes*, "The Odd Couple," 83.

25. *Forbes*, "The Odd Couple," 83.

26. Statistics were provided by the Membership Department of the Investment Company Institute.

27. Avi Nachmany, "Perspectives," *Windows into the Mutual Fund Industry* (February 2006): 2.

28. Investment Company Institute, *2007 Fact Book*, 93.

29. John Brooks, *The Go-Go Years: The Drama and Crashing Finale of Wall Street's Bullish 60s* (1973; rpt., New York: John Wiley, 1999), 127–28.

30. Henriques, *Fidelity's World*, 139.

31. Brooks, *The Go-Go Years*, 139.

32. Ibid.

33. Buffet's warnings are discussed in Maggie Mahar, *Bull! A History of the Boom and Bust: 1982–2004* (New York: HarpersBusiness, 2003), 38.

34. Donald C. Cook, "Recent Developments Concerning Mutual Funds," speech, Fourth Annual National Mutual Fund Conference, New York, September 17, 1952; Andrew Downey Orrick, "A Regulator Looks at the Mutual Fund Industry," speech, Ninth Annual Mutual Fund Conference, New York, October 2, 1957; and Allan A. Conwill, "The Minority Menace to Mutual Fund Selling," speech, New York Group of the Investment Bankers Association of America, Rye, April 23, 1963.

35. U.S. Securities and Exchange Commission, *Report of the Securities and Exchange Commission on the Public Policy Implications of Investment Company Growth,* House Report no. 2337, 89th Cong., 2d Sess. (1966), 224 and 225.

36. The creation of Vanguard is discussed in detail in Robert Slater, *John Bogle and the Vanguard Experiment: One Man's Quest to Transform the Mutual Fund Industry* (Chicago: Irwin, 1997).

37. Ibid., 26–27.

38. Ibid., 68.

39. Carter, "Mutual Investment Funds," 716. *Time,* "The Prudent Man," 75.

40. David Silver, "An Interview with David Silver," part 2, Virtual Museum and Archive of Securities and Exchange Commission and Securities Industry Historical Society, April 21, 2006, from http://www.sechistorical. org/museum/oralhistories/interviews/silver.php, 14; and Cook, "Recent Developments Concerning Mutual Funds."

41. Wharton School of Finance and Commerce, *A Study of Mutual Funds,* House Report no. 2274, 87th Cong., 2d sess. (1962), 3.

42. U.S. Securities and Exchange Commission, *Report of the Special Study of the Securities Markets of the U.S. Securities and Exchange Commission to the House Commerce Committee,* House Doc. no. 95, 88th Cong., 1st sess., part IV (1963), 169–212.

43. U.S. Securities and Exchange Commission, *Public Policy Implications of Investment Company Growth.*

44. Silver, "Edited Transcript," 21.

45. Gerard Manges, "The Investment Company Amendments Act of 1970: An Analysis and Appraisal after Two Years," *Boston College Industrial and Commercial Law Review,* 14, no. 3 (February 1973): 387.

46. John D. Rea and Brian K. Reid, "Trends in the Ownership Cost of Equity Mutual Funds," *Perspective,* 4, no. 3 (November 1998), 14.

47. The only extensive law review article on the 1970 amendments is Manges, "The Investment Company Amendments Act," which does not present the author's views. Seligman, *Transformation of Wall Street,* 363–82, discusses the history and provisions of the 1970 amendments, including his own criticisms and those of others.

48. Division of Investment Management, *Protecting Investors,* 291–346.

49. Seligman, *Transformation of Wall Street,* 382.

50. The exemptions are discussed in a number of works, including Mason and Roth, "SEC Regulation of Life Insurance Products," 522–27; Robert H. Mundheim and Gordon D. Henderson, "Applicability of the Federal Securities Laws to Pension and Profit-Sharing Plans," *Law and Contemporary Problems,* 29, no. 1 (Summer 1964): 820; and Division of Investment Management, *Protecting Investors,* 123–33.

51. Sarah Holden, Peter Brady, and Michael Hadley, "401(k) Plans at Age 30: A 25-Year Retrospective," *Research Perspective,* 12, no. 2 (November 2006).

52. Division of Investment Management, *Protecting Investors*, 178–79.

53. Bonnie Bauman, "Collective Funds Gain on Mutual Funds in 401(k)s," May 10, 2006, from http://www.ignites.com.

54. Pamela Perun and C. Eugene Steurle, "From Fiduciary to Facilitator: Employers and Defined Contribution Plans," in *The Evolving Pension System: Trends, Effects, and Proposals for Reform*, eds. William G. Gale, John B. Shoven, and Mark J. Warshawsky (Washington, DC: Brookings Institution Press, 2005), 197.

55. Investment Company Institute, *Report of the Advisory Group on Personal Investing* (Washington, DC: Investment Company Institute, 1994).

56. *Rosenfeld v. Black*, 445 F.2d 1337 (2d Cir. 1971), cert dism'd, 409 U.S. 802 (1972).

57. Investment Company Institute, *2001 Investment Company Fact Book* (Washington, DC: Investment Company Institute, 2001), 63.

58. Information as to fund families, the five largest funds, and five largest groups in 1970 was provided by the Research Department of the Investment Company Institute.

59. Sales information was provided by the Research Department of the Investment Company Institute.

60. Morningstar, *Stocks, Bonds, Bills, and Inflation*, 286 and 292.

Chapter 4

1. Investment Company Institute, *2007 Fact Book*, 93.

2. John Rea and Richard Marcis, "Mutual Fund Shareholder Activity during U.S. Stock Market Cycles, 1944–95," *Perspective*, 2, no. 2 (March 1996): 10.

3. *Business Week*, "What Ails the Mutual Fund Industry," 50.

4. Investment Company Institute, *2007 Fact Book*, 95.

5. Eric John Abrahamson and Grant Alger, *Persistence and Perspective: Franklin Templeton Investments; The First Sixty Years* (San Mateo, CA: Franklin Resources, 2007), 46. Pitti is quoted in *Business Week*, "What Ails the Mutual Fund Industry," 47.

6. Abrahamson and Alger, *Persistence and Perspective*, 45.

7. Donald Saltz, "Thinking in Terms of $100 Billion," *Washington Star*, December 12, 1975.

8. Reprinted with the permission of Simon & Schuster Adult Publishing Group from Joseph Nocera, *A Piece of the Action: How the Middle Class Joined the Money Class* (New York: Simon & Schuster, 1994), 76.

9. Ibid., 77–84.

10. Ibid., 84–88.

11. Investment Company Institute, *2007 Fact Book*, 95.

12. David Silver, "The Washington Scene," keynote address, Investment Company Institute 1982 General Membership Meeting, Washington, DC, May 20, 1982.

13. Letter dated November 13, 1975, from David Silver, Senior Vice President and General Counsel, Investment Company Institute, to Lewis J. Mendelson, Assistant Director, SEC Division of Investment Management Regulation, U.S. Securities and Exchange Commission, SEC File no. S7–568.

14. Securities Act Release no. 5836 (1977).

15. Jeffrey L. Rodengen, *New Horizons: The Story of Federated Investors* (Fort Lauderdale, FL: Write Stuff Enterprises, 2006), 63.

16. Investment Company Act Release no. 13380 (1983).

17. Efforts by bank regulators to impede money market funds are discussed in Matthew P. Fink, "Money Market Funds: A New Financial Product in the Age of Deregulation," *Mutual Funds Forum,* January 1980, 3–20.

18. *Hearings on Money Market Mutual Funds,* Subcommittee on Financial Institutions of the Senate Committee on Banking, Housing and Urban Affairs, 96th Cong., 2d sess. (1980).

19. The history of the credit controls is presented in Stacey L. Schreft, "Credit Controls: 1980," *Economic Review,* Federal Reserve Bank of Richmond (November/December 1990): 25–55. The reports about bank and S&L associations' plans are in Merrill Brown, "Banks, S&Ls Unite to Stop Money Market Funds Rise," *Washington Post,* March 11, 1980; and Laura Gross, "Bank, S&L Leaders Beginning to Talk of Joining to Fight Nonbank Rivals," *American Banker,* March 11, 1980, 1–15.

20. It is unclear whether the state attacks were orchestrated by the American Bankers Association in Washington or were spontaneous. Nocera, *A Piece of the Action,* 199.

21. The Utah story is set forth in Nocera, *A Piece of the Action,* 199–206.

Chapter 5

1. The history of the tax-exempt fund legislation is set forth in Alfred P. Johnson, "Municipal Bond Mutual Funds: An Idea Whose Time Has Come," paper presented at the Municipal Finance Officers Association Pre-Conference Seminar, Atlanta, April 16, 1977; and Cohen, *A Lawyer's Life,* 595–603.

2. Bullock, *Story of Investment Companies,* 168–69.

3. A good description of Stein's style is set forth in Henriques, *Fidelity's World,* 196–97.

4. Investment Company Institute, *2008 Fact Book* Washington, DC: Investment Company Institute, 2008), 146.

5. The Tax Reform Act of 1976 provided favorable tax treatment for funds receiving interest that is exempt from tax under section 103(a) of the Internal Revenue Code, the section that generally provides tax exemption for municipal bond interest. However, tax-exempt money market funds also bought HUD Project Notes, which derived their tax exemption from the Housing Act of 1937, not from section 103(a). Corrective legislation to rectify this glitch was passed by both houses of Congress and went to President

Ronald Reagan for his signature. But there was a second glitch. The president also was about to sign another bill, one dealing with the issuance of tax-exempt obligations by Native American tribes. The two bills were worded so that if the president first signed the Native American bill and then the mutual fund bill, both bills would take effect. But if he signed the mutual fund bill and then the Native American bill, there was a technical argument that the Native American bill repealed the mutual fund language. The Treasury Department was aware of the issue, but the president signed the bills in the wrong order. This necessitated a third piece of legislation deeming that the Native American bill had been signed before the mutual fund bill. Cohen, *A Lawyer's Life*, 598–603.

6. Vanguard Group, "Indexing: 25 Years and Counting" (Valley Forge, PA: Vanguard Group, 2006).

7. John C. Bogle, *Common Sense on Mutual Funds: New Imperatives for the Intelligent Investor* (New York: John Wiley, 1999), 114–15.

8. Vanguard, "Indexing." Bogle, *Common Sense*, 115–16.

9. Vanguard, "Indexing." Bogle, *Common Sense*, 115–16.

10. Investment Company Institute, *2008 Fact Book*, 154.

11. Altruist Financial Advisors, "ETFs vs. Index Mutual Funds," 2006, from http://www.altruistfa.com/etfs.htm. Joe Morris, "Bogle and Malkiel Take on Index Alternatives," June 28, 2006, from http://www.ignites.com. Joe Morris, "Bogle and Siegel Tangle on TV," August 22, 2006, from http://www.ignites.com.

12. The 1933 act and the history of mutual fund advertising rules are discussed in Division of Investment Management, *Protecting Investors*, 352–61.

13. Don G. Campbell, "Restrictive Ads Hobble Growth of Mutual Funds," *Mutual Funds Forum*, April 1976, 5–11.

14. Investment Company Act Release no. 7475 (1972).

15. Investment Company Institute, "Casey Suggests Securities Act Might Be Changed to Broaden Mutual Fund Advertising Rules," *Mutual Funds Forum*, October 1972, 5.

16. Lewis J. Mendelson, "The SEC's Investment Company Advertising Rules: Why and How They Have Been Changed," *Mutual Funds Forum*, December 1974, 13.

17. Securities Act Release no. 5591 (1975); emphasis added.

18. Investment Company Institute, "Casey Suggests," 5. Roberta S. Karmel, "Mutual Fund Advertising," *Mutual Funds Forum*, April 1978, 1–18.

19. Investment Company Institute, *Annual Report 1977* (Washington, DC: Investment Company Institute, 1977), 16.

20. Investment Company Institute "Mutual Fund Advertising and the First Amendment," *Mutual Funds Forum*, July 1978, 19–20. Karmel, "Mutual Fund Advertising," 2.

21. Securities Act Release no. 6116 (1979).

22. Brian K. Reid and John D. Rea, "Mutual Fund Distribution Channels and Distribution Costs," *Perspective*, 9, no. 3 (July 2003): 16.

23. Statement of David Schenker, *House Hearings*, 112. Jaretzki, "The Investment Company Act of 1940," 324–25.

24. U.S. Securities and Exchange Commission, "Statement on the Future Structure of the Securities Markets," *BNA Securities Regulation and Law Reporter*, 137, pt. 2 (February 1972): 7.

25. Mutual Liquid Assets, SEC No-Action Letter (1976).

26. Investment Company Act Release no. 10862 (1976).

27. Investment Company Act Release no. 11414 (1980).

28. Joel H. Goldberg and Gregory N. Bressler, "Revisiting Rule 12b-1 under the Investment Company Act," *Review of Securities & Commodities Regulation*, 31, no. 13 (July 1998): 150.

29. Ibid.

30. Investment Company Institute, "How Mutual Funds Use 12b-1 Fees," *Fundamentals*, 14, no. 2 (February 2005).

31. Investment Company Institute, *2007 Fact Book*, 95.

32. Information as to the five largest funds and the five largest fund groups in 1980 was provided by the Research Department of the Investment Company Institute.

33. Investment Company Institute, *2007 Fact Book*, 95.

34. Slater, *John Bogle and the Vanguard Experiment*, 98.

35. Reid and Rea, "Mutual Fund Distribution Channels," 16.

Chapter 6

1. Investment Company Institute, "The U.S. Retirement Market, First Quarter 2009," *Research Fundamentals*, 18, no. 5–Q1 (August 2009), 11.

2. Cohen, *A Lawyer's Life*, 239.

3. Richard M. Corbett, *Pension Trends and the Self-Employed* (New Brunswick, NJ: Rutgers University Press, 1961), 27.

4. John F. Kelly, "Keogh Sales Opportunity Unlimited," *Mutual Funds Forum*, special issue, 1974, 4.

5. *Barron's*, "Win with Keogh," June 9, 1969, 3–18.

6. Cohen, *A Lawyer's Life*, 536.

7. Statistics for 1967, 1970, and 1980 are from Investment Company Institute, *1981 Mutual Fund Fact Book* (Washington, DC: Investment Company Institute, 1981), 47; *Barron's*, "Win with Keogh," 3; Norman E. Mains, "The Keogh Plan Universe," *Mutual Funds Forum*, October 1974, 1; and David Silver, "Retirement Planning with Mutual Funds," *Mutual Funds Forum*, January 1978, 1.

8. James A. Wooten, *The Employee Retirement Income Security Act of 1974: A Political History* (Berkeley: University of California Press, 2004), 39.

9. Matthew P. Fink, "Institute Activity in Pension Reform," *Mutual Funds Forum,* special issue, 1974, 12–13.

10. Investment Company Institute, *1981 Fact Book,* 47.

11. Investment Company Institute, "The U.S. Retirement Market, First Quarter 2009," 9.

12. Sarah Holden, Kathy Ireland, Vicky Leonard-Chambers, and Michael Bogdan, "The Individual Retirement Account at Age 30: A Retrospective," *Perspective,* 11, no. 1 (February 2005): 16.

13. Investment Company Institute, "The U.S. Retirement Market, First Quarter 2009," 4.

14. Letter dated June 21, 1976, from Matthew P. Fink, Associate Counsel, Investment Company Institute, to Morton Klevan, Acting Counsel Fiduciary Responsibility, Plan Benefit Security Division, U.S. Department of Labor.

15. The history of the universal IRA is set forth in Cohen, *A Lawyer's Life,* 621–24.

16. Silver, "Edited Transcript," 34–35.

17. Statistics on IRA contributions are from Holden, Ireland, Leonard-Chambers, and Bogdan, "The Individual Retirement Account," 4–5. Statistics on median income are from Jonathan Skinner, "Individual Retirement Accounts: A Review of the Evidence," *Tax Notes,* 54, no. 2 (January 13, 1992): 204.

18. Holden, Ireland, Leonard-Chambers, and Bogdan, "The Individual Retirement Account," 5–6.

19. Reprinted with the permission of Simon & Schuster Adult Publishing Group from Nocera, *A Piece of the Action,* 293.

20. Peter Brady and Sarah Holden, "The U.S. Retirement Market, 2006," *Research Fundamentals,* 16, no. 3 (July 2007), 6.

21. Statistics are from Holden, Ireland, Leonard-Chambers, and Bogdan, "The Individual Retirement Account," 16; and Investment Company Institute, "The U.S. Retirement Market, First Quarter 2009," 4. Nocera, *A Piece of the Action,* 286.

22. The history of 401(k) plans is set forth in Cohen, *A Lawyer's Life,* 223–34; and John M. Vine, "Cash or Deferred Arrangements: What's the Beef? What's at Stake?" *Virginia Tax Review,* 5, no. 4 (Spring 1986): 855–910.

23. Ted Benna, "401(k) Plans: From Inception to the Present Day," in *The Handbook of Employee Benefits: Design, Funding and Administration,* ed. Jerry S. Rosenbloom, 6th ed. (New York: McGraw-Hill, 2005), 685.

24. Statistics are from Sarah Holden, Peter Brady, and Michael Hadley, "401(k) Plans: A 25-Year Retrospective," *Research Perspective,* 12, no. 2 (February 2006), 3; and Investment Company Institute, "The U.S. Retirement Market, First Quarter 2009," 7.

25. Wooten, *The Employee Retirement Income Security Act,* 278.

26. Ibid., 278–79.

27. Benna, "401(k) Plans," 695.

28. Perun and Steurle, "From Fiduciary to Facilitator," 197.

29. Ibid.

30. American Enterprise Institute for Public Policy Research, Transcript, "The Regulation of Mutual Funds: Competition with Other Investment Vehicles for Retirement Savings," January 3, 2006, from http://www.aei.org/events/filter.all,eventID.1223/transcript.asp, 7–8.

31. Ibid., 8.

32. Investment Company Institute, *2007 Fact Book,* 77; and Investment Company Institute, "The U.S. Retirement Market, First Quarter 2009," 8.

33. Investment Company Institute, "The U.S. Retirement Market, First Quarter 2009," 14.

Chapter 7

1. Fowler, *American Investment Trusts,* 25.

2. Edwin J. Perkins, *Wall Street to Main Street: Charles Merrill and Middle Class Investors* (Cambridge: Cambridge University Press, 1999), 226–29. Reprinted with permission of Cambridge University Press.

3. Terry Robards, "Merrill Lynch to Acquire Edie," *New York Times,* April 30, 1969.

4. Jeffrey M. Laderman and Geoffrey Smith, "The Power of Mutual Funds," *Business Week,* January 18, 1993, 64.

5. Arthur Zeikel, "Presentation at Retired Partners Meeting, Palm Springs, California," March 1, 1997, in author's files.

6. Daniel P. Wiener, "Falling Short," *U.S. News & World Report,* April 8, 1991, 63.

7. Laderman and Smith, "The Power of Mutual Funds," 64.

8. "Paine Webber's Mitchell Hutchins Backs off Retail Business," Ignites.com, October 11, 2000, from http://www.ignites.com.

9. The 1991 percentage is from Wiener, "Falling Short," 63. The 2006 percentage was provided by the Membership Department of the Investment Company Institute.

10. The observer was James Gerald Smith, "Banking and the Stock Market," in *Facing the Facts: an Economic Diagnosis,* ed. James Gerald Smith (New York: G. P. Putnam's Sons, 1932), 157.

11. Flynn, *Investment Trusts Gone Wrong!,* 69.

12. The events through 1976 are discussed in Martin E. Lybecker, "Bank-Sponsored Investment Management Services: A Legal History and Statutory Interpretative Analysis," part 1, *Securities Regulation Law Journal,* 5, no. 2 (Summer 1977): 110–64; part 2, *Securities Regulation Law Journal,* 5, no. 3 (Autumn 1977): 195–258.

13. Ibid., 204.

14. 301 US 617 (1971).

15. Statistics were provided by the Membership Department of the Investment Company Institute.

16. American Enterprise Institute for Public Policy Research, transcript, "Is There a Better Way to Regulate Mutual Funds? The Bogle Critique of the Mutual Fund Industry," May 9, 2006, from http://www.aei.org/events/filter.all,eventID.1317/transcript.asp 37.

Chapter 8

1. Household statistics are from Sarah Holden and Michael Bogdan, "Trends in Ownership of Mutual Funds in the United States, 2007," *Research Fundamentals,* 16, no. 5 (November 2007). Other statistics are from Investment Company Institute, *2007 Fact Book,* 93 and 95.

2. Brian Reid, "Growth and Development of Bond Mutual Funds," *Perspective,* 3, no. 2 (June 1997): 4. Brian Reid, "The 1990s: A Decade of Expansion and Change in the U.S. Mutual Fund Industry," *Perspective,* 6, no. 3 (July 2000): 7 and 9.

3. Reid, "The 1990s," 4.

4. Ibid., 5.

5. Holden, Brady, and Hadley, "401(k) Plans," 3 and 15.

6. Holden, Ireland, Leonard-Chambers, and Bogdan, "The Individual Retirement Account."

7. Investment Company Institute, *2007 Fact Book,* 95.

8. Reid and Rea, "Mutual Fund Distribution Channels," 16.

9. Division of Investment Management, *Protecting Investors,* 334.

10. The headlines are quoted in Nocera, *A Piece of the Action,* 280–81; and Mahar, *Bull!,* 167.

11. Gerald E. Corrigan, "Are Banks Special?," Federal Reserve Board of Minneapolis, 1982 Annual Report Essay.

12. Statement of William Cary, Chairman, U.S. Securities and Exchange Commission, *Hearings on Common Trust Funds—Overlapping Responsibility and Conflict in Regulation,* Subcommittee of the House Committee on Government Operations, 88th Cong., 1st sess. (1963), 20.

13. Kaufman, "Structural Changes in the Financial Markets," 7, 8, and 13.

14. Richard Marcis, Sandra West, and Victoria Leonard-Chambers, "Mutual Fund Shareholder Response to Market Disruptions," *Perspective,* 1, no. 1 (July 1995). Eli M. Remolana, Paul Kleiman, and Debbie Gruenstein, "Market Returns and Mutual Fund Flows," *Federal Reserve Bank of New York Economic Policy Review* (July 1997): 33–52.

15. Steven Mufson, "White House Eyes Community Lending Aid," *Washington Post,* May 15, 1993. Richard M. Rosenberg, "Community Reinvestment: The Next Step," speech, Federal Reserve Bank of Dallas

Community Reinvestment Conference, Dallas, August 24, 1993. Linda Corman, "Spreading the Burden," *Financial Planning's Bank Investment Marketing* (January/February 1994): 38.

16. Letter dated May 26, 1993, from Mary L. Schapiro, Acting Chairman, U.S. Securities and Exchange Commission, to Frank N. Newman, Undersecretary for Domestic Finance, U.S. Department of the Treasury.

17. HR 1289, Community Reinvestment Modernization Act of 2007, 110th Cong., 1st sess., 2007.

18. Jack M. Whitney II, Address Before the Investment Company Institute, New York, May 3, 1962.

19. Investment Company Act Release no. 13044 (1983). Comment letter dated May 12, 1983, from Matthew P. Fink, Senior Vice President and General Counsel, Investment Company Institute, File no. S7–960.

20. Arthur Levitt, "Protecting the American Investor: A New Partnership," speech, North American Securities Administrators Association Fall Conference, Orlando, September 29, 1993.

21. Joel Seligman, "Should Investment Companies Be Subject to a New Statutory Self-Regulatory Organization?" *Washington University Law Quarterly*, 83, no. 4 (2005): 1115–26.

22. Ibid., 1124.

23. Landis, *The Administrative Process*, 30.

Chapter 9

1. Brandeis, *Other People's Money*, 92 and 104.

2. Schwed, *Where Are the Customers' Yachts?*, 209.

3. Investment Company Act Release no. 13436 (1983). Comment letter dated January 14, 1985, from Thomas D. Maher, Assistant General Counsel, Investment Company Institute, File no. S7–34-84. Investment Company Act Release no. 16244 (1988).

4. Investment Company Act Release no. 23064 (1998).

5. Securities Act Release no. 8861 (2007).

6. The advocacy groups included Fund Democracy, the Financial Planning Association, Consumer Federation of America, National Association of Investors Corporation, and the American Federation of Labor and Congress of Industrial Corporations.

7. Jason Zweig, "Why Your Fund Manager May Work Better in the Dark," *Money* (March 1998): 50–51.

8. "Funds Ignore Internet, Feed Investors Stale Data," Editorial, *USA Today*, July 7, 2000.

9. Securities Act Release no. 8393 (2004).

10. Investment Company Act Release no. 11379 (1980). Investment Company Act Release no. 13049 (1983).

11. Kathryn B. McGrath, "Good Compliance Is Good Business," keynote address, 1985 ICI/SEC Procedures Conference, Washington, DC, October 31, 1985.

12. Letter dated March 11, 1986, from David Silver, President, Investment Company Institute, to Kathryn B. McGrath, Director, Division of Investment Management, U.S. Securities and Exchange Commission.

13. Investment Company Act Release no. 15315 (1986). Comment letter dated December 22, 1986, from Matthew P. Fink, Senior Vice President and General Counsel, Investment Company Institute, File no. S7–23-86. Investment Company Act Release no. 16245 (1988).

14. The Pilgrim saga is set forth in Susan E. Kuhn, "Time to Sell Your Mutual Fund Today?" *Fortune*, March 6, 1995, 98–112.

15. Letter dated May 21, 1993, from Craig S. Tyle, Vice President–Securities, Investment Company Institute, to R. Clark Hooper, Vice President–Advertising/Investment Companies Regulation, National Association of Securities Dealers. Securities Exchange Act Release no. 34354 (1994).

16. Letter dated December 14, 1987, from Stanley P. Judd, Senior Special Counsel, Division of Investment Management, U.S. Securities and Exchange Commission, to various mutual fund companies.

17. Letter dated January 15, 1990, from Matthew P. Fink, Senior Vice President and General Counsel, Investment Company Institute, to Kathryn B. McGrath, Director, Division of Investment Management, U.S. Securities and Exchange Commission, and letter dated January 29, 1980, from Ms. McGrath to Mr. Fink.

18. Letter dated October 19, 1995, from Paul Schott Stevens, General Counsel, Investment Company Institute, to R. Clark Hooper, Vice President Advertising/Investment Companies Regulation, National Association of Securities Dealers. Comment letter dated October 15, 1997, from Craig S. Tyle, General Counsel, Investment Company Institute, NASD Regulation Request for Comment 97–50.

19. Letter dated May 8, 2000, from Craig S. Tyle, General Counsel, Investment Company Institute, to Annette L. Nazareth, Director, Division of Market Regulation, U.S. Securities and Exchange Commission, and Paul F. Roye, Director, Division of Investment Management, U.S. Securities and Exchange Commission. Letter dated August 17, 2000, from Colette D. Kimbrough, Chair, SIA Investment Company Committee, to Ms. Nazareth and Mr. Roye.

20. Charles Dickens, *Bleak House* (New York: Oxford University Press, 1991), 4.

21. Aaron Lucchetti, "Fidelity Faces Rally by AFL-CIO," *Wall Street Journal*, July 31, 2002.

22. Securities Act Release no. 8131 (2002).

23. John J. Brennan and Edward C. Johnson III, "No Disclosure: The Feeling is Mutual," *Wall Street Journal*, January 14, 2003.

24. Jonathan R. Laing, "Never Say Never, Or How Safe Is Your Money Market Fund?," *Barron's*, March 26, 1990, 6–27.

25. Investment Company Act Release no. 18005 (1991).

26. Laing, "Never Say Never," 7.

27. Shannon D. Harrington, "Money Fund Sponsors May Be under Most Stress Ever, Moody's Says," *Bloomberg.com*, November 19, 2007, from http://www.bloomberg.com/apps/news?pid=newsarchive&sid=a21z 9rkb1ZRs.

28. Investment Company Act Release no. 16244 (1988).

29. Securities Exchange Act Release no. 30897 (1992).

30. Chet Currier, "It's High Time to Right the Wrong of 12B-1 Fees," *Seattle Post- Intelligencer*, February 21, 2004.

31. Lori Pizzani, "Debate Grows on Closed Funds' 12b-1 Fees," *Bank Investment Consultant*, September 2003.

32. Ibid.

33. Stan Luxenberg, "Will 12b-1 Fees No Longer Be?" *Registered Rep.*, May 1, 2005.

34. Division of Investment Management, *Protecting Investors*, 327.

35. Securities Act Release no. 9128 (2010).

36. Investment Company Act Release no. 11421 (1980).

37. Investment Company Institute, *An Investment Company Director's Guide to Oversight of Codes of Ethics and Personal Investing* (Washington, DC: Investment Company Institute, July 2000).

38. Brett E. Fromson, "Fund Managers Own Trades Termed a Potential Conflict," *Washington Post*, January 11, 1994. Tom Petruno, "Hard Questions for Fund Industry," *Chicago Sun-Times*, January 18, 1994.

39. Paul Starobin, "Fragile Nest Egg?," *National Journal* (May 7, 1994): 1066.

40. Ibid., 1062.

41. Susan Antilla, "Fund Managers Testing the Rules," *New York Times*, January 23, 1994.

42. Investment Company Institute, *Report of the Advisory Group on Personal Investing*.

43. Chairmen Levitt's and Dingell's remarks are quoted in letter dated May 23, 1996, from Matthew P. Fink, President, Investment Company Institute, to Arthur Levitt Jr., Chairman, U.S. Securities and Exchange Commission. Amy L. Goodman and Richard C. Marshall, Editorial, "A Quieter Time for the Fund Industry," *Investment Lawyer*, 2, no. 4 (April 1995): 2.

44. Arthur Levitt, "From Security to Self-Reliance: American Investors in the 1990s," speech, Investment Company Institute 1996 General Membership Meeting, Washington, DC, May 22, 1996. "Funds and Games," Editorial, *Economist*, September 14, 1996, 14.

45. Statement of David Schenker, Chief Counsel, SEC Investment Trust Study, *House Hearings*, 109–10; emphasis added.

46. Examples of early exemptive rules requiring approval by directors are rule 17f-1 (custody), 1940; rule 10f-1 (underwritings), 1941; rule 17g-1 (fidelity bonding), 1947; and rule 10f-3 (underwritings), 1958. More recent rules include rule 17f-4 (securities depositories), 1977; rule 17a-8 (fund mergers), 1980; rule 2a-7 (money market funds), 1982; and rule 18f-3 (classes of shares), 1995.

47. Charles Gasparino, "Navalier Vote Curbs Power of Trustees," *Wall Street Journal*, June 18, 1997.

48. Letters dated February 17, 2003, and February 27, 2004, from Warren Buffett, Chairman of the Board, to the Shareholders of Berkshire Hathaway.

49. Stephen K. West, speech, 1980 General Membership Meeting of the Investment Company Institute, Washington, DC, May 1, 1980. Peter J. Wallison and Robert E. Litan, *Competitive Equity: A Better Way to Organize Mutual Funds* (Washington, DC: AEI Press, 2007).

50. Gary Gensler, Testimony before the Subcommittee on Capital Markets, Insurance and Government Sponsored Enterprises of the Committee on Financial Services, U.S. House of Representatives, March 12, 2003, from http://financialservices.house.gov/108.shtml. American Enterprise Institute for Public Policy Research, transcript, "Is There a Better Way to Regulate Mutual Funds: The Bogle Critique," 16.

51. Investment Company Institute, *Report of the Advisory Committee on Best Practices for Fund Directors: Enhancing a Culture of Independence and Effectiveness* (Washington, DC: Investment Company Institute, June 24, 1999).

52. Rea, "Trends in the Ownership Cost of Equity Mutual Funds," 14.

53. Julie Goodman, "Congress Expected to Spare Mutual Fund Structure," *Board IQ*, January 6, 2009.

54. Division of Investment Management, *Protecting Investors*, 282–89. Stephen K. West, "Is There a Better Way to Regulate Mutual Funds," paper presented to the Committee on Investment Management Regulation of the New York Bar, March 6, 2008.

55. Rachel Witmer, "ICI's Fink Predicts Problems Ahead if Hedge Funds Are Not More Regulated," *Bureau of National Affairs Securities Regulation and Law Report*, 32 (December 11, 2000): 1670. Letter dated April 30, 2003, from Craig S. Tyle, General Counsel, Investment Company Institute, File no. 4–476.

56. *Goldstein v. SEC*, 451 F.3d 873 (D.C. Cir. 2006).

57. Comment letter, dated August 4, 1992, from Craig S. Tyle, Vice President-Securities, Investment Company Institute, File no. S7-12-92, Investment Company Act Release no. 19105 (1992).

58. Ibid.

59. Submission of the Investment Company Institute in Response to NASD Regulation, Inc. Concept Release on the Use of Bond Mutual Fund Risk Ratings in Supplemental Sales literature, February 24, 1997.

60. Letter dated November 19, 1993, from Matthew P. Fink, President, Investment Company Institute, to Arthur J. Levitt, Chairman, U.S. Securities and Exchange Commission, in files of the Investment Company Institute.

61. Investment Company Act Release no. 25925 (2003). Investment Company Act Release no. 26299 (2003).

62. Julie Goodman, "Former Staffers Point to SEC Flaws as Agency Tackles Its Workforce," *Board IQ*, August 4, 2009.

63. U.S. Securities and Exchange Commission, News Release 95–50 (1995).

64. Goodman, "Former Staffers Point to SEC Flaws."

65. U.S. Chamber of Commerce, *Commission on the Regulation of U.S. Capital Markets in the 21st Century* (Washington, DC: U.S. Chamber of Commerce, March 2007), 134–35.

Chapter 10

1. John H. Hollands, "Governmental Regulation of the Distribution of Investment Company Shares," speech, Annual Convention of the National Association of Securities Commissioners, Biloxi, October 8, 1941.

2. Letter and memorandum dated December 29, 1994, "Inconsistent State Investment Company Requirements," from Tamara K. Cain, Assistant Counsel, Investment Company Institute, to William Beatty, NASAA Investment Companies Committee.

3. North American Securities Administrators Association, "Final Report of the 1984 Investment Companies Committee of the North American Securities Administrators Association," October 29, 1984.

4. North American Securities Administrators Association, "Resolution Adopted by the North American Securities Administrators Association," October 1991.

5. Ruth Simon, "How Washington Could Tip the Scales against Investors," *Money* (October 1995): 122–24.

6. Arthur Levitt, "The SEC and the States: Toward a More Perfect Union," speech, North American Securities Administrators Association, Vancouver, October 3, 1995.

7. Andrew Taylor, "Widely Backed Securities Bill Advances in Both Chambers," *Congressional Quarterly* (June 22, 1996): 1745–46.

8. Division of Investment Management, *Protecting Investors*, 103–18.

9. Committtee on Financial Institutions and Insurance Companies of the New York State Bar Association, "Regulated Investment Companies," *Tax Notes*, 21, no. 9 (November 28, 1983): 747. Tax Section of the American Bar Association, "Specifications for Simplification and Reform of the Federal Income Tax Treatment of Regulated Investment Companies," July 18, 1984. Tax Reform Act of 1986, Public Law 99–514, section 653(b).

10. Michael Siconolfi, "What Do You Get for Weathering Oct. 19? A Message from the IRS," *Wall Street Journal*, February 24, 1988. Kevin G. Salven, "Steinhardt's Aim at Small Investor Now Blurred by Obscure Tax Rule," *Wall Street Journal*, March 16, 1989.

11. Matthew P. Fink, keynote address, Mutual Funds and Investment Management Conference, Tucson, March 23, 1992.

12. Letter and memorandum dated June 21, 1976, from Matthew P. Fink to Morton J. Klevan; emphasis added.

13. 29 C.F.R. 2550.404c-1(b) (2)(i)(B)(1)(vi).

14. Letter dated February 12, 1992, from Matthew P. Fink, President, Investment Company Institute, to Lynn Martin, Secretary, U.S. Department of Labor.

15. Statement of Matthew P. Fink, President, Investment Company Institute, "On 401(k) Plan Expenses," before the Pension and Welfare Benefits Administration, U.S. Department of Labor, November 12, 1997.

16. Humberto Cruz, "More Details Could Help 401(k) Plans," *Chicago Tribune*, May 7, 2002. © Tribune Media Services, Inc. All rights reserved. Reprinted with permission.

17. Statement of Elizabeth Krentzman, General Counsel, Investment Company Institute, "On Disclosure to Plan Sponsors and Participants," before the ERISA Advisory Council Working Groups on Disclosure, September 21, 2004. Letter dated May 26, 2005, from Elizabeth R. Kretzman, General Counsel, Investment Company Institute, to Robert Doyle, Director, Office of Regulations and Interpretations, Employee Benefits Security Administration, U.S. Department of Labor.

18. Investment Company Institute, *2007 Fact Book*, 58 and 95.

19. Information as to the five largest funds and five largest complexes was provided by the Research Department of the Investment Company Institute.

20. Reid and Rea, "Mutual Fund Distribution Channels and Distribution Costs," 16.

21. Philip G. Kuehl, Senior Staff Consultant, Westat, "Executive Summary: 2001 ICI Membership Surveys," in files of the Investment Company Institute.

22. Investment Company Institute, *2007 Fact Book*, 8, 75, and 77.

Chapter 11

1. Mahar, *Bull!*, 301 and 325.

2. Ibid., 331.

3. John Waggoner, "10 Lessons from Mutual Fund Meltdowns," *USA Today*, October 3, 2001.

4. Lawrence A. Cunningham, "The Sarbanes-Oxley Yawn: Heavy Rhetoric, Light Reform (and It Just Might Work)," *University of Connecticut Law Review*, 36, no. 3 (Spring 2003): 924.

5. Ibid., 925.

6. Ibid., 917.

7. Kathleen Day and Jim VandeHei, "Congressman Urges Republican Lobbyist; Oxley Staff Pressuring Mutual Funds," *Washington Post*, February 15, 2003.

8. Information on the hearings can be found on the Web site of the House Financial Services Committee, http://financialservices.house.gov/108.shtml.

9. Ibid.

10. "Baker Bill Loses Most of its Bite," July 21, 2003, Ignites.com, from http://www.ignites.com

11. Eric W. Zitzewitz, "Who Cares about Shareholders? Arbitrage-Proofing Mutual Funds," *Journal of Law, Economics, and Organization,* 19 (October 2003): 245–80. An example illustrates the arbitrage problem. Assume that a U.S. fund investing exclusively in Asian securities has five shares outstanding and that based on closing prices in Asia the portfolio is worth $100. After the Asian markets close there is a 5 percent rally in U.S. markets. Experience indicates that Asian markets tend to follow U.S. markets, so the stocks in the fund's portfolio can be expected to rise when the Asian markets open the next day. Just before the NYSE closes, an arbitrageur places an order to buy one share of the fund. After the exchange closes, the fund calculates its NAV at $20 ($100 divided by five shares). Therefore, the arbitrageur pays $20 for the share. The next day, as expected, the portfolio rises 5 percent, and the arbitrageur places an order to redeem the share. The fund calculates its new nav at $20.83 ($105 in Asian securities plus $20 paid by the arbitrageur divided by six outstanding shares). The arbitrageur receives $20.83 for the redemption of one share. The fund is left with a portfolio of $104.17 ($125 minus $20.83) and five outstanding shares with a NAV of $20.83. Had the arbitrageur not appeared, the portfolio would have been worth $105, equal to a NAV of $21. Thus the arbitrageur made an $0.83 (4.15 percent) profit at the expense of the fund and its remaining shareholders.

12. Putnam Growth Fund and Putnam International Equities Fund, SEC No-Action Letter (publicly available February 23, 1981). Investment Company Act Release no. 14244 (1984).

13. Barry B. Barbash, "Remembering the Past: Mutual Funds and the Lessons of the Wonder Years," speech, 1997 ICI Securities Law Procedures Conference, Washington, DC, December 4, 1997. Investment Company Act Release no. 23064 (1998).

14. Geoffrey Smith, "Commentary; Funds: A Hidden Trick Investors Should Know About," *Business Week* (November 17, 1997): 41.

15. Barbash, "Remembering the Past."

16. Letter dated April 30, 2001, from Douglas Scheidt, Associate Director and Chief Counsel, Division of Investment Management, U.S. Securities

and Exchange Commission, to Craig S. Tyle, General Counsel, Investment Company Institute.

17. Investment Company Institute, *Valuation and Liquidity Issues for Mutual Funds: 2002 Supplement* (Washington, DC: Investment Company Institute, March 2002).

18. Stan Wilson, "Funds' Dilemma with Pricing, Timers Seen Getting Eye From SEC," *Fund Action* (October 21, 2001): 1.

19. Letter dated November 13, 2002, from Jana M. Cayne, Senior Counsel, Division of Investment Management, U.S. Securities and Exchange Commission, to Craig S. Tyle, General Counsel, Investment Company Institute.

20. Abrahamson and Alger, *Persistence and Perspective*, 183–84.

21. Attorney General Spitzer subsequently told me that he recounted the tennis court incident to reporters who asked for a humorous story about the scandals. It is the lead story in Daniel Kadlec, "Is Your Mutual Fund Clean?" *Time* (September 22, 2003): 46–48.

22. *State of New York against Canary Capital Partners, LLC, Canary Investment Management, LLC, Canary Capital Partners, LTD and Edward J. Stern*, N.Y. Sup. Ct., September 3, 2003.

23. Kenneth R. Gray, Larry A. Frieder, and George W. Clark Jr., *Corporate Scandals: The Many Faces of Greed* (St. Paul: Paragon House, 2005), 138.

24. Office of the New York State Attorney General, Press Release, "State Investigation Reveals Mutual Fund Fraud," September 3, 2003.

25. Investment Company Institute, Press Release, "ICI Statement on Today's Announcement by New York State Attorney General," September 3, 2003.

26. Letter dated September 4, 2003, from William H. Donaldson, Chairman, U.S. Securities and Exchange Commission, to Matthew P. Fink, President, Investment Company Institute.

27. Summaries of these and other cases are in Gray, Frieder, and Clark, *Corporate Scandals*, 133–62.

28. Spitzer's criticism of the SEC is quoted in Tom Lauricella, Deborah Solomon, and Gregory Zuckerman, "Mutual Funds Face Overhaul as Spitzer and SEC Fight for Turf," *Wall Street Journal*, October 31, 2003. Senator Fitzgerald is quoted in Rachel McTague, "Fitzgerald, Spitzer Blast Mutual Fund Industry, Call for Dramatic Governance Reforms," *Bureau of National Affairs Securities Regulation and Law Report*, 35 (November 10, 2003): 1875. Predictions that legislation would be enacted were made in Paula Dwyer, Amy Borrus, and Lauren Young, "The Coming Reforms," *Business Week* (November 10, 2003): 116; and Michael Schroeder, "Flurry of Mutual-Fund Laws on the Way," *Wall Street Journal*, November 19, 2003.

29. See Statements of John C. Bogle, Founder and Former Chief Executive, Vanguard Group, and Mercer E. Bullard, Founder and President, Fund Democracy, Hearing on Mutual Fund Trading Abuses, Before the

Subcommittee on Governmental Affairs of the Senate Committee on Financial Management, the Budget and International Security, November 3, 2003.

30. Shelby's views are set forth in Rachel McTague, "Mutual Funds at Center of Arena; Reform a Good Bet, but Scope Unclear," *Bureau of National Affairs Securities Regulation and Law Report*, 36 (January 26, 2004): 149; Richard Hill, "Shelby Wants Review of Fund Management, But Still Undecided about How to Legislate," *Bureau of National Affairs Securities Regulation and Law Report*, 36 (March 1, 2004): 388; and Rachel McTague, "Donaldson, Shelby on Same Wave Length: SEC Able to Handle Mutual Fund Reforms," *Bureau of National Affairs Securities Regulation and Law Report*, 36 (April 12, 2004): 661.

31. Writers who blame the SEC, NASD, or the institute include Gray, Frieder, and Clark, *Corporate Scandals*, 246–47; Paula Dwyer, "Breach of Trust," *Business Week* (December 15, 2003): 98–108; John C. Coffee Jr., "A Course of Inaction: Where Was the SEC When the Mutual Fund Scandals Happened?" *Legal Affairs* (March/April 2004): 46–49; and Stephen Labaton, "S.E.C.'s Oversight of Mutual Funds Is Said to be Lax," *New York Times*, November 16, 2003.

32. Lawrence Greene, "Interview with Lawrence Greene," Virtual Museum and Archive of Securities and Exchange Commission and Securities Industry Historical Society, July 7, 2005, from http://www.sechistorical.org/museum/oralhistories/interviews/greene-l.php.

33. Statistics are from Investment Company Institute, *2008 Fact Book*, 9, 10, 20, 22, 70, and 99–100. Information as to the five largest mutual funds and the five largest fund groups was provided by the Research Department of the Investment Company Institute.

Chapter 12

1. Martin Neil Baily, Robert E. Litan, and Matthew S. Johnson, *The Origins of the Financial Crisis* (Washington, DC: Brookings, November 2008), 11.

2. Ibid, 14.

3. John Cassidy, "Anatomy of a Meltdown," *New Yorker*, December 1, 2008, 52.

4. Edmund L. Andrews, "Fed Shrugged as Subprime Crisis Spread," *New York Times*, December 18, 2007.

5. Baily, *The Origins of the Financial Crisis*, 30.

6. Andrew J. Donohue, "Investment Company Act of 1940: Regulatory Gap between Paradigm and Reality?" speech, American Bar Association Spring Meeting, Vancouver, April 17, 2009.

7. *Financial News Online*, "Mutual funds in peril, study says."

8. Heather Landy, "Bleak Year Brought Almost No Winners," *Washington Post*, January 11, 2009. Scott Burns, "Mutual funds can serve as a pattern for our financial system," *Dallas Evening News*, March 15, 2009.

9. Investment Company Institute, *Report of the Money Market Working Group* (Washington, DC: Investment Company Institute, March 17, 2009), 53.

10. Group of Thirty, *Financial Reform: A Framework for Financial Stability* (Washington, DC: Group of Thirty, January 15, 2009), 60.

11. U.S. Department of the Treasury, *Financial Regulatory Reform: A New Foundation* (Washington, DC: Department of the Treasury, June 18, 2009), 12.

12. Investment Company Act Release no. 28807 (2009).

13. Anne M. Khademian, *The SEC and Capital Market Regulation: The Politics of Expertise* (Pittsburgh: University of Pittsburgh Press, 1992), 126.

14. U. V. Wilcox, *The Bankers Be Damned* (New York: Daniel Ryerson, 1940), 114 and 116.

15. Gary Weiss, *Wall Street Versus America: The Rampant Greed and Dishonesty that Imperil Your Investments* (New York: Penguin, 2006), 161.

16. Marty Jezer, "We Need a New Old Deal," *Common Dreams News Center*, November 21, 2003, from http://www.commondreams.org/egi-bin/print.egi?file=views03/1121-08.htm.

17. Weiss, *Wall Street Versus America*, xxiii.

18. Jim Puzzanghera and Walter Hamilton, "SEC failures spur calls for agency overhaul," *Los Angeles Times*, December 18, 2008.

19. U.S. Department of the Treasury, *Blueprint for a Modernized Financial Regulatory Structure* (Washington, DC: Department of the Treasury, March 2008). Committee on Capital Markets Regulation, *Recommendations for Reorganizing the U.S. Financial Regulatory Structure* (New York: Committee on Capital Markets Regulation, January 14, 2009).

20. Robert Schmidt and Jesse Westbrook, "U.S. May Strip SEC of Powers in Regulatory Overhaul," *Bloomberg.com*, from http://www.bloomberg.com/apps/news?pid=20601087&sid=amepJWiwJJNM&refer=home.

21. U.S. Department of the Treasury, *Financial Regulatory Reform*, 37–38 and 45–46.

22. Gail Marks Jarvis, "401(k) plans under scrutiny after Americans lose $600 billion in retirement savings," *Chicagotribune.com*, April 22, 2009, from http://www.chicagotribune.com/business/yourmoney/chi-tc-401k-gail-apr22,04007210.prin.

23. Doug Halonen, "401(k) plans could be facing total revamp," *Pensions & Investments*, October 27, 2009.

24. Daniel Solin, "The 401(k) skimming scam," *Daily Finance*, February 25, 2009, from http://www.dailyfinance.com/2009/02/25/the-401-k-skimming-scam/.

25. William G. Gale, J. Mark Iwry, David C. John, and Lina Walker, *Increasing Annuitization of 401(k) Plans With Automatic Trial Income* (Washington, DC: Brookings, June 2008).

26. Employee Benefit Research Institute, "401(k) Plan Asset Allocation, Account Balances, and Loan Activity in 2008," *EBRI Issue Brief #335* (October 2009).

27. *Gartenberg v. Merrill Lynch Asset Management, Inc.* 694 F.2d 923 (2d Cir. 1982), *cert. denied sub nom Andre v. Merrill Lynch Ready Assets Trust*, 461 U.S. 906 (1983).

28. *Jones v. Harris Associates LP*, 527 F.3d 627 (7th Cir. 2008).

29. *Jones v Harris Associates LP*, 130 S. Ct. 1418 (2010).

30. "Both Sides Claim Victory in Supreme Court Decision," March 31, 2010, *Ignites.com*, from http://www.ignites.com.

31. "Fund Fee Battle Resumes on Heels of Supreme Court Ruling," June 22, 2010, *Ignites.com*, from http://www.ignites.com.

Chapter 13

1. Stan Wilson, "ICI, Others Come out against SIA Proposal," *Fund Action*, May 10, 1999, 1–10. John Waggoner, "Protests Stop Mutual Funds Change Proposal," *USA Today*, June 16, 1999.

2. Benjamin Calvin Korschot, *A Lifetime of Investing* (Kansas City, MO: Richardson, 1997), 209.

3. Silver, "Edited Transcript," 58.

4. Rachel McTague, "As SEC Contemplates More Regulation of Hedge Funds, CFTC Counsel, Others Object," *Bureau of National Affairs Daily Report for Executives*, 95 (May 16, 2003), A-50; Kip Betz, "SEC's Campos Calls Upon Mutual Funds to Examine Risk Mitigation Approach," *Bureau of National Affairs Daily Report for Executives*, 92 (May 13, 2003), A-11; and Erin E. Arvelund, "Fund of Information: Let the Masses in," *Barron's*, May 19, 2003, F2.

5. Debra Cope, "As Funds Boom, Trade Group Chief Worries," *American Banker*, July 14, 1993, 10. Edward Wyatt, "For Mutual Funds, New Political Muscle," *New York Times*, September 8, 1996. Richard Wolffe, "Mutual Funds Lobby Escapes Cynicism," *Financial Times*, September 12, 1999.

6. Arthur Levitt, "60th Anniversary of the Investment Company Act and the Investment Company Institute," speech, Board of Governors of the Investment Company Institute, Washington DC, October 5, 2000.

7. Labaton, "S.E.C.'S Oversight." Dwyer, "Breach of Trust," 98.

Chapter 14

1. Morningstar, *2009 Ibbotson Stocks, Bonds, Bills, and Inflation Classic Yearbook*, 239, 245, and 251.

2. "All crises have involved debt that, in one fashion or another, has become dangerously out of scale in relation to the underlying means of payment." John Kenneth Galbraith, *A Short History of Financial Euphoria* (1990; rpt., New York: Whittle Books, 1994), 20.

3. Diana B. Henriques, "A Sense of History, a Feeling of Betrayal," *New York Times*, January 2, 2004.

4. James Allen, ed., *Democracy and Finance: The Addresses and Public Statements of William O. Douglas as Member and Chairman of the Securities and Exchange Commission* (New Haven, CT: Yale University Press, 1940), 59.

5. Ian Salisbury, "Some ETFs Fall Short on Pricing," *Wall Street Journal*, November 21, 2008; Richard Shaw, "As Arbitrage Falters, Bond ETFs Teeter," *Index Universe.com*, December 17, 2008, from http:///www.indexuniverse.com/sections/features/5068-broken-bond-etf-arbitrage.html?tmp; Michael Iachini, "ETFs: A Cautionary Tale," *Schwab Investing Insights*, January 2009; Eleanor Laise, "Bond ETFs Are Popular But Pricing Is a Problem." *Wall Street Journal*, October 6, 2009; Eleanor Laise, "Risks Lurk for ETF Investor," *Wall Street Journal*, February 1, 2010; and Ian Salisbury, "'Flash Crash' May Be Blemish for ETFs," *Wall Street Journal*, May 13, 2010.

6. The recent trend toward concentration in the mutual fund industry is discussed in Empirical Research Partners, "The Future of the Money Management Industry," September 25, 2009. The economic structure of the industry is discussed in John C. Coates IV and R. Glenn Hubbard, "Competition and Shareholder Fees in the Mutual Fund Industry: Evidence and Implications for Policy," AEI Working Paper no. 127, June 2006.

7. *Directorship*, "Whose Fund Is It, Anyway? A Practitioner's Guide to Better Mutual Fund Governance," *Directorship*, 32, no. 2 (February 2006): 15 and 13.

8. Ibid., 19.

Bibliography

Abrahamson, Eric John, and Grant Alger. *Persistence and Perspective: Franklin Templeton Investments; the First Sixty Years.* San Mateo, CA: Franklin Resources, 2007.

Allen, James, ed. *Democracy and Finance: The Addresses and Public Statements of William O. Douglas as Member and Chairman of the Securities and Exchange Commission.* New Haven, CT: Yale University Press, 1940.

American Enterprise Institute for Public Policy Research. Transcript, "The Regulation of Mutual Funds: Competition with Other Investment Vehicles for Retirement Savings," January 3, 2006, from http://www.aei.org/events/filter.all,eventID.1223/transcript.asp, 7–8.

Angly, Edward. *Oh Yeah?* New York. 1931, rpt; Burlington, VT: Fraser Publishing, 1988.

Ansberry, Timothy Peter. "The Investment Company Act of 1940." *Georgetown Law Journal,* 29, no. 5 (February 1941): 614–27.

Arvedlund, Erin E. "Fund of Information: Let the Masses in" *Barron's,* May 19, 2003, F2.

Baily, Neil, Robert E. Litan, and Matthew S. Johnson. *The Origins of the Financial Crisis.* Washington, DC: Brookings, November 2008.

Barbash, Barry B. "Remembering the Past: Mutual Funds and the Lessons of the Wonder Years." Speech, 1997 ICI Securities Law Procedures Conference, Washington, DC, December 4, 1997.

Bartholet, Paul. "Investment Companies and Their Regulation." *Blue Sky News,* December 1942, 4–8.

————. "Investment Funds' Second Decade Lays Foundation for Sound Growth." *Investment Dealers' Digest*, May 8, 1945, 75–101.

Benna, Ted. "401(k) Plans: From Inception to the Present Day." In *The Handbook of Employee Benefits: Design, Funding and Administration*, 6th ed., ed. Jerry S. Rosenbloom, 685–98. New York: McGraw-Hill, 2005.

Betz, Kip. "SEC's Campos Calls Upon Mutual Funds to Examine Risk Mitigation Approach" *Bureau of National Affairs Daily Report for Executives*, 92 (May 13, 2003): A-11.

Bogle, John C. "Marketing Mutual Funds in the 1970's." In *How to Start, Operate and Manage Mutual Funds*, ed. Lucile Tomlinson, 12–24. New York: President's Publishing House, 1971.

————. *Common Sense on Mutual Funds: New Imperatives for the Intelligent Investor*. New York: John Wiley, 1999.

Brady, Peter, and Sarah Holden. "The U.S. Retirement Market, 2006." *Research Fundamentals*, July 2007.

Brandeis, Louis D. *Other People's Money and How the Bankers Use It*. New York: Frederick A. Stokes, 1913.

Brooks, John. *The Go-Go Years: The Drama and Crashing Finale of Wall Street's Bullish 1960s*. 1973, rpt; New York: John Wiley, 1999.

Bullock, Hugh. "The Investment Company in 1945." Speech, Twenty-eighth Annual Convention of the National Association of Securities Commissioners, Chicago, November 17, 1945.

————. *The Story of Investment Companies*. New York: Columbia University Press, 1959.

Burton, H., and D. C. Corner. *Investment and Unit Trusts in Britain and America*. London: Elek Books, 1968.

Business Week. "What Ails the Mutual Fund Industry." March 3, 1973, 46–62.

Cabot, Paul C. "The Investment Trust." *Atlantic Monthly* (March 1929): 401–408.

Campbell, Don. G. "Restrictive Ads Hobble Growth of Mutual Funds." *Mutual Funds Forum*, April 1976, 5–11.

Campbell, William A. "The Investment Act of 1940: 'Reasonable and Intelligent.'" *Friends of Financial History*, 52 (Fall 1954): 14–18.

Carosso, Vincent P. *Investment Banking in America*. Cambridge, MA: Harvard University Press, 1970.

Carter, William D. "Mutual Investment Funds." *Harvard Business Review*, 27, no. 6 (November 1949): 715–40.

Cassidy, John. "Anatomy of a Meltdown," *New Yorker* (December 1, 2008): 48-63.

Coates, John C. IV, and R. Glenn Hubbard. "Competition and Shareholder Fees in the Mutual Fund Industry: Evidence and Implications for Policy." AEI Working Paper no. 27, June 2006.

Coffee, John C. Jr. "A Course of Inaction: Where Was the SEC When the Mutual Fund Scandals Happened?" *Legal Affairs* (March/April 2004): 46–49.

Cohen, Edwin S. *A Lawyer's Life: Deep in the Heart of Taxes.* Arlington, VA: Tax Analysts, 1994.

Committee on Capital Markets Regulation. *Recommendations for Reorganizing the U.S. Financial Regulatory Structure.* New York: Committee on Capital Markets Regulation, January 14, 2009.

Committee on Financial Institutions and Insurance of the New York State Bar Association. "Regulated Investment Companies." *Tax Notes,* 21, no. 9 (November 28, 1983): 747.

Conwill, Allan F. "The Minority Menace of Mutual Fund Selling." Speech, New York Group of the Investment Bankers Association of America, Rye, April 23, 1963.

Cook, Donald C. "Recent Developments Concerning Mutual Funds." Speech, Fourth Annual Mutual Fund Conference, New York, September 17, 1952.

Cope, Debra. "As Funds Boom, Trade Group Chief Worries." *American Banker,* July 14, 1993, 1–11.

Corbett, Richard M. *Pension Trends and the Self-Employed.* New Brunswick, NJ: Rutgers University Press, 1961.

Corman, Linda. "Spreading the Burden." *Financial Planning's Bank Investment Marketing* (January/February 1994): 38–41.

Corrigan, Gerald E. "Are Banks Special?" Federal Reserve Bank of Minneapolis, 1982 Annual Report Essay, 1982.

Cunningham, Lawrence A. "The Sarbanes-Oxley Yawn: Heavy Rhetoric, Light Reform (and It Just Might Work)." *University of Connecticut Law Review,* 36, no. 3 (Spring 2003): 915–88.

de Bedts, Ralph F. *The New Deal's SEC: The Formative Years.* New York: Columbia University Press, 1964.

Directorship. "Whose Fund Is It, Anyway? A Practitioner's Guide to Better Mutual Fund Governance." *Directorship,* 32, no. 2 (February 2006): 10–19.

Division of Investment Management, U.S. Securities and Exchange Commission. *Protecting Investors: A Half Century of Investment Company Regulation.* Washington, DC: Government Printing Office, May 1992.

Donohue, Andrew J., "Investment Company Act of 1940: Regulatory Gap between Paradigm and Reality?" Speech, American Bar Association Spring Meeting, Vancouver, April 17, 2009.

Douglas, William O. *Go East, Young Man: The Early Years; The Autobiography of William O. Douglas.* New York: Random House, 1974.

Dwyer, Paula. "Breach of Trust." *Business Week* (December 15, 2003): 98–108.

Dwyer, Paula, Amy Borrus, and Lauren Young. "The Coming Reforms." *Business Week* (November 10, 2003): 116–17.

Fink, Matthew P. "Institute Activity in Pension Reform." *Mutual Funds Forum,* special issue, 1974, 12–13.

———. "Money Market Funds: A New Financial Product in the Age of Deregulation." *Mutual Funds Forum,* January 1980, 3–20.

———. Keynote address, Mutual Funds and Investment Management Conference, Tucson, March 23, 1992.

———. "The Strange Birth of the SEC." *Financial History,* 86 (Summer 2006): 16–19.

Fisher, Irving. *The Stock Market Crash—And After.* New York: Macmillan, 1930.

Flynn, John T. *Investment Trusts Gone Wrong!* New York: New Republic, 1930.

———. *Graft in Business.* New York: Vanguard Press, 1931.

Fowler, John Francis Jr. *American Investment Trusts.* New York: Harper and Brothers, 1928.

FundScope. "From Our Washington Correspondent." *FundScope,* 13, no. 3 (March 7, 1970): 27–32.

Galbraith, John Kenneth. *The Great Crash: 1929.* 1954, rpt.; Boston: Houghton Mifflin, 1997.

———. *A Short History of Financial Euphoria.* 1990, rpt; New York: Whittle Books, 1994.

Gale, William G., J. Mark Iwry, David C. John, and Linda Walker. *Increasing Annuitization of 401(k) Plans With Automatic Trial Income.* Washington, DC: Brookings, June 2008.

Goldberg, Joel H., and Gregory N. Bressler. "Revisiting Rule 12b-1 under the Investment Company Act." *Review of Securities & Commodities Regulation,* 31, no. 13 (July 1998): 147–52.

Goldschmidt, R. W., "Taxation of Investment Companies." Typed memorandum, October 26, 1937, to Paul P. Gourrich, in files of the Securities and Exchange Commission.

Goodman, Amy L., and Richard D. Marshall. Editorial, "A Quieter Time for the Fund Industry." *Investment Lawyer,* 2, no. 4 (April 1995): 2.

Gray, Kenneth R., Larry A. Frieder, and George W. Clark Jr. *Corporate Scandals: The Many Faces of Greed.* St. Paul: Paragon House, 2005.

Grayson, Theodore J. *Investment Trusts: Their Origin, Development, and Operation.* New York: John Wiley, 1928.

Greene, Lawrence. "Interview with Lawrence Greene," Virtual Museum and Archive of Securities and Exchange Commission and Securities Industry, July 7, 2005, from http://www.sechistorical.org/museum/oralhistories/interviews/greene-l.php.

Greenough, William C. *It's My Retirement Money: Take Good Care of It; The TIAA–CREF Story.* Homewood, IL: Irwin, 1990.

Griswold, Merrill. "Taxation of Investment Companies and Their Shareholders." Typed paper labeled "11th Draft, January 6, 1958," in files of Massachusetts Financial Services.

Grow, Natalie R. "The 'Boston-Type Open-End Fund'—Development of a National Financial Institution: 1924–1940." PhD diss., Harvard University, 1977.

Gross, Laura. "Bank, S&L Leaders Beginning to Talk of Joining to Fight Nonbank Rivals." *American Banker,* March 11, 1980, 1–15.

Group of Thirty. *Financial Reform: A Framework for Financial Stability.* Washington, DC: Group of Thirty, January 15, 2009.

Harr, Luther, and W. Carlton Harris. *Banking Theory and Practice.* New York: McGraw-Hill, 1930.

Henriques, Diana B. *Fidelity's World: The Secret Life and Public Power of the Mutual Fund Giant.* New York: Scribner, 1995.

Hill, Richard. "Shelby Wants Review of Fund Management, but Still Undecided about How to Legislate." *Bureau of National Affairs Securities Regulation and Law Report,* 36 (March 1, 2004): 388.

Holden, Sarah, Kathy Ireland, Vicky Leonard-Chambers, and Michael Bogdan. "The Individual Retirement Account at Age 30: A Retrospective." *Perspective,* 11, no. 1 (February 2005).

Holden, Sarah, and Michael Bogdan. "Trends in Ownership of Mutual Funds in the United States." *Research Fundamentals,* 16, no. 5 (November 2007).

Holden, Sarah, Peter Brady, and Michael Hadley. "401(k) Plans: A 25-Year Retrospective." *Research Perspective,* 12, no. 2 (February 2006).

Hollands, John H. "Governmental Regulation of the Distribution of Mutual Fund Shares." Speech, Annual Convention of the National Association of Securities Commissioners, Biloxi, October 8, 1941.

IDS Financial Services. *Investing in the Future: A Century of IDS.* Minneapolis: IDS Financial Services, 1994.

Investment Company Institute. "Casey Suggests Securities Act Might Be Changed to Broaden Mutual Fund Advertising Rules." *Mutual Funds Forum,* October 1972, 5.

———. *Annual Report 1977* (Washington, DC: Investment Company Institute, 1977).

———. "Mutual Fund Advertising and the First Amendment." *Mutual Funds Forum,* July 1978, 2.

———. *1981 Mutual Fund Fact Book.* Washington, DC: Investment Company Institute, 1981.

———. *Report of the Advisory Group on Personal Investing.* Washington, DC: Investment Company Institute, May 9, 1994.

———. *Report of the Advisory Group on Best Practices for Fund Directors: Enhancing a Culture of Independence and Effectiveness.* Washington, DC: Investment Company Institute, July 24, 1999.

———. *An Investment Company Director's Guide to Oversight of Codes of Ethics and Personal Investing.* Washington, DC: Investment Company Institute, July 2000.

———. *2001 Mutual Fund Fact Book.* Washington, DC: Investment Company Institute, 2001.

———. *Valuation and Liquidity Issues for Mutual Funds: 2002 Supplement.* Washington, DC: Investment Company Institute, March 2002.

———. "How Mutual Funds Use 12b-1 Fees." *Research Fundamentals* 14, no. 2 (February 2005).

———. *2007 Investment Company Fact Book.* Washington, DC: Investment Company Institute, 2007.

———. *2008 Investment Company Institute Fact Book.* Washington, DC: Investment Company Institute, 2008.

———. *Report of the Money Market Fund Working Group.* Washington, DC: Investment Company Institute, March 17, 2009.

———. "The U.S. Retirement Market, First Quarter 2009," *Research Fundamentals,* 18, no. 5-Q1 (August 2009).

Jaretzki, Alfred Jr. "The Investment Company Act of 1940." *George Washington University Law Quarterly,* 26, no. 3 (April 1941): 303–47.

Johnson, Alfred P. "Municipal Bond Mutual Funds: An Idea Whose Time Has Come." Paper presented to the Municipal Bond Finance Officers Association Pre-Conference Seminar, "Expanding the Municipal Bond Market," Atlanta, April 16, 1977.

Kadlec, Daniel. "Is Your Mutual Fund Clean?" *Time,* September 22, 2003, 46–48.

Karmel, Roberta. "Mutual Fund Advertising." *Mutual Funds Forum,* April 1978, 1–18.

Kaufman, Henry. "Structural Changes in the Financial Markets: Economic and Policy Significance." *Economic Review,* Federal Reserve Bank of Kansas City (Second Quarter 1994): 5–15.

Kelly, John F. "Keogh Sales Opportunity Unlimited." *Mutual Funds Forum,* January 1974, 4–15.

Khademian, Anne M. *The SEC and Capital Market Regulation: The Politics of Expertise.* Pittsburgh: University of Pittsburgh Press, 1992.

Korschot, Benjamin Calvin. *A Lifetime of Investing.* Kansas City, MO: Richardson, 1997.

Landis, James M. *The Administrative Process.* New Haven, CT: Yale University Press, 1938.

Levitt, Arthur. "Protecting the American Investor: A New Partnership." Speech, North American Securities Administrators Association Fall Conference, Orlando, September 29, 1993.

————. "The SEC and the States: Toward a More Perfect Union." Speech, North American Securities Administrators Association, Vancouver, October 3, 1995.

————. "From Security to Self-Reliance: American Investors in the 1990s." Speech, Investment Company Institute 1996 General Membership Meeting, Washington, DC, May 22, 1996.

————. "60th Anniversary of the Investment Company Act and the Investment Company Institute." Speech, Board of Governors of the Investment Company Institute, Washington, DC, October 5, 2000.

Life Insurance Management Association. *What You Should Know about Mutual Funds.* Hartford: Life Insurance Management Association, 1959.

Lybecker, Martin E. "Bank-Sponsored Investment Management Services: A Legal History and Statutory Interpretative Analysis," part 1, *Securities Regulation Law Journal*, 5, no. 2 (Summer 1977): 110–64; part 2, *Securities Regulation Law Journal*, 5, no. 3 (Autumn 1977): 195–258.

Mahar, Maggie. *Bull! A History of the Boom and Bust, 1982–2004.* New York: Harpers Business, 2003.

Mains, Norman E. "The Keogh Plan Universe." *Mutual Funds Forum,* October 1974, 1–9.

Manges, Gerard. "The Investment Company Amendments Act of 1975: An Analysis and Appraisal after Two Years." *Boston College Industrial and Commercial Law Review,* 14, no. 3 (February 1973): 387–436.

Marcis, Richard, Sandra West, and Victoria Leonard-Chambers. "Mutual Fund Shareholder Response to Market Disruptions." *Perspective,* 1, no. 1 (July 1995).

Mason, Paul J., and Stephen E. Roth. "SEC Regulation of Life Insurance Products—On the Brink of the Universal." *Connecticut Law Review,* 15, no. 3 (Spring 1983): 505–63.

McDonald, Harry A. "The S.E.C. Looks at Mutual Funds." Speech, First Annual Mutual Fund Conference, New York, June 18, 1949.

McGrath, Kathryn B. "Good Compliance Is Good Business." Keynote address, 1985 ICI/SEC Procedures Conference, Washington, DC, October 31, 1985.

McLaughlin, George V. Proceedings of the Twenty-Seventh Annual Convention of the National Association of Supervisors of State Banks, July 25, 1928.

McTague, Rachel. "As SEC Contemplates More Regulation of Hedge Funds, CFTC Counsel, Others Object." *Bureau of National Affairs Daily Report for Executives,* 95 (May 16, 2003): A-50.

————. "Fitzgerald, Spitzer Blast Mutual Fund Industry, Call for Dramatic Governance Reforms." *Bureau of National Affairs Securities Regulation and Law Report*, 35 (November 10, 2003): 1875.

————. "Mutual Funds at Center of Arena; Reform a Good Bet, But Scope Unclear." *Bureau of National Affairs Securities Regulation and Law Report*, 36 (January 26, 2004): 149.

————. "Donaldson, Shelby on Same Wave Length: SEC Able to Handle Mutual Fund Reforms." *Bureau of National Affairs Securities Regulation and Law Report*, 36 (April 12, 2004): 661.

Mendelson, Lewis J. "The SEC's Investment Company Advertising Rules: Why and How They Have Been Changed." *Mutual Funds Forum*, December 1974, 3–13.

Meredith, Douglas. *Life Insurance versus the Ups and Downs of Mutual Funds.* Montpelier, VT: National Life Insurance, 1960.

Moley, Raymond. *The First New Deal.* New York: Harcourt, Brace & World, 1966.

Morningstar. *2009 Ibbotson Stocks, Bonds, Bills, and Inflation Classic Yearbook.* Chicago: Morningstar, 2009.

Mundheim, Robert H., and Gordon D. Henderson. "Applicability of the Federal Securities Laws to Pension and Profit-Sharing Plans." *Law and Contemporary Problems*, 29, no. 1 (Summer 1964): 795–841.

Nachmany, Avi. "Perspectives." *Windows into the Mutual Fund Industry*, February 2006, 2.

Nocera, Joseph. *A Piece of the Action: How the Middle Class Joined the Money Class.* New York: Simon & Schuster, 1994.

North American Securities Administrators Association. "Final Report of the 1984 Investment Companies Committee of the North American Securities Administrators Association," October 29, 1984.

————. Resolution Adopted by the North American Securities Administrators Association," October 1991.

Orrick, Andrew Downey. "A Regulator Looks at the Mutual Fund Industry." Speech, Ninth Annual Mutual Fund Conference, New York, October 2, 1957.

Parrish, Michael E. *Securities Regulation and the New Deal.* New Haven, CT: Yale University Press, 1970.

Perkins, Edwin J. *Wall Street to Main Street: Charles Merrill and Middle-Class Investors.* Cambridge: Cambridge University Press, 1999.

Perun, Pamela and C. Eugene Steurle. "From Fiduciary to Facilitator: Employers and Defined Contribution Plans." In *The Evolving Pension System: Trends, Effects, and Proposals for Reform,* edited by William G. Gale, John B. Shoven and Mark J. Warshawsky, 191–206. Washington, DC: Brookings Institution Press, 2005.

Plummer, A. Newton. *The Great American Swindle Incorporated.* New York: A. Newton Plummer, 1932.

Punishell, Jaime, Ron Shevlin, and Tom Watson. "The End of Mutual Fund Dominance," Forrester Research, December 8, 2000.

Rea, John D., and Brian K. Reid. "Trends in the Ownership Cost of Equity Mutual Funds." *Perspective,* 4, no. 3 (November 1998).

Rea, John, and Richard Marcis. "Mutual Fund Shareholder Activity during U.S. Stock Market Cycles, 1944–95." *Perspective,* 2, no. 2 (March 1996).

Red Herring. "The Death of Mutual Funds," August 31, 2000, from http:// www.redherring.com/Home/268.

Reid, Brian. "Growth and Development of Bond Mutual Funds." *Perspective,* 3, no. 2 (June 1997).

———. "The 1990s: A Decade of Expansion and Change in the U.S. Mutual Fund Industry." *Perspective,* 6, no. 3 (July 2000).

Reid, Brian K., and John D. Rea. "Mutual Fund Distribution Channels and Distribution Costs." *Perspective,* 9, no. 3 (July 2003).

Remoloana, Eli M., Paul Kleiman, and Debbie Gruenstein. "Market Returns and Mutual Fund Flows." *Federal Reserve Bank of New York Economic Policy Review* (July 1997): 33–52.

Robinson, Dwight P. Jr. *Massachusetts Investors Trust: Pioneer in Open-End Investment Trusts.* New York: Newcomen Society in North America, 1954.

Robinson, Leland Rex. *Investment Trust Organization and Management.* New York: Ronald Press, 1926.

Rodengen, Jeffrey L. *New Horizons: The Story of Federated Investors.* Ft. Lauderdale, FL: Write Stuff Enterprises, 2006.

Roe, Mark J. "Political Elements in the Creation of a Mutual Fund Industry." *University of Pennsylvania Law Review,* 139, no. 6 (June 1991): 1469–511.

Rosenberg, Richard M. "Community Reinvestment: The Next Step." Speech, Federal Reserve Bank of Dallas Community Reinvestment Conference, Dallas, August 24, 1993.

Rottersman, Max, and Jason Zweig. "An Early History of Mutual Funds." *Friends of Financial History,* 51 (Spring 1994): 12–20.

Rouwenhorst, K. Geert. "The Origins of Mutual Funds." Yale International Center for Finance Working Paper No. 04–48, December 12, 2004.

Schreft, Stacey L. "Credit Controls: 1980." *Economic Review,* Federal Reserve Bank of Richmond, 6 (November/December 1990): 25–55.

Schwed, Fred Jr. *Where Are the Customers' Yachts? Or, a Good Hard Look at Wall Street.* New York: Simon and Schuster, 1940.

Scudder, Stevens & Clark. *History of Scudder, Stevens & Clark.* Boston: Scudder, Stevens & Clark, 1994.

Seligman, Joel. *The Transformation of Wall Street: A History of the Securities and Exchange Commission and Modern Corporate Finance,* 3rd. ed. New York: Aspen, 2003.

——. "Should Investment Companies Be Subject to a New Statutory Self-Regulatory Organization?" *Washington University Law Quarterly,* 83, no. 4 (2005): 1115–26.

Shaffner, Felix I. *The Problem of Investment.* New York: John Wiley, 1936.

Silberman, H. Lee. *50 Years of Trust: Massachusetts Investors Trust 1924–1974.* Boston: Massachusetts Financial Services, 1974.

Silver, David. "Retirement Planning with Mutual Funds." *Mutual Funds Forum,* January 1978, 1–13.

——. "The Washington Scene." Keynote Address, Investment Company Institute 1982 General Membership Meeting, Washington, DC, May 20, 1982.

——. "Edited Transcript of Interview with David Silver," part 2. Virtual Museum and Archive of Securities and Exchange Commission and Securities Industry, April 21, 2006, from http://www.sechistorical.org/museum/oralhistories/interviews/silver.php.

Simon, Ruth. "How Washington Could Tip the Scales against Investors." *Money,* October 1995, 122–24.

Simpson, Murray L., and Scott Hodes. "The Continuing Controversy Surrounding the Uniform Retail Price Maintenance Provisions of the Investment Company Act of 1940." *Notre Dame Law Review,* 44, no. 5 (June 1969): 718–31.

Skinner, Jonathan. "Individual Retirement Accounts: A Review of the Evidence." *Tax Notes,* 2 (January 13, 1992): 201–12.

Slater, Robert. *John Bogle and the Vanguard Experiment: One Man's Quest to Transform the Mutual Fund Industry.* Chicago: Irwin, 1997.

Smith, Geoffrey. "Commentary: Funds; A Hidden Trick Investors Should Know About." *Business Week* (November 17, 1997): 41.

Smith, James Gerald. "Banking and the Stock Market." In *Facing the Facts: An Economic Diagnosis,* ed. James Gerald Smith, 153–85. New York: G. P. Putnam's Sons, 1932.

Sobel, Robert. *The Great Bull Market: Wall Street in the 1920s.* New York: Norton, 1968.

Steiner, William Howard. *Investment Trusts: American Experience.* New York: Adelphi, 1929.

Thaler, Alan A. "Life Insurance Sales of Investment Company Shares." *Mutual Funds Forum,* April 1973, 6–7.

Twentieth Century Fund. *The Security Markets: Findings and Recommendations of a Special Staff of the Twentieth Century Fund.* New York: Twentieth Century Fund, 1935.

U.S. Chamber of Commerce, *Commission on the Regulation of U.S. Capital Markets in the 21st Century*. Washington, DC: U.S. Chamber of Commerce, March 2007.

U.S. Congress, House. *Report of the Committee Appointed Pursuant to House Resolutions 429 and 504 to Investigate the Concentration of Money and Credit*. 62d Cong., 3d sess., 1913.

———. Subcommittee of the Committee on Interstate and Foreign Commerce. *Investment Trusts and Investment Companies*. 76th Cong., 3d sess., 1940.

———. Subcommittee of the Committee on Government Operations. *Hearings on Common Trust Funds—Overlapping Responsibility and Conflict in Regulation*. 88th Cong., 1st sess., 1963.

U.S. Congress, Senate. Subcommittee of the Committee on Banking and Currency. *Investment Trusts and Investment Companies*. 76th Cong., 3d sess., 1940.

———. Subcommittee on Financial Institutions of the Committee on Banking, Housing and Urban Affairs. *Hearings on Money Market Mutual Funds*. 96th Cong., 2d sess., 1980.

U.S. Department of the Treasury. *Blueprint for a Modernized Financial Regulatory Structure*. Washington, DC: Department of the Treasury, March 2008.

———. *Financial Regulatory Reform: A New Foundation*. Washington, DC: Department of the Treasury, June 18, 2009.

U.S. General Accounting Office. *Long-Term Capital Management: Regulators Need to Focus Greater Attention on Systemic Risk*. Washington, DC: Government Printing Office, 1999.

U.S. Government Accountability Office. *Increased Reliance on 401(k) Plans Calls for Better Information on Fees*. Washington, DC: Government Printing Office, 2007.

U.S. Securities and Exchange Commission. *Investment Trusts and Investment Companies, 1939–1942*. Washington, DC, 1939–1942.

———. *Report of the Special Study of Securities Markets of the Securities and Exchange Commission to the House Commerce Committee*, House Doc. no. 95, 88th Cong., 1st sess., Pt. IV, 1963.

———. *Report of the Securities and Exchange Commission on the Public Policy Implications of Investment Company Growth*, House Report no. 2337, 89th Cong., 2d sess., 1966.

———. Statement on the Future Structure of the Securities Markets. *BNA Securities Regulation and Law Reporter*, 137, pt. 2 (February 1972).

Vanderlip, Frank A. *Tomorrow's Money*. New York: Reynal & Hitchcock, 1934.

Vanguard Group, *Indexing: 25 Years and Counting*. Valley Forge, PA: Vanguard Group, 2006.

Vine, John M. "Cash or Deferred Arrangements: What's the Beef? What's at Stake?" *Virginia Tax Law Review*, 5, no. 4 (Spring 1986): 855–910.

Wallison, Peter J., and Robert E. Litan. *Competitive Equity: A Better Way to Organize Mutual Funds.* Washington, DC: AEI Press, 2007.

Weiss, Gary. *Wall Street Versus America: The Rampant Greed And Dishonesty That Imperil Your Investments.* New York, Penguin, 2006.

West, Stephen K. Speech, Investment Company Institute 1980 General Membership Meeting, Washington, DC, May 1, 1980.

———. "Is There a Better Way to Regulate Mutual Funds." Paper presented to the Committee on Investment Management of the New York Bar, March 6, 2008.

Wharton School of Finance and Commerce. *A Study of Mutual Funds.* House Report no. 2274, 87th Cong., 2d sess., 1962.

Whitney, Jack M. II. Address Before the Investment Company Institute, New York, May 3, 1962.

Wiesenberger, Arthur. *Investment Companies and Their Securities: 1942 Edition.* New York: Arthur Wiesenberger, 1942.

Wilcox, U.V. *The Bankers Be Damned.* New York: Daniel Ryerson, 1940.

Williams, Marshall H. *Investment Trusts in America.* New York: Macmillan, 1928.

Wilson, Stan. "ICI, Others Come out against SIA Proposal." *Fund Action,* May 10, 1999, 1–10.

———. "Funds Dilemma with Pricing, Timers Seen Getting Eye from the SEC." *Fund Action,* October 21, 2003, 1.

Winkelman, Barnie F. *Ten Years of Wall Street.* 1932, rpt.; Burlington, VT: Fraser Publishing, 1987.

Witmer, Rachel. "ICI's Fink Predicts Problems Ahead if Hedge Funds Are Not More Regulated." *Bureau of National Affairs Securities Regulation and Law Report,* 32 (December 11, 2000): 1670.

Wooten, James A. *The Employee Retirement Income Security Act of 1974: A Political History.* Berkeley: University of California Press, 2005.

Yogg, Michael R. *Passion for Reality: Paul Cabot and the Boston Mutual Fund.* Xlibris, 2006.

Zitzewitz, Eric W. "Who Cares about Shareholders? Arbitrage-Proofing Mutual Funds." *Journal of Law, Economics, and Organization,* 19 (October 2003): 245–80.

Zweig, Jason. "Why Your Fund Manager May Work Better in the Dark." *Money* (March 1998), 50–51.

Index